The Garden
of Gratitude

By
Rabbi Shalom Arush

Director of Chut Shel Chessed Institutions

Author of:

The Garden of Emuna

The Garden of Peace

The Garden of Yearning

In Forest Fields

Women's Wisdom

The Garden of Riches

And other books

Translated by:

Rabbi Lazer Brody

Iyar, 5771

In all matters relating to this book, please contact:

Chut Shel Chessed Institutions

Shmuel HaNavi St. 13

POB 50226, Jerusalem, Israel

Telephone 972-52-224-0696 or 972-2-581-2210

Distribution:

Tel: 972-52-224-0696

www.myemuna.com

ISBN: 978-965-7502-03-7

Printed in Israel

Rabbinical Approbations

The following are excerpts from the approbations that this generation's leading rabbinical figures wrote for *Shaarav B'Todah*, the original Hebrew version of **The Garden of Gratitude**:

***The Garden of Gratitude** is the work of an artist, the Prince of Torah, the brilliant and pious Rabbi Shalom Arush, may he merit long and happy days, who has assembled in his purity a golden treasure of emuna and ethics.*

Rabbi Ovadia Yossef
Rishon Letzion and President of
The Council of Torah Sages

Anyone who is privileged to purchase this wonderful book will undoubtedly see the best of this world and the next, and attain both riches and happiness...

Rabbi Eliezer Berland
Rosh Yeshiva of *Shuvu Banim Breslev*, Jerusalem

The author has succeeded in elaborating this cardinal principle – anyone who reads and learns this book will undoubtedly mitigate all stern judgments and enjoy happiness all the days of his life.

Rabbi Naftali Moskowitz, the Melitzer Rebbe

*My heart rejoiced when I saw the book **The Garden of Gratitude**.*

Yehuda Zev Lebowitz
Author of *Or Levi – Ziv Yehuda*

Contents

The Book of Life • Self-Pity and Complaints • A Stiff-Necked People • He Will Say of our Weeping, "Enough" • Be a Good Person • The Nullification of All Troubles • Terrible Ingratitude • The Source of All Good • Rectification of the Bitter Exile • Miracles • Self-Assessment • The First Task • The Challenge of the Redemption • Yearning • Thankful for Everything • Longing, Not Sadness • Their Light Will Guide Us • The Honor of G-d • Who is Just? • The Notebook • G-d is in Our Midst • Recognize Hashem

Why Didn't You Sing Praises? • Remembering Hashem's Loving-Kindness • Remember and Give Thanks • Love Your Neighbor as Yourself • The Obligation of Thanks • Important Reminders • A Paper Cup • A Point of Gratitude • Good Points • The Basics • Don't Be Lazy • Take Nothing for Granted • The Value of Giving Thanks for Everything • Sing to Him • The Sound of Music • A Truly Great Wonder • Write the Song • The Prominence of Song • Study • See the Abundance • Redemption of the World

The Greatest Gifts • Good News • Giving Thanks is Salvation • No More Pain • To Learn the Good • Get Up and Sing! • "This Time I Praise" – Just This Time? • On What Types of Seemingly Bad Do We

Chapter Five: The Little Things Count................................ 174

Chapter Six: Rectifying our Lives...................................... 212

Chapter Seven: Miracle Stories.. 246

With Hashem's Loving Grace

If everyone would heed the true tzaddik, follow in his path, and steadfastly believe in Hashem – in particular, that everything that happens is for our ultimate good; if everyone would constantly give thanks and praise to Hashem, whether under good circumstances or not, as it is written: 'In Hashem (expressing G-d's attribute of loving-kindness) I will praise His word, in Elokim (expressing G-d's attribute of judgment) I will praise His word,' surely all the troubles and all the exiles would be completely nullified and the complete redemption would take place!

Rabbi Natan of Breslev
Likutei Halachot, Laws of Unloading and Loading, 4

Author's Foreword

We praise Hashem, our beloved Creator, and sing of His glory. We thank You, Hashem our Master, for enabling us to express our endless gratitude to You.

Our sages teach that when the Third and final Holy Temple will be rebuilt in Jerusalem – speedily and in our days, amen - all the sacrifices of old will be nullified except for the *Korban Todah* – the Thanksgiving offering. This offering brings us continuously closer to Hashem, level after level. Even now, when we don't yet have our rebuilt Holy Temple, we can still attain a lofty measure of proximity to the Almighty by constantly expressing our gratitude. Gratitude, more than anything else, brings the world to a state of perfection.

The exalted act of expressing gratitude hastens the redemption in a merciful manner and prevents the Armageddon-type doomsday scenarios of the End of Days. Not only does it bring the all-inclusive redemption for Israel and the world, but each individual's personal redemption as well. Even in the world's present state, giving thanks is the master key that unlocks the doors of every blessing imaginable. Prayers of gratitude are always readily accepted.

This book explains how to make a quantum leap in your personal and spiritual growth – through gratefulness! The attribute of gratitude is a prerequisite to true happiness and success in interpersonal relations, especially marriage. Gratitude invokes miracles such as seemingly impossible recovery from illness and phenomenal deliverance from debt.

Gratitude not only opens closed gates of salvation, but also opens the locked and bolted gates. Opening bolted gates is different than opening closed gates. How? A person might not deserve a certain blessing; in that case, his prayers would encounter a closed door. But when a person accumulates spiritual debits as a result of misdeeds, the gates through which blessings flow are locked and bolted. Those locked and bolted gates of abundance and salvation open wide once there is gratitude.

This is how it works: Spiritual debts are the result of the Heavenly Court's accusations against a person. The intent of the accuser is to prevent the accused from receiving - not to stop the accused from giving. So when a person desires to give rather than receive, the accuser can't say anything. As such, the Heavenly Court cannot prevent even the worst transgressor from expressing gratitude, for gratitude is a gift. Who can repel a person who doesn't ask anything but simply desires to give a gift to the King?

This concept is not new; it's just been concealed for many years. We do not even grasp the full power and significance of gratitude, which invokes tremendous salvation for a person! If one sees that life is a brick wall or a dead end – he should realize that learning to give thanks is the key to a new tomorrow. Once a person learns to thank the Almighty for everything – even for life's deficiencies - then every gate suddenly opens. Expressions of gratitude reach the Almighty directly; no intermediary or spiritual force dare obstruct a "gift" that's intended for the King of Kings. The grateful person finds himself in close proximity to Hashem and receives salvations even without asking, because in Hashem's presence, there is no deficiency.

King David says (Psalms, 100:4), "Come to His gates in gratefulness, to His courtyards with praise." This verse hints to the idea that by coming to the Almighty's gates with gratefulness, we can enter those gates. In continuation of our internationally acclaimed best-selling life guides **The Garden of Emuna**, **The Garden of Peace** and others, we've entitled this book, **The Garden of Gratitude**. With gratitude, you will see how your life takes on the exquisite beauty of a tropical garden.

I would like to thank my cherished wife who stands always at my side, Miriam Varda. She deserves the credit for all my achievements. I am incapable of describing her greatness, wisdom, and selflessness. No one could dream of a more loyal and supportive partner. May her reward be complete both in this world and the World to Come, and may she derive limitless joy and gratification from our offspring, seeing them and subsequent generations living lives of Torah and emuna in truth and in simplicity.

Lavish thanks go to my Rabbi and teacher, HaRav Eliezer Berland, Shlit'a, from whose sweet waters I drink. May it be the will of Hashem that his days and years be lengthened in goodness and sweetness, in good health for himself and for his family, and may he see his teachings spread to his many students and students of students.

To my precious sons and precious daughters, to my precious sons-in-law and precious daughters-in-law, thank you from the depths of my heart. To those loyal members of our Yeshiva's community who give so much of themselves in the administration and running of the *Chut Shel Chesed* Institutions, and to all those who devote days and nights to our outreach programs - without their active help, it would not be possible to carry the weight of my responsibilities. May it be His will that they should grow in Torah and service of Hashem, and they should merit to see generations of children and children's children walking in the path of Torah and emuna.

Many thanks to my staff and students who assisted in the preparation of this book: Recorders, editors, typists, the internet staff, printers, and distributors. Special thanks go to my dear pupils Rabbi Yaakov Hertzberg and his wife Esther, may Hashem bless them, who merited from Above to help me compose my books.

My blessings and appreciation go to my faithful pupil, Rabbi Eliezer Raphael (Lazer) Brody, for the translation of this book and for his tireless dedication in spreading my teachings around the globe.

"And I will raise a prayer to the Living G-d" that all who read this book will merit to be inspired and aroused to pursue the path of gratitude. May all who read this book establish a steadfast connection with Hashem, and may all their suffering be nullified. May they see the coming of Moshiach and the building of the Holy Temple, and the ultimate redemption of mankind, speedily, and in our days, Amen.

Translator's Foreword

The Garden of Emuna – the first exquisite flower of Rabbi Shalom Arush's literary garden – is now a multi-language international bestseller that graces the bookshelves of millions of households around the world. **The Garden of Emuna** has been virtually the first book ever to show how to develop a personal relationship with the Creator, and demonstrate how emuna affects every phase of our daily lives. Rabbi Arush has succeeded in bringing the Hebrew word *emuna* to the forefront of global consciousness.

The Garden of Emuna is an entrance level course in spiritual and self-awareness. Life without it is like driving a car in China without being able to read the road signs in Chinese. Indeed, hundreds of readers have written that they would have never been able to find their way in this world without **The Garden of Emuna**.

As we all know, the road to happiness is strewn with formidable obstacles and grueling challenges. Rabbi Arush's newest book, **The Garden of Gratitude**, is an amazing yet surprisingly simple and effective guide in dealing with the most difficult obstacles and challenges. With the Almighty's loving grace, we're pleased to present this rare self-help blossom to the English-speaking reader.

In the coming pages, the reader will learn the secret of gratitude as well as its intrinsic power. Rabbi Arush presents the reader with a practical methodology for dealing with seemingly hopeless situations.

Rabbi Arush's teachings are not merely flowery prose for parlor tea parties; they have been proven successful time and again "under fire." During my thirteen years as Rabbi Arush's English mouthpiece, pupil, and understudy – and more specifically, in my travels around the globe in recent years spreading Rabbi Arush's teachings – I've seen people overcome terminal illnesses by implementing the advice that now appears in this book. I've also seen couples whom physicians deemed totally infertile become parents by following the invaluable lessons of the coming pages.

Emuna – the pure and complete belief in the Almighty – is above nature. Gratitude, as we're about to learn, is the greatest expression of emuna. Gratitude therefore has the power of invoking Divine intervention and blessings that transcend nature. Simply speaking, those who express their gratitude to the Almighty experience miracles.

I've never seen a counselor or therapist with Rabbi Arush's record of success in helping those who seek his advice. Rabbi Arush's teachings are girded firmly in the foundations of Talmudic and Jewish esoteric thought, and yet they're crystal clear and reader-friendly. Any person who implements Rabbi Arush's advice is bound to see major changes for the better, not only emotionally and spiritually, but physically and materially as well.

With Hashem's loving guidance, I have tried my utmost to preserve the flavor, intent, and beautiful simplicity of Rabbi Arush's original style. Even so, any deficiency in this book is surely that of the translator and not of the author. My sincere thanks and blessings go to (alphabetically) Rachel Tzipporah Avrahami, Shelli Karzan, Julie (Gila) Levi, Gita Levy and Miriam Maor for their unbelievably dedicated assistance in making **The Garden of Gratitude** a reality.

I wish to express my deepest gratitude to Rabbi Shalom Arush himself, who so selflessly has illuminated my mind and soul with his noble teachings. May Hashem bless him, his family, and his pupils with the very best of spiritual and material abundance always.

Yosef Nechama, General Director of Breslev Israel Communications, is my steadfast partner in spreading Rabbi Arush's teachings worldwide. His constant support and encouragement are priceless assets for which I'm ever so grateful. May Hashem shower him and his family with the best of blessings always.

My cherished wife Yehudit deserves the credit for this book and for everything else I do. May Hashem bless her with long and happy days, success, and true joy from all her offspring, amen.

With a song of thanks to the Almighty and a prayer that all of mankind may soon call His name,

Lazer Brody, Ashdod, Adar Aleph 5771

Chapter One:
The Path to Redemption

Everyone awaits the Redemption. Everyone wants to know what he can do to end the long exile and hasten salvation. Much has been said on this topic, but here we will learn the most fundamental cause of this bitter exile. By rectifying it, we can anticipate the imminent arrival of Moshiach.

The Book of Life

To find out what this important cause is and what needs to be rectified, we must reflect on what the Torah says about the first redemption from Egypt. From that prodigious event, we can learn what will bring about the final redemption which we yearn for every day.

The Torah is neither a history book nor a story book, G-d forbid. It is an instruction manual for our lives. Every single item written in the Torah is there to teach each and every person what Hashem wants from us. Thus, the Hebrew root of the word Torah means "instruction." The Torah instructs those who learn it and shows them the path they should take. This is why we want to discern what the Torah relates about the exodus from Egypt, and the People of Israel's desert sojourn and eventual entry into the Land of Israel. If we draw the proper conclusions, we will understand what pitfalls to avoid and what we need to amend as we strive for the final redemption.

Self-Pity and Complaints

From the very beginning of the redemption process, when Moses came to free Israel from Egyptian slavery - and throughout the forty years they were in the desert until their entry into the Land of Israel - the Children of Israel complained.

This behavior resulted in the positive commandment to remember every day how much we infuriated G-d with our complaints from the very beginning of the redemption in Egypt: "Remember, do not forget all that you angered Hashem your G-d in the desert, from the day that you left the Land of Egypt until you came to this place, you have been rebels against G-d" (Deuteronomy, 9). Israel's negative character trait of complaining was the main factor that angered Hashem.

Anyone who carefully reflects on the Torah portions that deal with the redemption from Egypt sees that time and again the Torah describes the complaints of the People of Israel in all sorts of situations and trials that they endured.

The first example is from the dawn of the redemption, when Moses first asked Pharaoh to let the People of Israel out of Egypt. Pharaoh refused, and instead intensified his decrees. Immediately, the Children of Israel complained against Moses and Aaron, and blamed them for making things worse, saying accusingly: "May G-d see you and judge, that you have made us abhorrent in the eyes of Pharaoh and the eyes of his servants, giving a sword in their hands to slay us" (Exodus, 5: 21).

Not only did they not thank Moses for his efforts to redeem them and for risking his life going to Pharaoh on their behalf, they blamed him for their intensified slavery. If they would have had some measure of gratitude, they would have appreciated Moses' efforts and understood it was only natural that Pharaoh would not want to release slaves that worked so well for free. After all, it's highly unlikely that Pharaoh would simply give in and say to Moses, "Fine –

they can go!" Pharaoh's angry reaction was a necessary part of the redemption process.

This lack of appreciation was, in itself, the reason for the intensification of the exile. If the People of Israel had overcome their ingratitude from the start and thanked Moses instead of complaining – they would immediately have been redeemed.

The next example: after a series of awesome plagues, the People of Israel left Egypt by virtue of G-d's mighty hand. When Pharaoh chased them, they complained: "Are there no graves in Egypt that you took us to die in the desert? What have you done to us, to take us out of Egypt? This is just what we said to you in Egypt: Leave us alone and we will serve Egypt, for it is preferable to us to serve Egypt than to die in the desert..." (Exodus, 14).

We can understand that the situation was dangerous and frightening; the sea was in front of them and the Egyptians behind them. But certainly everything was orchestrated by the Creator, Who was fully aware of the level of difficulty of this test of faith. He in His divine wisdom willed that the Children of Israel be tested; they had the potential to overcome this trial.

The difference between successfully withstanding the trial and failing it was dependent only on their level of gratitude. Did they recognize and fully appreciate G-d's miracles up until then, or deny them, G-d forbid? Gratitude is not contingent on lofty spiritual heights, but rather on something very basic. A decent human being will express gratitude and not forget all the kindnesses that G-d performs for him every single day, much less outright miracles.

A person must never forget a kindness or favor that anyone performed for him. The People of Israel should have remembered the myriad of miracles and wonders that G-d executed, namely the Ten Plagues and everything that followed. They should have recognized and appreciated how tirelessly Moses worked on their behalf for the exodus from Egypt and subsequent redemption. Moses, after all, was in danger no less than they were. They should have said to him: "Moses, our teacher. Thank you very much for all that you have done for us, but the situation is difficult and frightening. Help us! Guide us!" Instead, they complained, proving that they lacked basic decency; it was this ingratitude that was their downfall.

Obviously, one couldn't expect the Children of Israel – recently emancipated slaves - to attain the level of faith where they could perceive that a seemingly dire situation was for their ultimate benefit. This level was too high for them at such an early stage in their redemption. Under slavery by the idolatrous Egyptians, they had sunk to a low level of spiritual impurity, where Divine light was deeply concealed. However, they could have expressed some level of appreciation and offered thanks to Hashem, as well as Moses. At the very least, they could have refrained from complaining and denying the good that Hashem and Moses had done for them. After all, they saw fantastic miracles with their very own eyes throughout the period of the Ten Plagues!

Had the People of Israel been appreciative, they would immediately have witnessed even greater miracles.

Instead, the Children of Israel said, "It is preferable to us to serve Egypt."

Humans tend to be fooled by the falsehood that surrounds them. As such, the Children of Israel resigned themselves to a life of slavery. If they had sought the essence of truth, they would have agreed to die one thousand deaths rather than continue to live in the wanton atmosphere and crushing servitude of Egypt. Furthermore, if they had developed the character trait of gratitude, they would have understood that it is preferable to die one thousand deaths and not to deny the kindness that Moses had performed for them.

If the People of Israel had pondered the truth objectively, they would have realized that Moses did a tremendous amount on their behalf. Their predicament was not his fault. On the contrary, it was a trial for them – a test to see if they would appreciate his kindness or disregard it, G-d forbid.

The next instance of ingratitude came after the splitting of the Red Sea. The nation had gone a few days without water until they came to a place called Marah. But the water there was bitter and undrinkable, "And the nation complained to Moses, 'What will we drink?'"

They should have said: "Thank you very much for all of your efforts on our behalf until now. Please pray for us, so that we will have water." Why did they complain? Because they had no desire for redemption. They did not want to elevate themselves from their state of darkness and spiritual concealment into a life of emuna. They left Egypt reluctantly, as if they were doing Moses a favor. Subsequently, every time something did not work out for them, they complained: "We told you not to take us out! We did you a favor by leaving Egypt! And now look at us…"

With no desire for something, there is no dedication or self-sacrifice; any difficulty becomes a seemingly insurmountable challenge and a cause for complaint.

Exile is a situation in which people do not desire the truth; they are willing to forfeit their bona fide mission in life in exchange for some comfort - even food or water. They misconstrue liberty as the fulfillment of all their material desires and comforts. But true liberty is the desire to fulfill one's mission and purpose in this world. Exile is life with no purpose. Liberty is life with purpose.

Here's another example of ingratitude. After Moses sweetened the water in Marah, the Children of Israel continued their journey to the Wilderness of Zin. They also lamented there, "And the entire Congregation of the Children of Israel complained against Moses and Aaron in the desert and the Children of Israel said to them, 'Would it only be that we would have died at the hand of G-d in the land of Egypt, when we sat on the pot of meat, when we ate bread until we were satiated. For you have brought us out to this desert to kill this entire congregation by starvation…'" (Exodus, 16).

Once again we see how they were willing to give up redemption just to fill their stomachs! The true state of redemption is explained in the *Mishna*: "Eat bread with salt and drink water with measure and sleep on the ground." The truly free person receives his vitality – his sense of "living" - from his ultimate purpose in life. He is free from his bodily needs and constant urges. The person who seeks his sense of living from physical lusts – nothing more than fantasy – is enslaved to his transient and sorely limited body. There is no slavery worse than that.

The main source of Hashem's sorrow is from our improper actions – when we do not act like decent humans. A decent human is grateful for everything that is done for him. A person may have to accept the fact that he is so corporeal and attached to his bodily lusts that he does not want to be redeemed. But the least he can do is say thank you; he can always turn to G-d and say: "Hashem, help me be grateful and express my gratitude. Please have mercy on me."

A Stiff-Necked People

The aforementioned examples illustrate a frightening national tendency: after the Nation witnessed miracles and wonders that had never been seen or experienced before – neither in quantity nor quality – immediately upon encountering some sort of trial or difficulty, they complained! Instantaneously, after the awesome salvations, the Nation denied Hashem's goodness and the fact that He redeemed them from crushing slavery to true liberty. This history of national ingratitude stems from selective national amnesia – forgetting Hashem's endless wonderful favors for His people.

Take for example the test of Marah, where the Children of Israel could not find drinking water for three days. This incident occurred immediately after all the plagues in Egypt and the astounding miracle of the splitting of the Red Sea. The mighty Egyptian army was routed without a single Israelite lifting a finger in combat. But despite the awe-inspiring Divine intervention they witnessed, straight away the Children of Israel complained about their difficulties. Rashi explains (Rashi on Exodus, Chapter 15) that G-d gave them a test of faith and saw their stubbornness in approaching Moses with disrespect. They should have asked, "Request mercy for us so that we may have water to drink." Instead, they complained.

Rashi teaches us here that approaching Moses respectfully and asking him to pray for mercy is a completely acceptable action. But when the Children of Israel complained, they manifested their bad character traits of ingratitude and stubbornness. Rashi's explanation highlights the fine line between a request for mercy – which is both permissible and desirable - and a complaint, which Hashem despises.

Prayer in the form of complaint is not only not answered; it stimulates even more harsh judgments, Heaven forbid.

The Code of Jewish Law explains that if a person merely thinks that his prayers should be answered, he already awakens judgment on himself. If a person relies on his merits and does not beseech G-d's kindness despite his lack of merits, his deeds are thoroughly reviewed. This is especially true in the case of a person who makes demands or complains.

He Will Say of our Weeping, "Enough"

The examples above are just a portion of the complaints recorded in the Book of Exodus. The complaint that broke the proverbial camel's back was the baseless crying of the People of Israel upon hearing the words of the spies. The spies slandered the Land of Israel in the Book of Numbers (Parshat Shelach Lecha). "Then the Holy One, Blessed Be He said: You have cried for no reason, I will give you something to cry about for generations!" The needless crying triggered a devastating punishment: Thousands of years of terrible exile, replete with suffering and hardship.

The punishment that the Creator decreed on the Jews because of the sin of the spies is shocking. Do the People of Israel throughout the generations really deserve such retribution just because they baselessly cried for one night? The destruction of two Holy Temples and the subsequent unspeakable torture and deaths of millions that have plagued the Jews throughout this prolonged, arduous exile? Is that Divine justice?

Our own generation deals with troubles in clusters: terrible marital problems, diseases, traffic accidents, terror, and dire economic problems, may G-d have mercy. These are just the tip of the iceberg of this generation's tribulations. Are the trials because the People of Israel needlessly cried once? Is that really so awful? After all, what did they do? They didn't engage in debauchery, nor did they worship idols. All they did was cry. Must they suffer such reproof generation after generation? There is no sin in the Torah that invokes even a fraction of such bitter punishment!

The answer is amazingly simple: Hashem despises ingratitude more than any other sin. He can't stand self-pity, either. Hashem is fully aware that people have evil inclinations and that they are encumbered by lusts. While disdained, these human faults don't come close to the bad trait of ingratitude. Look at all the kindness that Hashem does for a person: He gives him life, showers him with goodness, and uplifts him from the sewers of promiscuity and bodily lusts. Hashem frees a person from the slavery of body and spirit. Hashem personally operates every part of us. Hashem feeds us every meal. After all the years filled with G-d's salvation, that person is still crying? Baseless tears? Hashem then teaches that complaining and needless crying are the worst forms of behavior. Hence, the punishment for baseless crying is the greatest one of all.

The main reason that the punishment for crying needlessly in the desert continues is because we are still crying and complaining to this day. We continue to cry and complain about everything that doesn't go exactly according to our wishes.

Today's exile is not because of G-d's anger thousands of years ago in the desert. It is because the Creator desires that we rectify this sin and completely uproot ungratefulness from our midst. As long as we have not rectified this negative trait, the exile and all its travails continue. In other words, we are not being punished for our tears in the past, but for the fact that we are still crying. In light of this, Hashem's words: "I will give you something to cry about for generations," mean that as long as the People of Israel cry, stern judgments, or *dinim*, are awakened, just like *dinim* the crying in the desert invoked. Therefore, if the Jews would uproot this terrible trait, the redemption would come immediately.

Be a Good Person

Why are ingratitude, baseless crying and not saying thank you the most serious sins that carry the bitterest punishments?

Even without Torah and its commandments, normal human decency obligates a person to appreciate what others do for him or her and express gratitude! Every person, with no exception, is required to be a fair and decent human. To paraphrase our sages, basic decency is a prerequisite for Torah.

We feel hurt and slighted when others deny the kindnesses and favors that we do for them. In fact, nothing upsets us more than ingratitude. Rabbi Akiva teaches, "Do not do to another what you, yourself, dislike." If we find ingratitude so unsightly, then why should any of us be ungrateful to Hashem?

Hashem is perturbed when people veer from the path of simple logic. Good manners are necessary for maintaining a normal, healthy society. Simple logic and common sense carry a person directly to the commandments of Torah.

Any human who is honest with himself – non-Jew and Jew alike – will ultimately seek the path of Torah, just as our holy patriarchs perceived the entire Torah through their powers of observation and contemplation. Straightforward logic dictates that a society cannot function properly in a climate where murder, thievery, dishonesty, and adultery are rampant. These are all prohibitions of Torah, the logic of which any decent person can comprehend.

The more that a person ignores common sense, the more he perturbs Hashem. A stark example of this is drug users, whose punishment – even in this world – is severe. They lose their humanity and many of them die terrible deaths after much suffering.

Many ask: What's the big deal about getting high every once in a while? The *once in a while* frequently becomes a wicked master by the name of *addiction*. A slave to substances cannot be a servant of Hashem. Additionally, most addicts – especially functioning ones – deny that they are addicted. Substance usage defies common sense in that it destroys mind, body and soul. As such, a person's willful self-destruction angers the Creator more than any other sin and arouses strict Heavenly judgments.

The same is true of ingratitude. When a young child denies the good given him, his parents are angered, despite the fact that he is small and still lacks understanding. Stop and think: who do we crown as a good and well-bred child? The one who knows how to say thank you...

Ingratitude is the collective negative trait of mankind. Our sages relate that even animals express appreciation, as the Torah says, "The ox knows its owner and the donkey the footsteps of its master" (Isaiah, 1:3).

Thus, if a person lacks gratitude, he can't plead, "I didn't learn Torah, I didn't know any better." Gratitude and expressing thanks are the most basic of human ethics.

Lack of gratitude leads to all types of tribulations in this world, including illness, divorce, and child-rearing troubles, Heaven forbid.

So much of our contemporary suffering is the result of our yet-to-be rectified sin of baseless crying. We cry and complain and the exile only gets longer and longer. Our main job is to uproot this despicable trait of ingratitude. We must pursue the path of thanks and gratefulness to attain our imminent redemption.

The Nullification of All Troubles

With the above in mind, we can now understand Rebbe Natan's message quoted at the beginning of the book: "If everyone would heed the true tzaddik, follow in his path, and steadfastly believe in Hashem - namely, that everything that happens is for our ultimate good; if everyone would constantly give thanks and praise to Hashem, whether under good circumstances or not, as is written: 'In Hashem (expressing G-d's attribute of loving-kindness) I will praise His word, in Elokim (expressing G-d's attribute of judgment) I will praise His word,' surely all the troubles and all the exiles would be completely nullified and the complete redemption would take place!"

This excerpt is a fundamental lesson that should never be forgotten. Rather, it should be engraved upon our hearts! Rebbe Natan promises that if we express gratitude, our suffering and exile will be nullified and we will merit the complete redemption.

Don't forget that the entire exile and its accompanied tribulations were the consequence of Israel's baseless crying. To amend this, we must eradicate any blemish of ingratitude and self-pity, replacing them with thanks for, gratitude to, and praise of Hashem.

Teshuvat hamishkal means *equivalent rectification*. Simply speaking, it's the principle of measure-for-measure in rectifying a misdeed. In order to correct our ancestors' needless crying in the desert, we must now, measure-for-measure, thank Hashem profusely for our troubles. Not a simple feat, but doing so is a cogent statement of our emuna; namely, we believe there is no bad, since Hashem does everything for our good.

Even if others have difficulty seeing Hashem's loving-kindness in our troubles, we must nonetheless focus on Hashem's good in all that happens to us.

Terrible Ingratitude

The root of a person's chronic crying, sadness, depression, despair and dissatisfaction is his lack of gratitude. He doesn't realize that he should be grateful for all the good that Hashem does for him and thank Hashem profusely all the time. Such people focus on the empty half of the cup - what they lack. As such, they are seldom satisfied. Their feelings of perpetual ingratitude blind them to Hashem's good intentions in all the seemingly negative circumstances that befall him.

Hashem rescued the Jewish people from slavery, taking them out of the house of bondage with wonders and miracles. Even so, they chided Moses and said: "Leave us alone and let us return to serve Egypt!" What was so great about Egypt? The forced labor in the desert sun? The beatings? The humiliation? What did they miss so much that they wanted to go back? The watermelon? The pumpkins, zucchini and garlic? For all this they preferred continued enslavement in Egypt?

The Children of Israel's illogical and inexplicably disrespectful attitude toward Moses stemmed from ingratitude - failing to see the good that was given to them.

Throughout world history, the root of all evil has been ingratitude. Adam was grossly ungrateful to Hashem when he sinned and said, "The woman who You gave me gave it to me and I ate" (Genesis, 3:12). Adam could have said: "The woman gave me and I ate." Why did he have to add the words "who You gave me"? It was as if he was accusing Hashem, "You are guilty for giving me this woman who constantly seduces me to sin…" From Adam until this very day, all of our sins, transgressions, crimes and failures result from ingratitude.

A grateful person never complains and is never depressed. His heart is full of appreciation for Hashem and all others, such as his spouse, employer, or teachers. He especially recognizes all the good that G-d did, does and will do for him. He is always saying thank you.

The Source of All Good

We now know that the root of all evil is ingratitude and the root of all good is gratitude. A grateful person is a good person. He acknowledges the goodness that others do for him. He thanks everyone and wants everyone to succeed.

This type of outlook is especially beneficial at home between husband and wife. When a spouse thanks the other for every small thing, their home is surely a haven of pleasantness and peace; they live a truly good life.

Gratitude begins with a person's upbringing. Was he brought up to be the wicked Haman, an ingrate who thinks he has everything coming to him and that everyone – including his parents – must bow to his wishes and serve him? Or was he brought up to say "thank you" for everything and understand that he's not automatically entitled to whatever he wants?

The primary rule for parents in child-rearing is teaching their children to say "thank you." This way, children learn to recognize and appreciate whatever they get, and not take things for granted. From the child's most tender age, parents should insist that the child express gratitude. The child should learn that if there's no expression of gratitude, he won't receive what he desires. Failure to teach children gratefulness results in spoiled, selfish, and insufferable children.

Our sages emphasize, "He who denies the kindness done by his friend will ultimately deny the kindness done by G-d." If we do not develop our gratitude towards Hashem's messengers, who we see with our own eyes in the flesh, we cannot really be grateful to G-d - the source of all the abundance that comes to us through those messengers. Furthermore, when a person does not feel gratitude toward the messengers, it is really because he does not want to feel gratitude toward the Sender. Thus, a person who denies the kindnesses done by his friend will certainly deny the kindnesses done for him by Hashem.

When a person walks around depressed, all the good that was given to him is revoked. Additionally, he is rendered unfit to serve G-d. Why? He thinks that he deserves all his heart's desires and cries about everything he lacks; therefore, he is far from the truth. If he would observe all of Hashem's kindnesses performed for him every second, he would not cry nor be sad. He would simply be happy, praising Hashem and ascending both spiritually and physically.

Rectification of the Bitter Exile

We have learned something shocking: the Creator of the world decreed this long exile, laden with so much suffering, sorrow and bloodshed, only because the Jewish people have developed a historical pattern of crying for no reason. They've been ungrateful.

Sure, the truth hurts, but please pay close attention to this fundamental fact: The People of Israel needlessly cried during the sin of the spies! Now here's the good news. Since now we know what sin causes us to continue to be in exile, now we also know how to repent. Once we stop crying and start expressing our thanks, we will have rectified the baseless crying that resulted from the spies' infamous sin.

Whenever a person cries and complains about anything in life, he perpetuates the blemish of the People of Israel in the desert.

If we feel that the punishment for baseless crying is too harsh, we must know that it is precisely measure-for-measure. The Gemara teaches us that Hashem leads a person on the path that he chooses. If a person wants to cry, Heaven gives him ample reason to do so. But he can also decide that he will begin to give thanks for everything! Surely then Hashem will then give him plenty of reasons to say thank you.

The choice is ours.

Miracles

Whoever contemplates the exodus from Egypt cannot but be awed that the People of Israel witnessed amazing miracles. The heavens opened and they saw G-d's Throne of Glory; they received the Torah by achieving a level of prophecy; the Clouds of Glory kept them warm and protected from the chill of the desert night; during the day, the same clouds shaded them from the burning sun and cooled them; their clothing did not wear out; and they ate *manna*, the Heaven-sent bread that was fully absorbed by the body, producing no waste whatsoever. With all these miracles and loving-kindnesses, how could it be that they did not change? After all, wouldn't you change if you experienced just a few miracles or a few Divine revelations?

Unfortunately, a person doesn't usually change even if he has seen miracles. If the People of Israel did not return to Hashem after all the miracles they witnessed, we can surely conclude that people do not inevitably return to Hashem after seeing miracles. Miracles can trigger a greater awareness of G-d, but to actually repent from the depths of one's heart and completely subjugate one's evil inclination, a person has to work on himself. This entails abundant prayer, beseeching Hashem for assistance, taking a serious accounting of one's spiritual state, and repentance. One must invest daily time and effort in personal prayer and self-assessment (see **In Forest's Fields** by this author for more information).

Self-Assessment

"A rebuke enters deeper into a man of understanding than a hundred lashes into a fool," said King Solomon in Proverbs 17:10.

Rabbi Yochanan, the Talmudic Sage, quoted Rabbi Yossi: "One twinge of guilt in the heart of man is better than a number of lashes."

In other words, a person who initiates his own repentance and subjugates himself before the Creator needs no more than rebuke to mend his ways. But a fool who lacks self-assessment has no idea why he suffers. He fails to wake up despite repeated prodding from Above.

The main focus of a person's spiritual service is to never forget any kindness that any person has done for him. Such kindnesses are really gifts from the Creator.

The main sin that traps mankind is the sin of pride; a person thinks that he has everything coming to him and that he does not have to thank anyone – not even Hashem, Heaven forbid. Thus, one's personal prayer energies should be directed to attaining gratitude in all its aspects and giving thanks with all one's heart.

Not even Torah study helps a person change if it is not accompanied by constant prayer, self-assessment and repentance – even if one is learning from the greatest rabbi. In the desert, the People of Israel heard the Torah from the Holy One, Blessed Be He, Himself. What an awe-inspiring thought! They learned Torah from the greatest rabbi and prophet of all times – Moses. They were not burdened by, nor busy with, other things - an excuse that many people use today to explain why they do not learn Torah or repent. On the contrary, they learned a tremendous amount of Torah during those forty years in the desert. There were no bank statements, grocery bills or mortgages. They didn't have to do laundry. They didn't have to sew because the clothing grew to fit the ever-changing sizes of the children. They didn't have to go to work or pay federal, municipal and property taxes. Everyone was free for the exclusive study of Torah, including the women. And learn Torah they did – but it didn't change them!

If a person doesn't make a concerted effort toward character improvement, the Torah that he learns will not change him. The main point of learning Torah is to translate it into action. Hashem also commanded us to incorporate what we learn into our hearts, as He wrote in the Torah: "And you shall know today and internalize it into your heart" (Deuteronomy, 4:39). G-d commands us to apply what we learn to our Divine service, which is prayer and self-betterment.

A person who sees that he has not sufficiently bettered himself should not aim his blame at bad luck, or a lack of talent or ability. He must realize that he simply didn't work hard enough. He should also not think that if he would only witness miracles, he would change. A person does not change by seeing miracles unless he awakens his soul and draws practical conclusions as to how to improve his ways. Our sages say: "If you work hard and get results, you can believe it. If you did not work hard and get results – don't believe it." Neither miracles nor Torah learning alone will change a person without his own intense efforts at self-improvement.

The First Task

A person's first task in self-improvement is to avoid all whining, complaining, needless crying, sadness and despair as if they were the Bubonic Plague. He would be well-advised to internalize the lessons of this book, focusing on devoting at least a third of his daily personal prayer session to expressing his gratitude for Hashem's numerous blessings. Such efforts will surely uproot all forms of discontent.

The Challenge of the Redemption

Many people forget Hashem's countless past favors and kindnesses as soon as life slightly veers from the comfort zone. When they encounter difficulties, they become upset and full of complaints, bearing a long list of grievances and reasons to be ungrateful.

In contrast, those who always recognize Hashem's kindness, and express gratitude to the Creator even when something doesn't work out as planned, avoid the pitfalls of sadness and depression. On the contrary - they are so grateful that they're embarrassed to ask the Creator to fill their own needs. When they do ask, they do so with humility and a heart filled with joy and gratitude, understanding that they're requesting a free gift that they don't necessarily deserve.

But what if the path to both personal and general redemption is difficult and strewn with challenges? Instead of crying, a person must focus on every moment's miracles. Why take the oxygen we breathe or a healthy heart for granted? We must never stop thanking Hashem as long as our hearts continue to beat.

The Torah relates: "The man Moses was the most humble of men."

Gratitude is the character trait that stems from humility. When a person sees how good Hashem is to him and how much He gives him, he becomes more humble and thinks: "Me? Who am I? Do I deserve all that Hashem gives me?" He even feels embarrassed and grows that much more humble.

The more a person is ungrateful and thinks he is entitled to everything, the more he becomes arrogant. He'll never be satisfied; whenever he receives something, he thinks:

"What? This is all I get? I deserve much more!" This is the result of the *klipa*, the negative spiritual influence of Haman and Amalek.

Humility is the predominant character trait of Moses. Rabbi Yaakov Abuchatzeira, of blessed and saintly memory, writes that the humility of Moses can overcome the Evil Inclination. One who invests time and effort in striving to be a grateful person will ultimately attain humility, which in turn will help him defeat his Evil Inclination.

The grateful person who realizes that Hashem is endlessly good to him is almost embarrassed to ask Him for anything. But when he does ask for something, he does so humbly and submissively. Such a person's prayers are readily answered.

Ingratitude and sadness are the result of selfishness and an inflated sense of entitlement – when a person thinks that the entire world owes him something, as was the case with the wicked Haman. Dissatisfaction and discontent are normally rooted in ungratefulness. Therefore, strengthening gratitude has a direct, positive effect on improving one's mood.

Yearning

As long as we lack our rebuilt *Beit Hamikdash*, the Holy Temple in Jerusalem, we must feel genuine sorrow over its destruction. *Tikkun Chatzot*, or midnight lamentations, is our prescribed daily prayer for expressing our yearning for the Holy Temple.

During the three weeks leading up to Tisha B'Av (the ninth day of the Jewish month of Av) – the days in which the destruction took place - we increase our mourning. On Tisha B'Av, the grief is at fever pitch; we fast, sit on the floor, cry and recite lamentations.

The Gemara says that from the time of the destruction of the Holy Temple it is forbidden for a person to laugh with all his heart in this world. However, this does not mean that we should be sad, G-d forbid.

A person must know how to serve Hashem at every time, and what the proper service is in a particular circumstance.

To paraphrase Ecclesiastes, at a time when one must be happy, he should be happy; at a time when one must cry, he should cry. Even when a person cries, he must be careful to cry for the right reasons. His tears should be tears of yearning and not of grievance and complaint. One must be very careful not to fall into the trap of baseless weeping, which causes all destruction.

Our Sages' directives to remember the destruction did not imply that we should sulk or be somber, G-d forbid. They intended to remind us to strive to rectify the reasons for the destruction, to know what we lost through our sins and to long for Hashem. The main point is to repent and remedy the root cause of the destruction.

As we've learned, the main cause for the ultimate destruction was baseless crying. Certainly, our Sages would not direct us to repeat the sin that led to such a severe punishment. On the contrary, the repentance for this sin is to stop our baseless weeping, to constantly feel thanks and gratitude and to rejoice in all that Hashem does for us. The main way to repent is to learn to say thank you.

Thankful for Everything

The Talmud in Tractate Sukkah talks about Raban Gamliel, Rabbi Elazar ben Azaryah, Rabbi Yehoshua and Rabbi Akiva – four holy *Tannaim* – who walked down the road and heard the uproar of the Romans from a distance of hundreds of miles. There was so much joy and cheer in Rome that it could be heard as far away as the Land of Israel. Upon hearing the commotion, Raban Gamliel, Rabbi Elazar and Rabbi Yehoshua cried, while Rabbi Akiva rejoiced and laughed.

"Why are you happy?" his friends asked.

"And why are you crying?" Rabbi Akiva answered.

"How can we not cry when those idol worshippers rejoice while our Holy Temple is burned?" they answered.

"That's the very reason I'm so happy," Rabbi Akiva replied.

"Please explain," they said.

"If we see that transgressors of G-d's will enjoy so much success and happiness – how much more joy and success will be relished by those who perform His will? Certainly, the Nation of Israel will ultimately merit tremendous joy - infinitely more than the joy the Romans are experiencing now," Rabbi Akiva explained.

Rabbi Akiva was adamant to see only the good in every situation, including the aftermath of the Holy Temple's destruction. He even saw the good in the fact that those who angered Hashem could enjoy happiness and success. He managed to extract the positive message from any situation. He realized – in the case of the Romans - that if those who anger Hashem receive so much revealed good, one can only imagine the blessings that will come, in due time, for those whose actions gratify Hashem.

We learn from Rabbi Akiva that although we are commanded to cry over the destruction of the Holy Temple, we should only do so during the midnight prayer (*Tikkun Chatzot*) and on

Tisha B'Av. Those times aside, we should be strictly happy – always.

The Talmud relates that these four great sages continued walking and reached Mount Scopus, overlooking the site of the Holy Temple. They stood there and tore their clothing as a sign of mourning. (This law is still performed today: anyone who views the destroyed site of the Temple after not seeing it for thirty days must make a tear in his clothing, similar to a person mourning for a relative, Heaven forbid).

The sages saw a fox coming out of the place where the Holy of Holies had stood. They began to cry. But Rabbi Akiva, once again, rejoiced and laughed.

"Now what are you happy about?" they asked him.

"And what are you crying about again?" Rabbi Akiva retorted.

"How can we not cry?" they asked. "The place of which it is written 'And the foreigner who nears it will be put to death' now has foxes walking through it – and we shouldn't cry? And you, what are you laughing about?"

Rabbi Akiva said to the sages: "As long as the prophecy of destruction was not fulfilled I was concerned that the prophecy of redemption would also not be fulfilled. But now that the destruction has indeed taken place, we can be sure that the prophecy of Zachariah will also be fulfilled, and there will be a great salvation and complete redemption, happiness and joy for the Jews. That is why I am happy and laughing."

When Rabbi Akiva's friends heard this, they exclaimed: "Akiva, you have comforted us! Akiva, you have comforted us!"

Longing, Not Sadness

Rabbi Akiva shows us how a servant of G-d must look at the world. Everything must be in its proper measure and proper time. Certainly, Rabbi Akiva did not mourn the Temple any less than the other holy sages. But he knew when to cry and when to rejoice. When he did cry, it was not out of ingratitude, sadness nor despair. His tears were tears of longing.

Let's think for a moment. Do we miss the Holy Temple? If we really want to rebuild it, then why do we continue crying?

If we truly lamented the loss of our Holy Temple, it would have already been built. Our sages teach us that if the Holy Temple is not built in our generation, then it's as if it were destroyed in our generation.

How can that be?

Hashem certainly doesn't want the Holy Temple destroyed again, so He won't rebuild it for us until we are worthy. To merit the Holy Temple, we must return to the path of truth and faith. Every person must strive to do his or her part to avoid being an agent of delay in the full redemption of our people, and in the rebuilding of our Holy Temple. We can achieve this by strengthening our emuna and enhancing our gratitude to Hashem for everything He does – the good and the seemingly otherwise.

We can cry justifiable tears because of our sins, which delay the rebuilding of the Holy Temple, or over the painful fact that the Jewish people and the world at large are shrouded in heavy spiritual darkness. But after one has finished crying, he must be happy and shift into a more constructive mode.

Even on Tisha B'Av – when one laments for hours – he must be careful not to fall into the pit of sadness.

By being happy, a person not only strengthens his own emuna, but he also has the ability to help others strengthen themselves as well. In turn, he plays a role in hastening the rebuilding of the Holy Temple.

Their Light Will Guide Us

Nothing could extinguish the fire in Rebbe Natan of Breslev's heart or his yearning for Hashem. Only two things made him cry his eyes out: the destruction of the Holy Temple and the loss of the generation's Tzaddik, the righteous spiritual leader and guide.

On Tisha B'Av, Rebbe Natan would go down to the cellar following the evening prayers, and wouldn't re-emerge until the following afternoon. He would cry incessantly over the destruction of the Temple all night and half the next day.

When Rebbe Nachman passed from this world, Rebbe Natan, his prime disciple, felt the loss of Rebbe Nachman deep in his heart. For him, the death of the tzaddik was comparable to the destruction of the Holy Temple.

It is vital to come close to the tzaddik, whose light is so crucial. The tzaddik of the generation is tantamount to the Moses of the generation; losing the tzaddik is therefore akin to losing Moses.

Rebbe Natan knew the depth of the loss – firsthand - when the tzaddik's light was extinguished. But after he cried and mourned, he moved into a positive, happy and productive mode, devoting his life to spreading the tzaddik's teachings. It is never permissible for a person to be sad, for sadness stems from the "dark side" of spirituality – the antithesis of holiness. Even on Tisha B'Av and during mourning, Heaven forbid, we have no license to align ourselves with the dark side. Sure, we have prescribed times for mourning and weeping, but we shed our tears as an expression of our pain, and not as a result of sadness, G-d forbid.

There are situations in life that cause us pain. We are certainly allowed – even encouraged – to express our pain, especially in personal prayer. But with emuna, we know that Hashem does everything for the best, so we not only accept our pain without sadness, we even thank Hashem for it. We'll elaborate much more on this concept later in this book, G-d willing.

There is no place in Judaism for sadness. A person should not be sad for even one second of his entire life. Sadness is heresy, and a denial of one of the main principles of emuna – the pure and simple belief in Hashem - that everything is for the best and that there is no evil in the world. For in the final accounting, there are no exceptions.

The Honor of G-d

The sin of baseless crying is so terrible that it causes a desecration of Hashem's name and delays the revelation of G-d's monarchy over the world. The spiritual force of impurity known as Amalek conceals G-d's monarchy. Hashem, therefore, commands us to remember this evil influence and eradicate anything that is associated with Amalek. Our sages teach that G-d's throne and G-d's name seemingly lack completion until the memory of Amalek is obliterated.

Any Jew would be delighted to find Amalek and wipe out his name so that G-d's throne and name could be complete. But we must know that in order to obliterate any semblance of Amalek we must first wipe out the ungratefulness within our hearts, because a lack of gratitude stems from Amalek's dark-side spiritual influence!

Ask yourself: How is G-d's monarchy over the world discernable if the Nation of Israel – G-d's nation – is crying and complaining? A king whose nation is dissatisfied with his leadership and despondent – is that the monarchy of G-d, the Almighty and Omniscient? Is that a manifestation of Divine perfection? Of course not! There can be no greater disgrace for the monarchy of Hashem than a sad person. Sadness desecrates His name, Heaven forbid.

When a person is blue, it's as if he does not accept G-d's reign over the world and doesn't agree with His decrees and supremacy. It's as if G-d does not rule the world with justice, for His subjects have complaints. They are not satisfied with their King and disagree with His divine justice.

Who is Just?

A person who does not lovingly accept everything that happens to him in his life in effect makes a statement that he doesn't like the way Hashem governs the world; in other words, he thinks that Hashem treats him unjustly. The Heavenly Court regards such an attitude unfavorably. Accordingly, the Heavenly tribunal opens the files of the disgruntled, despairing or sad person and checks if there is truth to his complaint. Perhaps Hashem really did forget, Heaven forbid, to pay him for something? Perhaps, Heaven forbid, He really did not judge him justly? Merely suspecting Hashem of injustice is both insult and blasphemy.

Before we continue, here is an important spiritual principle to always keep in mind: G-d is always merciful, but the

Heavenly Court judges according to the letter of the law - and with no mercy.

Let's see now what happens to the person who has complained. The Heavenly Court microscopically examines the complainer's file. After much scrutiny, the truth becomes readily apparent in the Heavenly Court: Not only are the person's complaints against G-d unfounded, but the very opposite is true. This person has a substantial slate of outstanding spiritual debts resulting from his transgressions, for which he has not yet been tried because Hashem, in His infinite mercy, has delayed judgment. Hashem has been giving this person multiple chances to rectify himself (which the person has not yet done). When the Heavenly Court discovers this, it tries the person according to the letter of the law, mercilessly demanding punitive measures for every tiny misdeed. Now his troubles really begin.

This is the reason why a person's prayers are ineffective when he cries and complains. All his requests, prayers and supplications return empty-handed. All the Heavenly gates, doors and windows are closed before him. Perhaps an angel is even sent to re-plaster all the walls to ensure that there will not be the slightest crack through which the complainer may get a word in. Everything is completely sealed before him. "You like to cry," the Heavenly Court says to him, "so we will provide you with reasons to keep crying" (Heaven forbid). "Don't worry; we have all the tools necessary to help you cry as much as you want…"

On the other hand, when a person lives his life with gratitude, all the Heavenly gates, doors and windows are open before him. Perhaps an angel is even sent to tear down the walls so that there should not be any hindrance from blocking his thanks from ascending before G-d. "You like to give thanks?" the Heavenly Court says to him. "We will give you plenty to be thankful for. We will make sure that you will not stop praising G-d and giving thanks."

The Notebook

If you would like to see all the good and kindness that G-d bestows upon you and fill your life with thanks, here's a useful suggestion: start a notebook and write down all the kindnesses and small miracles that Hashem does for you. Then, thank Him for every detail that you have recorded. Anybody who does this will be automatically filled with joy. He will discover that life is full of the Creator's kindness and that his notebook is not large enough to record all of the good that G-d sends his way. Furthermore, he will experience more and more miracles and wonders in his life.

With a thankfulness notebook, a person can taste paradise in this world. Hashem forgives all the sins of those grateful people who are happy with their lot and accept everything that happens to them with love. He even forgives those sins that the Torah considers unforgivable. That's not all - a person's willful sins turn into merits because his gratitude brings him to teshuva out of love.

The book **Netivot Olam** states that Hashem forgives the sins of a person who accepts everything that happens to him with happiness and adoration – measure for measure. It's as if G-d says, just as this person accepts the way that I conduct the world with love, so I accept his behavior with love.

G-d is in Our Midst

Gratitude to Hashem completely nullifies the impure spiritual force of Haman and Amalek. The *klipa* of Amalek receives its sustenance when the Jewish people do not accept what happens to them with love. Then it gains the power to torment Israel, Heaven forbid. Our sages say that Amalek is the "whip of rebelliousness" against the Jewish people. When they do not lovingly accept the small amount of bitterness that they have coming to them because of their sins, then they have to suffer much greater bitterness.

What is the root of Amalek? Where did he come from? Amalek appeared when the Children of Israel asked in the desert, "Is G-d in our midst or not?" Such a question is the lowest level of disgrace and ungratefulness. After 50 plagues that befell the Egyptians (or two hundred or two hundred and fifty according to varying opinions in the Passover *Haggadah*), after the giving of the Torah at Mount Sinai - when G-d's voice was heard and phenomenal revelations were experienced - how could they still ask if G-d was in their midst or not?

The Midrash says that as soon as they asked that question, Amalek appeared. Since they lacked faith in G-d, He sent Amalek to attack them so that they would be forced to cry out for His help, and subsequently see once more that He is with them. But on a deeper level, the root of their lack of faith was actually ingratitude.

When a person sees Hashem's good and thanks Him, he actually sees Hashem. He would never think of asking if G-d is there or not. The intrinsic root of Divine concealment is consequently ingratitude.

Recognize Hashem

If a person does not work on being grateful, and if he doesn't have a notebook filled with all of G-d's kindnesses, then instead of seeing G-d through the service of gratitude, he must see G-d through troubles that will necessitate his calling out to Him. The ingrate then only brings pain and suffering to his body and soul.

The Zohar says that if the Nation of Israel had lovingly accepted the decree to wander in the desert for forty years, then immediately at the end of that time, they would have entered the Land of Israel and merited the complete redemption. However, they did not accept the decree with love; instead, they complained and grumbled – and the exile has been lengthened until now.

The same is true for every individual. When a person does not accept his own personal "exile" – his tribulations and low moments - with love, he prolongs his own suffering. But when he accepts his circumstances with love, his troubles vanish, and he also receives wondrous gifts from Above.

Hashem always wants the very best for every person.

Chapter Two:
Miracles and Wonders

Praise and gratitude are the purpose of creation, since true gratitude is the loftiest level that one can attain.

The book **Dibrot Eliyahu** recounts the story of Jacob's battle with Esau's angel. In the morning, the angel said to Jacob: "Let me go, because I must return to Heaven to sing my song of praise."

Jacob responded to the angel: "I will not let you go until you bless me."

And the angel blessed him: "Your name will no longer be Jacob. Instead it will be Israel."

The *Dibrot Eliyahu* then asks: The angel did not bless Jacob, but simply changed his name to Israel. Where is the blessing? He explains that when re-arranged, the Hebrew letters of the word Israel spell *shir-el*, which means *song of G-d*. The angel's blessing was that Jacob would attain the spiritual heights in which he would always be singing to G-d: "In every situation, no matter what will happen, you will sing to G-d. And if you do this, you will be on the loftiest level possible in this world!"

The ultimate purpose of the Nation of Israel is to sing and praise G-d, as is written in Isaiah (43:21): "I have formed this nation for Myself, so that they will tell My praise." In other words, G-d created the Nation of Israel so that they would tell the world about all His wonders, thank Him and praise Him.

For example, we experienced extraordinary miracles in the recent war in Gaza. It is a mitzvah to publicize them. There were many obvious miracles; missiles that missed their marks in ways that cannot be naturally explained. Even the Arabs admitted to this miraculous phenomenon. One of the heads of the Hamas terrorists was asked in an interview how he explains the fact that their missiles did not hit their targets. The terrorist answered: "Listen. Nowadays, you don't have to aim. Everything is automatic and computerized. Our missiles are the most sophisticated around, computerized and equipped with state of the art GPS. All you have to do is put in your coordinates and the missile will fly to its exact destination. But what can we do if the G-d of Israel moved the missiles off their route and protected His children, the Jews?" This was a great sanctification of G-d's Name. All the nations of the world saw that Hashem was fighting for Israel.

Another miracle occurred in a factory in Ashdod. Every time that the air-raid sirens would go off, all the workers would run to a particular room that was considered the safest. During one of the missile attacks, the siren did not work, and the workers did not run to the safe room. That time, the missile hit that very room and completely destroyed it. If the siren had worked, all those workers could have been killed, G-d forbid.

It's great to recount miracles, and there is certainly no lack of miracles to tell. But human nature is such that a person does not experience a true spiritual awakening from stories of miracles that happened to others. If at all, he will experience a spiritual awakening when he personally experiences Divine intervention. Even the impression of miracles that one personally experiences can be diminished by forgetfulness, agnosticism and pessimism - when a person refuses to believe or fails to see the positive side of a given situation.

Why Didn't You Sing Praises?

King David was chosen by to be G-d's anointed, the Moshiach, mainly because he devoted extensive time to prayer and praise of G-d – more time than any other righteous person. That is why King David is called "the pleasant singer of Israel." In his famous Book of Psalms, King David calls upon the entire Nation of Israel and the entire world: "Sing to G-d! Praise Him! Sanctify His Name! Tell of His wonders! Let us go and praise G-d, let us shout for joy to the Rock of our salvation! Let the entire earth shout for joy to G-d!" The entire Book of Psalms is filled with King David's message to all mankind: Sing to G-d, praise Him and thank Him.

Was the time that King David devoted to prayer detrimental to his Torah learning? Certainly not, Heaven forbid. The Talmud testifies that the entire Torah was like an open book before him and that all his decisions in Jewish law became accepted legislation. The Talmud further states that King David learned more Torah in one night than a veteran student can learn in one hundred years! The Midrash relates that King David learned Torah with such devotion that when the Angel of Death came to take his soul, he had to figure out how to get King David to stop his learning, because he could not get near him as long as he was learning Torah. Nevertheless, King David became the Messianic predecessor by virtue of his songs of praise and not in the merit of his Torah learning. His songs of praise testify to his prowess in the inner dimension of the Torah: the ability to know G-d, to thank Him, to praise Him, and to sing to Him.

True Torah is conducive to emuna, enhancing a person's faith and his ability to see G-d's loving-kindness in all events. Building and reinforcing emuna is the ultimate purpose of the Torah. If one's intention in learning Torah doesn't include the desire to enhance his emuna, particularly his emuna in Divine Providence - what is called in Hebrew *hashgacha pratit* - then he is missing the entire point of his Torah study.

During the period of King Hezekiah, Torah study surpassed every other era in Jewish history. However, the Hezekiah-era Torah study did not bring the redemption. This was despite the fact that the men, women, and children of the Nation of Israel in King Hezekiah's time knew the Torah inside and out. However, their learning didn't fuel their emuna nor move them to sing G-d's praises for the huge miracles that they saw, such as the miraculous defeat of the Assyrian army.

Everyone learned Torah in the days of King Hezekiah. The Talmud relates that the Sages of the time searched the entire Land of Israel and could not find one small child who was not an expert on the laws of ritual purification – today considered the most difficult set of laws in all of Judaism! Nowadays, even leading Torah sages don't fully understand all the nuances of ritual purification. When Sancherib came to destroy Jerusalem, King Hezekiah plunged a sword into the ground at the entrance to the Study Hall so that the Jews learning Torah there would not leave. Indeed, Sancherib's entire army was destroyed in a supernatural way, without a single Jew leaving the study hall. Hashem waged the war.

So if the Jews of that time so fiercely clung to the Torah, why didn't the redemption arrive in Hezekiah's days? The Talmud says that G-d wanted to make Hezekiah the Moshiach, His anointed. With all His learning and righteousness, Hezekiah failed to qualify because he did not regularly sing in praise to Hashem!

In light of everything that Hashem did for them, King Hezekiah and the entire Nation of Israel should have sung praises to G-d long before they witnessed the miraculous downfall of Sancherib. And certainly a song of praise was in order on the night that an angel of G-d smote the Assyrian military camp surrounding Jerusalem – all 185,000 Assyrian officers, not to mention all the soldiers under their command. If the Nation of Israel did not sing G-d's praises after such revealed miracles, it was a sure sign that they had still not achieved the ultimate goal – emuna, the pure and complete faith in G-d. They had not yet emerged from the spiritual husk of grievance and ingratitude. Thus, it was impossible to bring the redemption in their time!

Remembering Hashem's Loving-Kindness

A wonderful book called **Chazak V'amatz** explains in the name of the **Sefer Haredim** that recalling G-d's loving-kindness is a positive Torah commandment. Every time that a person recalls an instance of loving-kindness that G-d did for him, he is fulfilling a positive commandment. We learn this from the Torah verse, "And you shall remember the way that Hashem your G-d led you these forty years in the desert...and He fed you the manna, your clothing did not wear out..." (Numbers, 8:2-5). The Torah commands the Jewish people to remember the acts of loving-kindness that G-d performed for us thousands of years ago, when we were in the Sinai desert. G-d shepherded us through the desert and guarded us, gave us manna to eat and led us with complete miracles; He even saw to it that our clothing would not wear out. Not only that, but the children's clothes and sandals would grow with them as a display of Hashem's phenomenal and living Divine Providence.

If we fulfill a positive Torah commandment by remembering the loving-kindness that G-d did for our forefathers thousands of years ago, then certainly when we remember G-d's daily loving-kindness to us in the here and now, we fulfill a positive mitzvah many times over.

Our Sages require us to recite a chapter of Psalms daily that recalls G-d's loving-kindness: "A song of ascent to David, if not for G-d Who is with us?" (Psalms, 124). If not for G-d, where would we be? Israel's very existence is above nature. Certainly our existence in the Land of Israel is way above the laws of nature. Every moment that we live in relative quiet is a great and wondrous miracle. G-d turns the worlds upside down so that the Nation of Israel can have a quiet day.

Every day we must remember that were it not for G-d, as King David said, life would swallow us up. This world would swallow us up alive! Every day that someone remembers Hashem's all-encompassing loving-kindness – not only for the entire Nation of Israel but for each of us individually – and appreciate the myriad of general and personal miracles that He performs for us every second, they fulfill a positive Torah commandment.

Remember and Give Thanks

The Torah commands every Jew to remember ten archetypical Biblical events. Not only are we commanded to remember them, but we must remember the loving-kindness that G-d showered upon us in each of these events and thank Him for it.

The following short commentary on the Ten Remembrances should help us to focus on what miracles to thank G-d for when we recite the verses:

1. **The Exodus from Egypt** – To remember Hashem's loving-kindness and all the miracles and wonders that He performed when He redeemed the Jewish people from slavery, made us a nation, gave us the Torah, and more. The remembrance of the exodus from Egypt is the fundamental remembrance upon which all others and our entire existence as a nation are founded. As such, every person must thank G-d for the exodus from Egypt with all his heart, and then imagine himself being redeemed from Egypt and say to G-d: "Thank You very much, G-d, for taking us out of Egypt. Thank You for splitting the Red Sea for us. Thank You for accompanying us through the desert with the seven clouds of glory. Thank You!"

2. **Shabbat** – We must thank Hashem every day for Shabbat. G-d told Moses, "I have a fine gift stored in My treasure house, and Shabbat is its name, go and tell them (Israel)." We must thank G-d every day for Shabbat and the Jewish holidays. How can we not say thank you for such wonderful gifts? True, we can never thank G-d enough for these gifts, but at least we should be grateful every day.

3. *Manna* – We must thank G-d for the *manna*, the Heaven-sent bread that He fed us in the desert, for the quail and for the well of water that accompanied Israel throughout their desert trek. Not only did the *manna* fall from the heavens to feed Israel on a daily basis, but it also brought abundance down to earth with it. When we thank G-d for the *manna*, we should also thank Him for the sustenance that G-d provides for us every hour of every day. We must

also strengthen ourselves with faith and confidence that it is G-d Who provides our sustenance. We must know that it is G-d's job to provide and man's job to serve Him and if necessary, G-d will once again shower us with *manna* from heaven.

4. **Amalek** - Amalek first attacked Israel when they asked a question that stemmed from ingratitude: "Is G-d in our midst or not?" A person who is not an ingrate sees Hashem's loving-kindness every moment and would never ask such a question. When reciting this remembrance we should focus on belief that G-d protects and watches over us constantly. He is always with us, showering us with His goodness. We should never ask if G-d is in our midst or not. Instead, we should always see His goodness and thank Him for His boundless kindness.

Ingratitude is a manifestation of the dark-side spiritual force of Amalek. The main point of the commandment to remember Amalek is to remember not to be ungrateful and to thank G-d for everything. To erase the memory of Amalek means to erase our ungratefulness and complaints. Every time that we remember Amalek we should focus on not being ungrateful. By blotting out the ingratitude in our character, we blot out Amalek.

5. **Receiving the Torah on Mount Sinai** – We must thank Hashem for the Torah every day! We can never thank G-d enough for the Torah, but at least we should thank Him daily and say: "Thank You, G-d for giving us the holy Torah at Mount Sinai and thank You for the commandments that we receive anew every day."

6. **Angering G-d in the desert, particularly with the Golden Calf** - One way to understand this remembrance

is that we must thank Hashem for His patience, especially for the fact that He did not pour out His wrath upon us, but rather divided the punishment for the Golden Calf into smaller installments. We must also thank G-d for His patience with us now and say: "Thank You, G-d, for Your patience with all my sins and for the fact that You still love me."

The main point of this remembrance is to recall how much we angered G-d with our unnecessary crying and complaints from the very beginning of the redemption from Egypt, as the Torah testifies: "Remember, do not forget how you angered Hashem your G-d in the desert from the day that you left the land of Egypt until you came to this place, you have been rebellious against G-d" (Deuteronomy, 9:7).

7. **Hashem's foiling of Balak and Bilam's plot against our ancestors, so that we may know His righteousness** – Clearly, we must remember G-d's loving-kindness and goodness; how He protects us from our enemies' plots minute by minute, even without our awareness. Balak and Bilam circled the Camp of Israel, looking for a way to carry out their evil plot, while the Nation of Israel did not even know the great danger that it was facing.

With this remembrance in mind, we must thank Hashem, Who alters nature in order to save His nation, as in the desert. Thanks to Divine intervention, neither Balak's sorcery nor Bilam's curses had any effect on Israel.

Surely we must thank the Creator for everything that He does for us every moment, even when we have no idea what our enemies are planning against us. In every generation a new enemy rises to destroy us, and the Holy One, Blessed be He saves us from their grasp.

8. **Miriam the Prophetess in the desert** – We must remember that Hashem gave us our mouths and the power of speech for the purpose of thanking Him, as it is written: "I have formed this nation for Myself, so that they may tell My praise" (Isaiah, 43:21). Immediately before reciting the *Amidah* prayer, we say: "G-d, open my lips so that my mouth may tell of your praises." We certainly do not want Hashem to open our lips and mouths so that we can complain, cry and speak ill of others.

9. **G-d gives us strength to succeed** – We must thank Hashem for all of our successes in every facet of our lives. We must not be ungrateful or arrogant, thinking that our achievements are due to our personal prowess.

10. **Jerusalem** – We must remember why Jerusalem was destroyed - the needless crying that resulted in the destruction of the two Holy Temples – for which we still cry to this very day.

In summary, all the remembrances teach us to develop our gratitude. If we remember all the kindness that Hashem performed for our ancestors, we will certainly remember the kindness that He has performed for each one of us individually. We can also add our own personal remembrances and thank Him daily for significant blessings in our lives. For example, a husband can thank G-d for his wife, the wife for her husband, both of them for their parents, their children, and their rabbi, and so forth.

For fifteen years, the Seer from Lublin spent an hour a day thanking G-d for bringing the soul of his mentor Rabbi Elimelech of Liszansk down to this world. Fifteen years!

We must thank G-d all day long for the tzaddikim who bring us close to Him. When I heard this story about the Seer from Lublin, may his blessed memory intercede on our behalf, it became even clearer to me how much we must thank Hashem for the tzaddikim who illuminate our path.

Love Your Neighbor as Yourself

The entire Torah is filled with ethics that teach us how to rid ourselves of selfishness and pride, and instead attain humility. The Talmud tells of a non-Jew who wanted to convert. He came to Rabbi Hillel requesting that he teach him the entire Torah while standing on one leg. Rabbi Hillel replied that the main rule of the Torah is, "What is hateful to you, do not do to your friend." A person hates when others deny all the good that he has done for them. The Torah detests ingratitude. We must remember any and all favors that others do for us and express our gratitude for them.

A person's prime effort toward self-improvement should focus on shedding selfishness and learning to think about others. Rabbi Akiva said, "Love your neighbor as yourself – this is a main rule in the Torah." In other words, a main rule of the Torah is to avoid selfishness.

The Obligation of Thanks

The first word that a person utters when he wakes up in the morning is 'thanks': "I give thanks before You, living and eternal King, that You have returned my soul to me with compassion; great is Your faithfulness." Just as we begin our day with thanks, we should continue our entire day with thanks. The words "thank you" should be at the tip of our tongues all day. We should end our day with thanks, as well.

Giving thanks is not optional. It is compulsory! This is reflected in the text of our daily prayers: "Therefore we are obligated to thank you." "Therefore it is the obligation of all creatures before you, Hashem our G-d…to thank and praise…" Giving thanks is an obligation!

Many people learn about thanking G-d and do not understand just how fundamental it should be in our lives. They think that saying thank-you is just good manners or the honorable thing to do. But it's much more! Giving thanks is a primary obligation and the way to establish a true connection with the Creator. Every person must contemplate daily all the blessings that G-d bestows on him, and then express our thanks profusely.

Important Reminders

The morning preliminary prayer service begins with the *L'olam* prayer, which contains important reminders that we should carry in our hearts all day long:

A person should always fear Heaven in private as in public…

When a person is with others, he is more apt to act like a completely righteous person. But when he is at home – well, that's a different story altogether. As soon as he leaves his friends and enters his home, he completely changes. In this prayer, G-d reminds us that our behavior in private should reflect at least as much fear of Heaven as our public behavior.

And admit the truth and speak truth in his heart, and arise early and say: "Master of the Universe, we do not rely on our righteousness as we lay our supplications before You, but on Your great mercy."

A person with a morsel of integrity admits the obvious: he deserves nothing. He relies only on the mercy of the Creator for health, sustenance, and everything else in life. Truth and humility go together, for as soon as a person casts his arrogance aside, he realizes, "What are we, what are our lives worth, what is our righteousness, what is our strength, what is our bravery…"

For all the brave are as naught before You,

The mightiest heroes are powerless against Hashem during their lifetimes, and even more so after they pass on to the cemetery.

And the famous are as if they never existed,

So many famous people are like a splash in a bucket - while they're alive, they make waves, but once they're no longer here, they're completely forgotten.

And the wise men as if they have no knowledge and the people of understanding as if they have no intelligence, for all their deeds are emptiness

As long as a person is not seeking or involved in his or her ultimate purpose, everything is emptiness. It is all meaningless. A brave person is nothing, a famous person is as if he never existed, and all the smart and wise people are as if they have no knowledge or intelligence. But once a person is seeking, or involved in, his ultimate purpose, everything takes on great importance. We see with our own eyes how the memory of Torah scholars lives on, how people tell stories about them and study the books that they authored. We never forget them. They are still alive in our midst. The Gemara says that their lips move in their graves every time that we quote them.

Only the life of a person who is not seeking or involved in his ultimate purpose can be considered meaningless, as the prayer continues:

Because the superiority of a person over an animal is naught –

There is no difference between a person and an animal. Actually, an animal's situation is much better, because it lives without worries. Did you ever see a lion working as a welder or a horse driving a bus? Did you ever see a tiger reserving a wedding hall or a giraffe worried about paying his bills? A person who is not seeking or involved in his true mission in life, yet seeks only the amenities of the material world would be much happier as a worry-free animal…

Because there is no advantage to a man over an animal, because everything is nothingness,

A person who lives for the inconsequential pleasure-seeking material world - which all is meaningless – lives a life that is not only no better than the life of an animal, but is actually worse. He wastes physical and emotional efforts trying to attain inconsequential amenities that have nothing to do with his true purpose in life. An animal, at least, does what it is supposed to do.

However, a person who lives to fulfill his purpose in this world, who lives for his soul, is in a completely different place. As the prayer continues:

Except for the pure soul, which is destined to give an accounting before Your throne of glory!

The pure soul will give an accounting of all its deeds. It is eternal and has no connection to the nothingness of this world. After we have asserted that this world is nothingness, we once again thank G-d for our lives in this world:

But we are Your nation, the children of Your covenant, the children of Abraham, who loved You, to whom You vowed on Mount Moriah; the seed of Your son, Isaac, who was bound on the altar; the congregation of Your chosen son Jacob, who, because of the love that You loved him and the joy that You rejoiced in him, You called his name Israel and Yeshurun...

Because our lives have a purpose, they are a cherished gift for which we must certainly thank G-d. This leads us to the next part of the prayer:

Thus we are obligated to thank You and praise You and glorify You and give praise and thanks to Your Name,

We are obligated! The prayer does not say, "What a good idea to thank You," or "It is worthy to thank You." It is not a recommendation – it is an obligation!

We say every morning in the preliminary prayers: "Thus we are obligated to thank You and praise You and glorify You and give praise and thanks to Your Name. How fortunate we are, how good is our lot and how pleasant our fate." How fortunate we are that early in the morning and at night we are in the synagogues and study halls and twice daily say with love: "Hear o Israel, Hashem is our G-d, Hashem is One!"

A Paper Cup

As soon as we recognize our ultimate purpose and contemplate the spiritual gifts that Hashem has given us, we realize that we must thank G-d. Without His spiritual gifts, it would be irrelevant to say that we are obligated to thank Him, since nothing will remain of the physical portion of our lives. If all the abundance that G-d gives a person would be strictly material and relevant to this world, then we would thank Him a bit for our daily sustenance. Just as there's a major difference between a disposable cup and an heirloom silver goblet, we are obligated far more to thank Hashem for our souls and the spiritual side of our lives than we are for the material side of our lives, which is ever so temporary like a paper cup.

Every success in this world is frivolity. Take the greatest people in this world, like a renowned statesman, a famous genius, or a vastly wealthy corporate magnate – as soon as their time on earth is up, they are no better than a disposable paper cup. Nothing will remain of them.

How many people remember the anniversary of the deaths of national leaders? Does anybody light a candle for them, pray at their graves or quote them? On the other hand, we still remember and long for the tzaddikim. After hundreds or even thousands of years, they are still alive – even more alive than when they were in the flesh. The holy Zohar writes that after his death, a tzaddik is more involved in this world than when he was physically alive. The Talmud also states that tzaddikim are greater after they die than when they are alive.

I was in Morocco at the graves of ancient tzaddikim. People still frequent their resting places regularly and care well for them. They feel the presence of the tzaddik at their gravesites, and they pray and learn the tzaddik's Torah teachings there. Their prayers are answered – not just on the anniversary of the tzaddik's death, but all year round.

A Point of Gratitude

Looking at the beautiful spiritual gifts in this world, we realize that we have so much to live for and so much to be thankful for. Our obligation of thanks to Hashem is therefore much more than good manners or proper etiquette.

A young married man who lived in a non-observant community once came to ask my advice. He was overcome with sadness. He asked me: "What can I do to change my life?"

"First of all, work on being happy," I said to him. When I saw the astonished expression on his face, I understood that he didn't believe that he could be happy in his situation. So I showed him some of the good points in which he can rejoice: "Thank G-d, you observe Shabbat and you don't eat *chametz* (leavened products) on Pesach. You built a *succah* this past Succot, and you put on *tefillin* this morning – you should be jumping for joy!" Every tiny mitzvah, every miniscule spiritual endeavor, each and every syllable of Torah learned, and a single word of prayer is a reason to rejoice, especially when considering the unimaginable rewards that such spiritual endeavors earn. As such, we are truly obliged to thank G-d for the wonderful opportunities He gives us to serve Him and to perfect our souls by way of the Torah and mitzvot.

In their prayers, the Sephardim also add: "We are obligated to sing praises before You." We are obligated to sing to G-d! This is no nuance, for very Shabbat, we all recite the moving *Nishmat Kol Chai* prayer, which says: "For it is the obligation of the created being to sing praise before You." This reminds us that we're not doing G-d a favor by saying "thank You," as if it were some act of special devotion or piety on our part. Indeed, gratitude is the bare minimum repayment for the myriad of blessings that we enjoy each moment.

Good Points

This leads us to a new idea that we must fully internalize: Rebbe Nachman writes (Likutei Moharan, I:282) that a person must identify his own good points and rejoice in them. He must search for every meritorious deed that he performed and be happy about it.

In the *Nishmat* prayer we say: "For it is the obligation of all created beings before You to give thanks." There is an obligation to thank, praise and glorify G-d. Thus, Rebbe Nachman's advice to look for our own good points is more than a simple recommendation. It is also an obligation. We should realize that every meritorious deed that we have performed is a gift from G-d! We are subsequently obligated to thank Him and rejoice in the good deed that He has enabled us to do.

The Basics

Gratitude guards us against taking our many blessings for granted. We must therefore accustom ourselves to thanking G-d for every tiny blessing in our lives that might seem routine, but is actually the product of Divine Providence and G-d's infinite compassion. In this way, faith and gratitude purify and uplift our hearts.

The Silent *Amidah* Prayer says: "We thank you and tell your praises - for our lives that are in Your hands…" This is general thanks for our lives. "And for our souls that are deposited with You." This is thanks for our souls, deposited in the hands of G-d, as King David writes in the Bok of Psalms, "In Your hands I deposit my spirit." After that, we thank G-d specifically for all His daily miracles: "And for Your miracles that are with us daily." G-d does miracles every day, for everybody. It is our job to look for those miracles, thank G-d for them, write them down in a notebook so that we will remember them, and repeatedly thank Him for them. Recognizing and acknowledging Hashem's acts of loving-kindness are the basics of gratitude. Next we say: "And for Your wonders and goodness at all times, evening, morning and noon." We have reasons to thank G-d at every moment. We must teach and accustom ourselves to thank G-d for every detail of our lives, literally at every moment, never taking His loving-kindness for granted.

The truth is that the Creator is the Master of the World and everything we have is really His. He gives us the tools we need to perform our task in this world, and He gives us the ability to use those tools. Hashem could easily not supply us with those tools, or not give us the ability to use them. If a person uses someone else's belongings, he must thank the owner for their use. Since the Almighty is the Owner of all the world's belongings, we must thank Him for everything we have. A person who fails to thank G-d or believes that any given item actually belongs to him is living in a spiritual state of heresy, theft and falsehood. Every time we use any of the material possessions at our disposal, we must remember well that we are using something that Hashem has loaned us. Consequently, He deserves our thanks.

For example, when we turn on the faucet to wash our hands, we should thank G-d for the fact that there is a faucet with running water and that we don't have to draw water from the well in the backyard or from the river half a mile away. Since when is the convenience of running water in our own home something we should take for granted? How about clothes in the closet? If every husband thanked his wife for each ironed shirt, there wouldn't be marital problems in the world.

Thanking Hashem with a general "thanks for the clothing" isn't sufficient. We should really thank Him for every item – every shirt, trousers, sweater, blouse, skirt, and pair of shoes – nothing is too small or insignificant. When your feet are cold and wet in the dead of winter from walking in a snowstorm without boots or protective covering on your shoes, you know what a blessing a dry pair of socks can be. Why take them for granted? Such is the mindset of constant gratitude to Hashem.

Rebbe Nachman of Breslev worked on the attribute of gratitude even as a child. At mealtime, he wouldn't limit himself to the mandatory blessing before eating each type of food. In addition, he'd thank Hashem for every individual item: "Thank You, G-d, for the cucumber, thank You, G-d, for the tomato, thank You, G-d, for the cheese," and so forth.

What's wrong with a nice general "thank You, Hashem"? Why did Rebbe Nachman painstakingly thank Hashem for every individual item? General thanks are of course important, but they don't enhance our tangible feeling of Hashem's magnificent Divine Providence. General thanks leave us with general, abstract faith. But when we thank G-d for every detail, we really begin to feel Hashem's Divine Providence and His personal intervention in every facet of our lives. Consequently, we learn to recognize that even the most mundane items and events in our lives are none other than Hashem's loving Divine Providence over us.

Don't Be Lazy

When someone studies a subject, action must supplement theory. Optimally, one should first do an hour of personal prayer every day, half of which should be devoted to asking Hashem to learn true gratitude.

Next, make yourself a "miracle notebook." Carry around a pocket-size notepad and write down all the many miracles – big and small - that you see daily. This is very conducive to developing spiritual awareness because it accustoms a person to pay attention to G-d's wonderful Divine Providence and personal intervention in every phase of daily life. The more one thanks G-d for the miracles that He performs, the more one sees miracles, which will increase in frequency and strength. In no time, you will have filled up many miracle notebooks - reading the day's entries every night before you go to bed and thanking Hashem for the day's miracles will fill your heart with joy.

Here are a few examples of typical entries in miracle notebooks:

• You're driving on the freeway and the fuel gauge hits empty. The warning light goes on and you know that you only have two gallons of fuel left, which will suffice for another twenty miles or so. The nearest gas station is thirty-five miles away. You make it to the gas station.

• You suddenly realize that you accidentally put the wrong spice in the dish that you're preparing, and it comes out to be the tastiest thing you've ever cooked.

• You're driving in the middle lane during rush hour. A careless driver swerves into your lane, and there's nowhere to escape, since there are cars to the left and to the right of you. You slam on the brakes and brace for a collision, which amazingly and inexplicably never happens…

- For months, you've been trying to finalize an important deal that would have earned you a handsome commission. The deal falls through and you're left with nothing to show for all your hard work. A few days later, with no effort or initiative of your own, you get a phone call from Japan; in one hour, you seal a deal twice as large.

Undoubtedly, you have plenty of your own daily miracles.

Hashem leads a person on the path that he himself chooses. **When we choose to see the miracles and wonders that Hashem does for us, He shows us even more miracles and wonders.** The book **Peleh Yoetz** tells us that if a person experiences a miracle and sings a song of praise to Hashem, he gets another miracle as a reward, in accordance with what King David says in Psalm 50: "He who offers thanksgiving honors Me...I will show him the salvation of G-d." When a person says thank You, G-d shows him more and more salvation.

The holy Alshich cites the verse in Psalm 63, "Because Your loving-kindness is better than life, my lips will praise You," and explains that when we see G-d's loving-kindness and thank Him for it, we have enjoyed something that is better than life!

Take Nothing for Granted

Don't think that there is anything too small for which to thank Hashem. One of my students, having thanked Hashem profusely for a seemingly small favor, told me the following personal story:

One day he drove into a parking lot. The attendant was friendly and smiled at him. This student immediately thanked G-d: "Thank You G-d that this parking attendant smiled at me." Afterwards, he began to wonder if he wasn't getting carried away with thanking G-d. After all, the attendant was just being polite, or so he thought, and then he forgot about the entire incident.

The next day he had to park again in the same parking lot. The attendant suddenly got angry at him and began to shout at him and curse him for the way he parked. The student understood that this was a message from G-d for the doubt that he had entertained the previous day. He understood that it is not eccentric to thank G-d for the courteousness of others, for they can certainly act otherwise…

From this story we can learn to thank G-d for everything. We simply have to accustom ourselves to say thank you, just like we teach a child to say thank you. If you accustom yourself to thanking G-d for every small detail, you will get tremendous gratification. Gratitude is a lofty means of serving G-d that leads us to faith in Divine Providence, uprooting the heresy and ingratitude that conceal G-d's loving-kindness.

The Value of Giving Thanks for Everything

When a person gets used to thanking Hashem for everything, he overcomes the spiritual force of impurity known as the *klipa* (spiritual impurity) of Haman-Amalek. Haman was the greatest ingrate who ever lived. Since creation and until our own times, there was never a person upon whom G-d showered so much kindness and abundance as the ungrateful and wicked Haman, may his name be blotted out. G-d gave him fabulous wealth and 208 sons. All the citizens of King Ahashverosh's empire bowed down to him. He wore the king's royal ring and could make decrees at will. Yet he was neither grateful nor satisfied.

Haman exemplified just how much of an ingrate he was after Mordechai the Jew would not bow down to him. He gathered his family and friends and enumerated his great wealth and belongings, his plethora of sons and how there was nobody in the entire kingdom as honored as he. "The king has promoted me to the most important position in the empire," he boasted, "I actually rule over the entire world and even Queen Esther invited me to a royal feast with just her and the king. But all this is worthless to me because there is one Jew who doesn't bow down before me."

This is the epitome of the evil husk of ingratitude: as soon as something doesn't go as a person desires, he denies all the kindness that G-d did for him in the past and does for him at every moment. He essentially echoes Haman; because something did not work out for him, everything is worthless – all of Hashem's loving-kindness, all His goodness – they are all worth nothing because Haman – and those like him – didn't get exactly what they wanted.

The redemption hinges on gratitude to G-d. The long exile has been decreed upon us because of our ancestor's needless crying in the desert continues endlessly – not because of our ancestor's crying – but because of ours! We are still crying! If we stop crying and begin to thank G-d again and again, the redemption will come immediately. Even now, when some still cry and complain, those who begin thanking G-d will experience their own personal redemption.

Sing to Him

In his commentary on the Torah, Nachmanides writes that the entire purpose of the creation is so that the created beings will know their Creator and thank Him. Rebbe Nachman says (Likutei Moharan, II:2) that the greatest pleasure of the

World to Come is thanksgiving, since the Talmud says that in the future all the sacrifices will be nullified except for the sacrifice of thanksgiving.

The Hebrew word for Jews – *Yehudim* – means "those who give thanks." Thanking Hashem is our national spiritual task. The very essence of a Jew is thanksgiving. For this reason, when the Nation of Israel does not thank G-d, but instead whines and complains, stern judgments are awakened from Above. The Torah in the book of Deuteronomy states that the terrible troubles plaguing Israel are "Because you did not serve G-d, your G-d, with joy and good-heartedness." Even if a person stringently fulfills all the mitzvot - but without joy and a happy heart - he'll likely encounter severe tribulations. In the laws of *lulav*, Maimonides brings the above verse as proof that one who fails to serve Hashem happily is an ingrate who is deserving of punishment.

The Sound of Music

Please note, dear reader, that all the blessings and verses of praise in our liturgy are designed to accustom us and remind us – in the darkness of our physical world – that our entire purpose is to thank G-d, praise Him, sing to Him and glorify Him.

A person must sing to G-d, and even play music before Him if he can! Song brings enjoyment to every word of prayer, as does singing the blessings and verses of praise in a melody that encourages, inspires, and gladdens the heart. A person should also sing the Silent Prayer to oneself, since this enhances one's intent and joy, which are ever so conducive to effective prayer. Rebbe Nachman says (Likutei Moharan, I:42) that by singing in prayer, all harsh judgments are mitigated:

"'And He saw their sorrow when He heard their song' (Psalms, 106). Behold, through playing music, the severe judgments are sweetened. As the holy Zohar writes (Pinchas, 215): 'The rainbow is G-d's Divine Presence and the three colors of the rainbow are the (three) forefathers, and they are garments of G-d's Divine Presence. And when G-d's Divine Presence (the *Shechinah*) clothes herself in garments of light then "And I will see it to remember the eternal covenant" (Genesis, 9) and then "the anger of the King subsided" (The Scroll of Esther). This is like a king who became angry at his son, and when he saw the queen in garments of light he had mercy on his son.'"

The letters of prayer are G-d's Divine Presence, as is written in Psalms 51, "G-d, open my lips." The faculty of speech parallels G-d's Name, *A-donai*, which is the Name of G-d in this verse. *A-donai* is called a bow, as Rashi explains Jacob's words in Genesis 58, "with my sword and my bow" as referring to his prayers. The sound of music is the three colors of the rainbow. The voice contains the elements of fire, water and wind, which parallel the three Forefathers. The three Forefathers are the three shades of light in the rainbow. G-d's promise to look at the rainbow and remember His eternal covenant not to destroy the world with water, "And I will see it to remember the eternal covenant," is actually an allusion to the merit of the Forefathers.

A person who sings the letters of prayer in purity and clarity envelops G-d's Divine Presence - the letters - in garments of light. G-d sees the Divine Presence and his "anger subsides." This explains Rashi's commentary on the verse in Psalms 106 "when He heard their song." Rashi comments that G-d heard the song of Israel in the merit of our Forefathers. The song, which is the three shades of the rainbow, was sung with great clarity and purity, because the three colors of the rainbow are the Forefathers, as explained above. And they are the garments of G-d's Divine Presence. When the garments are alight with purity and clarity, this is called "the merit of the Forefathers." Then, "And I will see it to remember the eternal covenant" and then "And He decided not to punish them, in His great loving kindness" (Psalms 106), "And the wrath of the King dissipated" and the severe judgments are sweetened.

Music, especially prayer set to song, has phenomenal power in stimulating one's heart to yearn for Hashem. Rebbe Nachman's disciple Rebbe Natan would travel in a closed carriage while devoting himself to Torah study and prayer on the way. Once, his student Rebbe Shimon accompanied him. Rebbe Natan began to recite the morning prayers heavily, as if he were depressed, and then gradually began humming a happy tune. His joy steadily increased until he reached a level of tremendous enthusiasm. He sang to Hashem with such irresistible sweetness that the non-Jewish villagers along the way stopped working and began to chase after the wagon, yearning to hear the wondrous melody emanating from within it.

When Rebbe Natan reached the *Amida* - the Silent Prayer - he was so immersed in a state of clinging to G-d that his students had to remove him from the wagon on their hands and stand him before the wall of the wayside inn so that he could pray.

As they continued their journey, Rebbe Shimon asked his rabbi what had happened. Why was he deep in negativity at the beginning of his prayers, and how was he able to strengthen himself and become so joyous and enthusiastic?

Rebbe Natan answered: "At the beginning of my prayers, feelings of negativity and terrible sadness engulfed me.

Then I remembered what Rebbe Nachman said, that a person should revitalize himself with a song of joy – especially during prayer. So, I began to sing a joyous tune until I could say the rest of my prayers with tremendous joy."

A Truly Great Wonder

It's difficult to understand how prayer, composed of poetic songs of praise many of which King David wrote, is generally recited quickly and monotonously. The person praying does not even notice that he is contradicting himself. Here he is, calling upon the world to sing to G-d: "Thank G-d! Call out in His Name! Tell the nations of His deeds! Sing to Him! Tell of His wonders!" However, he himself does not sing to G-d, for either he lacks intent or his mind is wandering thousands of miles away.

We call upon the world and declare: "All the world, applaud Hashem!" Do we applaud Hashem ourselves, or hastily mumble the words of the prayers? Every day during the week we say, "Serve G-d with joy!" Can we pass the test of joyous prayer? It is downright hypocrisy to call upon the entire world to pray with joy when we don't do so ourselves.

If we would sing the blessings and Psalms that we say daily and happily give thanks and song to G-d, all the troubles and exiles would be nullified and the redemption would come. All the our hardships, illnesses, and tribulations come from lack of joy, thanksgiving and song. Our own lack of enthusiasm in the service of Hashem awakens the greatest accusations against us, Heaven forbid.

Write the Song

One who strives for perfection in prayer must of course learn Torah and do his utmost to observe its commandments. Yet the ultimate goal of Torah and mitzvot is to bring a person to the level of absolute gratitude to Hashem, where he constantly and joyfully praises His name.

As such, a person should also sing his Torah learning. The Torah itself is called *song*, as the Book of Deuteronomy says, "Write this song down in a book." Every person should find the melody that suits his Torah learning, his blessings, his Psalms, and his prayers.

The Prominence of Song

Rebbe Natan writes in a number of places in **Likutei Halachot** about the power of song and the lofty spiritual source from where it emanates. In the Laws of Marital Relations, law 4, he writes:

"The main point of clinging and closeness to G-d is with voices that are the aspect of the ten types of song. All the sounds in the world are included in these ten types of song. These sounds are the main channel through which Israel becomes closer to their Father in Heaven. All the prayers, songs, praises, supplications, requests, admissions of guilt and words of endearment and appeasement, and all the conversations that a person speaks between him and his Maker in personal prayer, etc., are all included in the ten types of song, which are the ten utterances with which the Book of Psalms was said. As our Sages say, 'with a song of praise, triumph,' etc."

Rebbe Nachman explains (Likutei Moharan, I: 205) that the ten chapters of Psalms in the *Tikkun Klali* are a rectification for nocturnal emissions.

The Book of Psalms includes all the different types of prayers and supplication. Most of the Book of Psalms is compiled of intense entreaties to G-d, beseeching Him to help and fulfill our requests, and to bring us out of the depths of our worldly lusts and frivolity. Side by side with these supplications, King David's Psalms are abounding with song and praise of G-d.

And all these holy paths and trails of the Book of Psalms are parallel to the ten different types of song. These different types of song are aspects of and represented by the different opening words of the various chapters of Psalms. They include all the supplications, songs and praises that the entire Nation of Israel – wherever they may be – sings to G-d. The main way to achieve closeness with G-d is through prayer, as Rebbe Nachman writes in Likutei Moharan (II: 84), "Know, that the main closeness and clinging of Israel to G-d is through prayer. We see, then, that the main closeness and clinging of Israel to G-d is through the holy voices of song, praise, prayers and supplications…melodies and music."

Study

The main subject of Torah study that fosters thanksgiving is the study of faith. Rebbe Nachman writes (Likutei Moharan, II: 2) that the main pleasure of the World to Come is thanksgiving and studying Jewish law, for through them a person becomes closer to G-d. The study of Jewish law has two aspects: one is the study of the simple meaning of the laws so that a person knows what he should and should not be doing. Observing Hashem's commandments and knowing how to fulfill them properly helps us know G-d more and more. For this reason, Rebbe Nachman said that a person is obligated to study Jewish law daily and that if a day goes by without the study of Jewish law, that day cannot be rectified. Elijah the Prophet promises that whoever studies Jewish law daily will merit the World to Come.

The second aspect of study of Jewish law is the study of the laws of emuna. Emuna enables us to traverse this world with inner peace and guides us on the path of returning to Hashem. We learn emuna from the true tzaddik, the righteous spiritual guide in each generation, who teaches us how to truly serve Hashem.

See the Abundance

King David cried to G-d, "Do not hide Your countenance from me!" G-d's "countenance" is His attribute of mercy and the abundance and loving-kindness with which He showers the world. King David asked G-d to never stop His mercy and loving-kindness. He beseeched Hashem to reveal His countenance and shower him with mercy, goodness and blessing. King David pleaded: "Do not hide Your countenance from me" – please Hashem, do not conceal Your mercy from me. Let me feel and see it.

Redemption of the World

A number of our Sages wrote that they hope not to be alive in the days that herald the Moshiach, since it will be a period of evil decrees and troubles. Rebbe Elimelech of Liszansk commented, "I am surprised at our Sages. With their holy sense of foresight, they were able to see the troubles in the days of Moshiach – but they didn't see that the soul of Rebbe Elimelech of Liszansk would come down to the world!"

Now we can express the same idea: Our Sages saw the troubles of the days of Moshiach – but they didn't see Rabbi Shalom Arush's CD **Stop Crying**! They didn't see this book! If they had seen them, they would have known that it is possible to bring Moshiach with smiles, thanksgiving, song and praise. They wouldn't have feared the days of Moshiach.

A life filled with thanks to Hashem will certainly bring salvation to the world and mitigate all harsh judgments. This must be the main focus of our service of G-d. We must uproot all complaining and ingratitude and work on expressing our thanks and praise to Hashem, thus hastening the complete redemption of our people. Redemption depends on gratitude and expressing our thanks. Life can be easy and pleasant – if we only learn to thank G-d.

Chapter Three:
It's All for the Best

Rebbe Nachman, of blessed memory, writes (Abridged Likutei Moharan, I:21): "All troubles, suffering, exiles, and all the lacking that a person feels, whether it is in financial income, or children, or physical health, etc. - all this only comes to a person according to their lack of spiritual awareness. And when a person perfects his spiritual awareness, then all of his shortcomings will be compensated for, as Rebbe Matla says, 'If you have acquired knowledge, then what are you lacking? And if you lack knowledge, then what have you acquired?'"

Rebbe Nachman did not write that only *certain* troubles come from a lack of spiritual awareness; he explains clearly that **all** troubles and **all** suffering come from a lack of spiritual awareness - literally! All exiles, as well as the tribulations of exile, are proportionate to a person's lack of spiritual awareness. Therefore, when we hone our spiritual awareness, we compensate for whatever we lack in life.

When a person perfects his emuna through the belief that everything is from Hashem and everything is for the best (in other words, true spiritual awareness), then he will never experience any pain, suffering, deficiency, or negative emotion.

The Greatest Gifts

Rebbe Nachman states (Likutei Moharan, I:65): "A person should know that this concept, the concept of 'One,' is an aspect of the world's very purpose. The prophet Zechariah (ch. 14) writes:

'On that day, Hashem will be One and His name will be One.'"

Our Sages refer to this quote from Zachariah and ask, "Is Hashem not One now? (Of course He is!) However, right now in this world we say the blessing 'Hashem is the true judge,' when something seemingly bad occurs, and we say the blessing, 'Hashem is good and does good' when something seemingly good occurs. However, in the future of 'that day,' everyone will bless on everything, 'Hashem is good and does good'" (Pesachim, 50).

Rebbe Nachman continues, "So it turns out that the concept of 'One' is the ultimate goal, and that goal is all good, since the purpose is only good. Even all the trials and tribulations and bad things that a person experiences, Heaven forbid - if he looks at the ultimate goal, then certainly they are not bad things at all – rather, they are great gifts! Without a doubt, all tribulations come intentionally from Hashem for a person's good, whether He sent these occurrences to remind a person to do teshuva, or whether to cleanse his sins. So, it turns out that all tribulations are actually great gifts, for Hashem's intent is certainly only for the good. If a person looks at all the negatives and difficulties that he has with this ultimate purpose in mind, i.e. the intent of the Almighty, he won't feel that he has any tribulations at all! Rather, he'll feel happy from the great gift that he will understand is the goal of these tribulations!"

Pay attention to what Rebbe Nachman writes - that all tribulations are great gifts. Not just "gifts" but "great gifts"! For example, when the Holy One, blessed be He, gives a person one hundred thousand dollars, this is a small gift. And when Hashem takes from him one million dollars, this is really a "great gift"! Sound ridiculous? Let's learn more.

Good News

When a person acquires the spiritual awareness that everything Hashem does is for his ultimate welfare and benefit, then he is able to make the blessing "Hashem is good and does good" on everything that happens to him. After Moshiach comes, when this knowledge will be easy to attain, we will no longer say the blessing: "Blessed is the true judge;" we will only say "Blessed is Hashem who is good and does good." With that in mind, here is a hypothetical example of a phone conversation after the full redemption:

The phone rings and Alan answers.

"Hello?"

"Hello."

"Yes, what can I help you with?"

"Your name is Alan?"

"Yes."

"We wanted to let you know that your ship has sunk…"

"Really? Thank You so much Hashem! Thank you, Sir, for this happy news!"

Alan begins to dance euphorically, and recites the blessing, "Blessed are You, our Lord, King of the universe, who is good and does good!" with much delight. Afterward, he puts on a lavish Gratitude Party, to which he invites the entire city.

When all the guests arrive, they ask, "What are we celebrating?"

Alan answers, "I made this party because my ship sunk, and all my possessions went down to the depths, and I am left without a red cent!"

When they all hear this explanation, no one is astonished. They all have the spiritual awareness that everything that occurs is for the very best, and that we bless on EVERYTHING "Hashem is good and does good."

The guests praise Alan, saying, "How fortunate are you! Blessed is Hashem! Thank G-d! How great it is that you have no more money. There is nothing better! How awesome is Hashem! Blessed is the good and Giver of good. Everything Hashem does is for the good. Give thanks!"

The above scenario seems totally bizarre to a person who believes there is evil in the world. But after Moshiach comes, everyone will realize that there is no such thing as evil or bad, so it will be completely normal to react like Alan and his friends.

We don't have to wait until Moshiach's arrival to understand right now that there is no evil in the world, and to give thanks to Hashem for everything.

A young man who became Torah-observant from our classes approached me and shared the following: "I have good news for you, Rabbi. They fired me at work! Now I'll have more time for *hitbodedut* (personal prayer). I thank Hashem for His loving-kindness! And I believe that whatever comes my way is for the very best."

This happened just when the young man was beginning to become observant. He had recently started attending classes and listening to our CDs, and here he was, already happy and thankful to Hashem for losing his job. If he would not have acquired this spiritual awareness, who knows what would have happened to him? He most likely would have come to me crying and complaining.

Saying "Hashem is good and does good" for everything that occurs, and giving thanks for it all, is truly the light of Moshiach. With spiritual awareness, we know that whatever Hashem does is for our ultimate good; therefore, we can thank Him for everything He does for us, whether or not we see the good in it. A person lacks joy and gratitude not because the reality isn't to his liking, but rather because he lacks spiritual awareness and emuna.

Giving Thanks is Salvation

The Gemara (Tractate Taanit, 8) tells us, "Rebbe Yehoshua Ben Levi says, 'All who accept their tribulations with joy bring salvation to the world.'" When a person accepts suffering with love and believes that the suffering is from Above, and thanks Hashem, he brings salvation not only to himself, but to the entire world as well.

This is an amazing and inspirational lesson that builds on what we have learned previously, namely, that a person who always says thank you saves himself. For truly, according to this Gemara the person who accepts his suffering with love brings salvation to the entire world– in his merit! This merit stems from the fact that he faced his suffering with joy.

Therefore, we must constantly strengthen ourselves in the path of recognizing that everything is good, that there is no evil in the world, and that everything Hashem does is always good. This is the true path of teshuva, and what is called *teshuvat hamishikal* – complete teshuva on the great sin of the mind believing that there is destruction and evil in the world.

No More Pain

We quoted Rebbe Nachman earlier as saying, "All bad things and suffering that a person goes through, G-d forbid…" Why did he say "G-d forbid" if everything is truly good?

Suffering is intended to arouse a person to seek Hashem, although Hashem prefers that a person seek Him on his own accord. A self-starter can attain spiritual awareness without any suffering or pain. However, when Hashem sees that a person remains in deep spiritual slumber, He sends him a wake-up call in the form of suffering. Hashem, as a loving Father in Heaven, doesn't like to do this for it causes Him pain - but it's preferable to letting a soul damage itself by straying so far away.

A person's suffering does not come from the "lack" that he thinks that his suffering comes from. In truth, this "lack" is sent from Hashem for his good. The suffering really comes from a person's lack of spiritual awareness and recognition that everything is really for the good. Consequently, a person feels pain because does not recognize that the "lack" is good and instead, feels that it is wrong.

A person with spiritual awareness realizes that his difficulties in life are not punishments, but rather stimulants designed to trigger spiritual growth and enhanced proximity to Hashem. With this in mind, he can sincerely thank Hashem for everything – good or seemingly otherwise - saying gladly, "Thank you so much, Hashem, for this particular tribulation which is helping me to come closer to You!"

To Learn the Good

Rebbe Nachman write further, "Truly there is no evil in the world, only absolute good. The pain that a person experiences, G-d forbid, is only because his spiritual awareness is taken away…"

To reiterate, Rebbe Nachman teaches that suffering comes through eliminating a person's spiritual awareness to the point that he cannot see the ultimate purpose, which is completely good. Subsequently, he feels pain and suffering. When a person has spiritual awareness, and can look towards the purpose, he will not feel any pain. We see this clearly when people internalize the lessons of our emuna broadcasts, CDs, and books; through them, they acquire spiritual awareness to know and believe that everything is for the good. As a result, they acquire the strength and spiritual stamina to withstand the trials of life.

Get Up and Sing!

Elijah the Prophet expounds on the passage from Lamentations 2:19, "Awaken and rejoice at night," commenting that the idea of singing and rejoicing expressed by the Hebrew word *rina* refers to giving thanks for suffering (Eliyahu Rabba, Parsha 18). A person must understand that suffering comes to cleanse his soul of the blemishes caused by his sins. "As such," Elijah says, "a person should get up in the middle of the night to bless, praise, and exalt Hashem's Holy Name."

King David says (Psalms, 119:62), "At midnight I will rise to praise You on Your righteous judgments." These judgments refer to stern judgments and suffering, which are all for a person's ultimate benefit.

Elijah the Prophet also teaches, "Everyone who gives thanks for their tribulations, and are happy with them, are given life in this world and in the Everlasting World to Come."

Rabbi Eliyahu Vidash writes in the landmark book, **Reishit Chochma** (Gate of Repentance, Chapter 3), "If it seems that suffering comes from the side of harsh judgment, realize that this is not true. Suffering only comes from the side of loving-kindness, as it says in Psalm 103, 'Merciful and gracious is Hashem, slow to anger and abundant in loving-kindness.' King Solomon says (Proverbs, Ch. 3), 'For whomever Hashem loves Hashem rebukes…' And, 'A person who spares his rod hates his child, and he who loves his child finds ways to reprove him.' And love is certainly from the side of loving-kindness…"

The Reishit Chochma explains that suffering comes from G-d's attributes of goodness and loving-kindness, in order to help us correct our souls and earn our portion in the World to Come. When we atone for any wrongdoing in this world, we are free to enjoy our rewards in the next world. Moreover, the pleasant life we lead with enhanced emuna and spiritual awareness is a wonderful reward that we can already enjoy in this world.

There are misdeeds that all of us do inadvertently, and as such, have yet to be corrected. The Zohar advises that by being happy with our tribulations in life, we can actually correct all the deeds that need rectification, even if we do not know about them!

"This Time I Praise" – Just This Time?

The Gemara states, "Rebbe Yochanan who learned from Rebbe Shimon Bar Yochai said, 'From the day Hashem created the world, there wasn't a person who praised Hashem, until Leah came to praise Him, as it says, 'This time I praise Hashem'" (Gemara, Berachot, 7b).

The Even Yisrael in his explanation on the Torah (Parshat Vayetzei) asks the question: "Is it possible that we can read this Gemara literally?" Can it really be true that no one praised Hashem until Leah? Abraham our forefather didn't praise Hashem? It's unbelievable – specifically since there is a requirement in religious law for a person to make the blessing, "Hashem is good and does good," after giving birth to a boy, and we know that Abraham kept the Torah in its entirety, even the rabbinic laws like Eiruv Tavshilin (Kiddushin, 82), certainly he blessed Hashem when he had a son! Many might be familiar with the Midrash that Adam sang, *Mizmor Shir L'Yom HaShabbos* (Psalm, 92) "It's good to praise Hashem!" when he saw that his efforts to repent were accepted. It's very hard to accept it literally that the great people before Leah didn't praise Hashem! Moreover, why didn't Leah praise Hashem for her previous sons?

The Gemara's intent is not to say that Leah was actually the first to praise Hashem for all the good that Hashem bestowed upon her. The forefathers surely praised Hashem for all His goodness and kindness as well. Additionally, Leah did praise Hashem before this for her children as each was born. Rather, the Gemara's intent is to teach us that Leah was the first to come and praise Hashem for her suffering - life's apparent bad.

Leah suffered many trials and tribulations. First, everyone said she was destined to marry the wicked Esau. She poured forth incessant prayers and supplications to avoid marry him, until her eyes became red and tired from all the crying. Laban, her own father, humiliated her when he tricked Jacob by substituting Leah for Rachel under the wedding canopy. Leah had to live with the anguish that her husband married her without initially desiring or loving her.

Therefore, until the birth of Judah, Leah was constantly in pain. She felt despised compared to her sister Rachel, whom Jacob wanted to marry in the first place.

Through these negative feelings, Judah was born - Leah's fourth son. By way of Judah, Leah received a greater portion of the Twelve Tribes than any of the other mothers! There were four mothers that were to birth Jacob's offspring, so each of them should have had three sons. Once Leah saw that she gave birth to a fourth son, she realized that everything really was for the best. All her suffering was for her ultimate benefit. By virtue of her humiliation and tribulations, she received a greater portion than the other mothers.

As such, Leah declared, "This time I praise Hashem! I praise You, Hashem, for all the pain I endured! The pain and suffering was certainly worth it for my four sons, from who shall emerge the Levites, Priests and Kings! Thank You, Hashem, for all the suffering! Thank You!"

Even more, Judah (*Yehuda* in Hebrew) literally means "one who thanks." The Hebrew word for Jews – *Yehudim* – means "those who will thank." Our very name as a people means that our national characteristic is giving thanks to Hashem.

On What Types of Seemingly Bad Do We Praise?

Once, someone asked the Maggid of Mezritch to explain to him the meaning of the Mishnah (Yoma, 9:5), "A person is obligated to make a blessing on the bad just as he is obligated to make a blessing on the good." The Maggid sent the person to ask this question to his impoverished student, Reb Zusha of Annipoli. The person made the journey, and told Reb Zusha that he had been sent from their Rebbe, the Maggid of Mezritch, to learn the meaning of the above Mishnah.

Reb Zusha - who wore tattered and patched clothing, lived in a shack, and barely had a daily morsel of bread - seemed bewildered. He said, "This is what the Maggid asks? That Zusha should explain this Mishnah specifically? This Mishnah is an enigma to me, because I've never experienced anything bad…"

How Lucky are You That You Saw Me Like This!

Rebbe Shimon bar Yochai was credited by the Gemara for the teaching that Leah was the first person to praise Hashem for the bad, since he himself knew the value of suffering. Rebbe Shimon bar Yochai was a fugitive fleeing from Roman oppression, forced into hiding for thirteen years in a cave. He existed on a diet solely of carob and water. By virtue of his suffering, he received the Divine inspiration and wisdom that he later recorded in the holy Zohar, his esoteric commentary on Torah that also serves as the basis of Kabbalah.

Lag B'Omer, the anniversary of Rebbe Shimon's exit from the physical world, is the largest celebrated *yartzeit* in the world! The Gemara (Tractate Shabbat, 33) explains that when Rebbe Shimon left the cave, he ran into his father-in-law, the holy tzaddik Rebbe Pinchas ben Yair, as he was going to the bathhouse. When Rebbe Pinchas saw Rebbe Shimon's skin all cracked and sore from being covered with sand inside the cave for thirteen years, he cried and said, "Woe is me that I have to see you like this!"

Rebbe Shimon responded, "How lucky are you that you see me like this! For if you hadn't, then you wouldn't have found me like this!" Rebbe Shimon meant that he would not have merited the great level of Torah knowledge he attained were it not for suffering in the cave. Rebbe Shimon bar Yochai was a holy sage even before he entered the cave, but when he emerged, he was on a pinnacle level of holiness.

The lesson we learn from both our matriarch Leah and from Rebbe Shimon bar Yochai is that we should thank Hashem for the seemingly bad as well as for the good; this is the key to happiness and emotional well-being. Any suffering we have will most certainly lead to a subsequent salvation. Therefore, we can already thank Hashem for the suffering, even before we see its intrinsic and ultimate good.

A woman once told me that she suffers terribly from her husband who is constantly depressed. Since I know the family, I knew she also had seven wonderful children, all Torah scholars of impeccable character. I reminded her about our matriarch Leah, and advised her to thank and praise Hashem for her good portion.

In my book **Women's Wisdom**, I note that when women suffer difficult marital problems, Hashem compensates them with exceptional children. Such rewards are typical for those who endure suffering. Therefore, when a person is tested in emuna, he should believe that Hashem does everything for the good and thank Hashem wholeheartedly.

One Cannot Touch What is Not His

There was once a man who owned a successful store in the outdoor market in central Jerusalem. The rent for the area was very high, but the prime location, along with the amount of business he received, was worth it.

One day, Hashem wanted to do this man a big favor, so He had someone else open a store similar to his right across the street. Even though in truth, a person cannot touch that which is not his, our dear store owner watched his sales dwindle, while the rent still remained high. Finally, his expenditures exceeded his income; at this rate, he would lose everything.

The man went Rabbi Beniahu Shmueli, may Hashem bless him, and told him his entire story, including the details of his diminishing income and the new competitor. The merchant was seething with anger and frustration.

Rabbi Shmueli said to him, "What has happened to you? Hashem did this to you – it's for the good! It's not the other guy, it's Hashem!"

The merchant couldn't accept this and protested, "What?!? Hashem? It's not Hashem, it's him!" However, he did have a bit of faith in Rabbi Shmueli, and asked, "What should I do?"

Rabbi Shmueli said, "Everything is for the good. Close your store here, and open it somewhere else where the rent is lower. You may not get what you're used to, but at least you will have an income. Accept this decree with love."

The merchant left angry and vexed, but he really had no choice, so he re-opened his store in a cheaper area, not far from Meah Shearim. Above the new store, a lonely old woman lived. The merchant realized that she was indeed lonely and took pity on her. He began to give her food and help with chores that were difficult for her. He became like a son and did everything for her, expecting nothing in return.

One day the old lady asked him to come upstairs because she wanted to tell him something. He was tired after a long work day, so he contemplated refusing her, but in the end he went up to her apartment. The lady began to tell him the story of her life, how she became a widow and lost her only son. Impatient, the merchant kept looking at his watch. The elderly woman said, "Stop looking at your watch! A little bit more patience. You have given me so much of your life - all I am asking for is one more hour…"

Then the woman got to the point. Her uncle passed away and bequeathed her five million dollars. Since she had no heirs, and since she saw how he was the only one that cared about her, she decided to bequeath the entire sum to him. She only asked that he buy a room in a yeshiva that would be in merit of her soul, and that there would always be learning in that room.

The merchant returned to Rabbi Shmueli to buy the room in his yeshiva. Rabbi Shmueli said, "Didn't you tell me you were losing everything?"

The merchant told the Rabbi the whole story. He realized that by virtue of following the Rabbi's advice, he merited tremendous wealth.

"You see," said Rabbi Shmueli, "everything is for the best! When we're being tested, we don't understand what's happening to us and why. Therefore, we must toss out our logic and cling to emuna that everything is for the best. We must praise Hashem wholeheartedly, and say 'Thank you Hashem that you gave me a good income for so many years, and thank you now for prodding me to move somewhere else.' Just be happy all the time, because a person must nullify his will before Hashem's Will, joyfully and wittingly."

The Loser Who Won

Similarly, there is a famous story about a millionaire who didn't even know how to write his own name, and used to sign his checks with a fingerprint. One day his secretary summoned up the courage (or the *chutzpah*) to ask him how it is possible that someone who can't even sign his own name could have become as successful as he. He answered,

"It's funny, but had I known how to write, I would not have become a millionaire. I'll tell you why…"

He grew up in a wreck of a home, and never learned to read and write. After much searching, he finally found work in a factory as a simple worker. One day the management decided that it was not acceptable to employ someone who didn't know how to read or write, so they laid him off. He received severance, and he left. Hashem helped this man, and even though he was left without work, he was satisfied with his lot, and believed with complete faith that everything was for the good.

He opened a small kiosk with his severance pay, and was successful selling newspapers and cigarettes. So he opened another kiosk and another until he became somewhat wealthy. He then decided to invest in a factory, and he struck it rich.

"So you see," concluded the wealthy man, "if I would have known how to write, I would have remained a simple worker at the factory, and would not be a millionaire now!"

The moral of the story – we can't see what Hashem sees, nor do we have even the tiniest capability to understand what Hashem is doing. But here's the good news – where our brains kick out, emuna kicks in! When we believe in Hashem, we can be calm, cool and collected, knowing that everything comes from Him and that everything is for our ultimate benefit. Hashem does only good. Do you know what that means? Really, there is no evil at all!

Look what happens when a person lacks emuna: He decides that it's NOT good to be fired, and his stress level goes through the roof. Such a person is miserable and worried. He agonizes, "They fired me! What will I do?" Such fretting is not exactly denying Divine Providence, but it leads to a downward spiral of anger, vengeance, and despair. How many sins of evil speech, jealousy, and worse will this person commit in the process, bringing more harsh decrees upon himself and the world? Such a person reacts irrationally, loses his emotional and even physical health, and virtually guarantees himself further suffering.

Emuna saves us from such a bleak scenario. Emuna enables us to continue functioning with self-composure. Emuna neutralizes the negative emotions that lead to ulcers, strokes, and cardiac arrests. Emuna is the only path to happiness and inner peace. With emuna, we don't have to shoulder the world's problems – we trust Hashem and let Him handle everything.

Even more, how many good deeds will such a person be able to do, and how much benefit will he derive from the light of those deeds done with emuna, both spiritually and materially?! How many negative decrees will be nullified for the entire world on behalf of this person's emuna?! He literally brings the redemption and has tremendous merit.

Who Tells Who?

There's a clever expression: "Don't tell Hashem that you have troubles; tell your troubles that you have Hashem." Tell your troubles, "You should know that I have Hashem, and in one moment, He can finish you off."

Divulging our problems to Hashem is fine, but it could lead to self-pity - the opposite of emuna. A person who knows that everything is for the best doesn't have self-pity. Instead of telling Hashem that we have troubles, we should tell ourselves that we have Hashem. Hashem loves us and does everything with our best interests at heart. He knows what's good for us much more than we ourselves do. Therefore, when we strengthen ourselves in emuna and thank Hashem for whatever problem or challenge we face, salvation comes in the blink of an eye.

With emuna, nothing scares us. Whenever a problem arises, we thank Hashem, assess ourselves, rectify whatever needs rectifying, and pray. If we respond to our troubles with emuna, then since emuna is above nature – Hashem responds accordingly and defies nature to solve our problems. The result is that we see miraculous solutions, because Hashem is constantly with us! This is the fantastic benefit of emuna and gratitude.

To Pray or Not to Pray?

The Gemara (Tractate Berachot, 34b) relates that the son of Rebbe Yochanan ben Zakai became ill. Rebbe Yochanan sent a message to Rebbe Chanina ben Dosa asking him to pray on his son's behalf. Rebbe Chanina ben Dosa put his head between his knees and prayed, and the son was healed. Rebbe Levi Yitzchak of Berditchev asked, "Why did Rebbe Chanina have to put his head between his knees? Why could he not have just exclaimed, 'Be healed!' and be finished? We know the concept of 'A Tzaddik decrees, and Hashem fulfills' – so why not here too?"

The Berditchever Rebbe responded that Rebbe Chanina ben Dosa was a highly spiritual person. His mind was always in the upper worlds where everything is good, and everything is seen as good. He would have seen that the boy's illness was for his eternal benefit, so how could he then pray for him to get better? Rebbe Yochanan ben Zakai came to Rebbe Chanina ben Dosa begging for mercy on behalf of his ill son. This roused Rebbe Chanina's mercy, so he decided to invoke mercy on the ill boy in a way that the boy would recognize as mercy. Since the child felt that being healthy was good, Rebbe Chanina "put his head between his knees," meaning that he lowered himself and entered the "head space" of this world. He did this deliberately in order to avoid seeing what was going on in the upper world; namely, that the boy's illness was actually for the good. In this way, Rebbe Chanina ben Dosa was able to pray for the ill child and help invoke both mercy and healing on this worldly level.

In the same vein, we can understand why we pray "Heal us" thrice daily in the *Shemonah Esrei* prayers. Why pray for ill people when it must be good for them to be sick? The answer is that when a person is sick, his suffering is due to one of four reasons:

1. To atone for his sins.

2. To atone for the sins of the generation.

3. To stimulate a person to self-assessment and subsequent teshuva.

4. To bring a person closer to Hashem.

If an illness triggers an atonement process that a person failed to initiate on his own, then the suffering is well worth the outcome. For that reason, we say the blessing "Heal us" after the blessing "Make us return in complete teshuva before You" and the blessing "Forgive us." Only after requesting forgiveness and teshuva is it appropriate to ask, "Heal us." Once we arise from our spiritual slumber and return to Hashem, Hashem no longer needs to implement wake-up calls such as illness and suffering.

Spiritual Awareness Mitigates Suffering

As mentioned in the beginning of the chapter, spiritual awareness mitigates the suffering of this world. Anyone who attains the level of spiritual awareness that everything is for the best does not suffer. This often painful material world is so much more bearable – even enjoyable - when we are able to accept everything that transpires in our lives with love.

Accepting Hashem's Rule with Humility

There is deep significance in thanking Hashem for the seemingly bad in a person's life. When a person thanks Hashem for the good in his life, he expresses his appreciation for this good, making the statement that he doesn't take Hashem's loving-kindness for granted. But when a person thanks Hashem for the less-desired occurrences and life's difficulties, he makes an even stronger statement that he lovingly and unconditionally accepts Hashem's sovereignty.

Love and unconditional acceptance of whatever Hashem does is a most admirable fulfillment of Jewish Law (Shulchan Aruch, Orach Chaim, 222:3) which states, "A person is obligated to say a blessing on the [seemingly] bad wholeheartedly, just as he would say a blessing on the good." In other words, such a person accepts Hashem's providence completely; this is a true expression of humility and the foundation of spiritual awareness.

Nothing mitigates harsh judgments like humility. Our Sages teach that by accepting life's tribulations and suffering willfully and with humility, we don't feel any pain from them.

In Rebbe Nachman's famous tale, *The Master of Prayer*, there was a warrior who would go around conquering lands, but with no desire for spoils or pay. All he wanted was that the locals should surrender to his domination. Once they surrendered, he was content.

The warrior is allegorical for *din*, the attribute of strict justice or stern judgment. As soon as a person humbles himself, the attribute of strict justice is immediately mollified and leaves the person alone. A prime reason that stern judgment befalls a person in the first place is to humble that person. Accepting the stern judgment while expressing gratitude with a full heart is a true manifestation of humility, which has the power to mitigate those judgments and invoke salvation.

The opposite also holds true: Someone who fails to accept suffering with humility cannot and will not express gratitude with a full heart; therefore, he has not humbled himself before Hashem. His discontent with Hashem's judgments is not only an unwillingness to accept the suffering but a statement of protest (even rebellion!) against Hashem. Such a person is in effect declaring, G-d forbid, "Hashem, I don't think that Your judgments are fair. I don't like the way You are running the world!" Needless to say, such an attitude not only makes the suffering all the more unbearable, but it invokes even more suffering.

One who cries and complains about suffering, especially in light of the fact that Hashem does everything for a person's ultimate welfare, can expect more suffering. Hashem says to such a person, "You're complaining when I'm actually doing everything for your ultimate best? Now I'll give you a real reason to complain!"

In contrast, when a person thanks Hashem with humility for his difficulties in life, Hashem says, "You're thanking Me for these tribulations? Now I'll give you a real reason to thank Me!" Soon, the humble and thankful person experiences miraculous redemption.

No Room for Doubt

'Doubt' in Hebrew is *safek*, with a numerical value of 240. 'Amalek,' one of the nicknames of the Evil Inclination, also has a numerical value of 240. We consequently learn that any doubt in our emuna comes directly from the Evil Inclination. Whenever the Torah alludes to Amalek, it is also referring to an attack on our emuna.

We must strengthen our emuna to the extent that we extinguish any doubt that Hashem runs the world. The very first principle of our faith states that Hashem alone did, does, and will do everything. Since everything He does is only for good, then believing that anything is otherwise is virtually a denial of Hashem, G-d forbid.

There are three types of heresy:

The first is pure atheism, where a person doesn't believe at all in Hashem.

The second type of heresy is a belief in a Higher Power, but a denial of Divine Providence. This is the denial that Hashem personally guides and governs our lives. This type of heresy is manifest by belief in happenstance and nature. It also leads to blaming others and/or self-persecution for life's setbacks and hardships.

The third type is belief in Hashem and Divine Providence, but denial that Hashem runs the world with complete loving-kindness and mercy.

By giving thanks to Hashem for everything in our lives – good and seemingly otherwise – we avoid all types of heresy. We must pray and seek Hashem's assistance that no bad thought or denial of Him should ever enter our minds. We should never refer to anything that happens in our lives as "bad," Heaven forbid. Rather, we should believe that everything is intrinsically good, and give thanks wholeheartedly as Jewish Law tells us to. We should say, "I certainly believe that everything is for the good, and that (insert problem here) is for my ultimate benefit. Thank You Hashem!"

The Reason for Salvation

There are many reasons and explanations for why thanking Hashem for one's suffering ultimately brings salvation.

First, gratitude invokes Divine compassion. We see this clearly in our own lives: Whenever someone thanks us from the heart, we want to do more and more for that person. Accordingly, someone who ignores or denies a favor we did for them destroys any desire we might have to help them ever again.

An additional reason that gratitude leads to salvation is found in the Talmudic rule (Makot, 10b) that a person is led down the path upon which he chooses to follow. If he believes that everything is for the good according to the principles of emuna, then the reality truly becomes good for him. Contrastingly and by the same token, if one mistakenly perceives that there is bad in this world, then he is treated according to his (lack of) emuna, and the bad not only becomes manifest - it becomes worse.

The third reason is that when a person gives thanks, he actively fulfills the goal of all creation. Rebbe Nachman of Breslev explains (Likutei Moharan, I:64), "Hashem created this world because of His mercy, and created the entire world in order to reveal His mercy." By believing that everything is good and thanking Hashem for everything, a person binds himself to the Creator in that he fulfills Hashem's ultimate goal for creating the universe. Hashem's mercy will always prevail over such a person and constantly increase.

The Slonimer Rebbe explains that when a person shows gratitude for suffering, he accepts the actions of Hashem. Measure for measure, Hashem then accepts the actions of that person as well, even if those actions are not so positive just as they are. And Hashem accepts them without judgment - only with love and mercy. This is yet another reason how salvation is brought to the world through acceptance and gratitude for difficulties.

Gratitude is in essence an admission that a person could not succeed without Divine assistance. It is very difficult for some people to say "thank you." Gratitude necessitates humility, since it is like saying, "Without your help, I could not have managed." Additionally, the spoiled person, the haughty person, and the person with a sense of entitlement will never express gratitude wholeheartedly, if at all. As such, ingratitude and arrogance always go together, while gratitude and humility also go hand in hand.

In light of the above, every time a person thanks Hashem, he is in essence admitting that he cannot get along without Him. This brings a person closer to the truth – to *Ein od Milvado* - "there is nothing without Him." We all need Hashem's help for every breath and every heartbeat, for without Him, there is nothing, period.

By recognizing all the good that Hashem does for us, we neutralize all sadness and depression. Gratitude leads to happiness, since grateful people are never bitter. On the other hand, bitter people are never grateful. They focus on what they lack, even if it's minor - all the more so if it's something major. The ingrate forgets all the good that Hashem does for him and forgets that there is no bad in this world. He sinks to sadness and oftentimes wastes valuable energy on self-pity, crying, and complaining.

The Real Protection

Let's observe the tests of faith that our forefather Jacob faced. His holy parents, Isaac and Rebecca, commanded him not to marry a local Canaanite girl, but to seek a bride from his mother's family in Padam Aram – what we know as Syria today. Hashem promised Jacob that He would guard him on his journey. So Jacob began his journey empowered with the merit of honoring his parents and with the express promise of Hashem to guard him.

But at the very beginning of the journey, Eliphaz (son of Esau) nearly killed Jacob, who had to ransom his own life by giving Eliphaz his every last cent.

What type of protection is this? Where's Hashem's promise, "And I will guard you wherever you go"? What happened to Jacob's additional merit of honoring his parents? Everything went topsy-turvy – what happened?

Did Jacob lose emuna from the bad that he encountered? Absolutely not! Jacob clung to simple faith; his belief and trust in Hashem were by no means conditional. By virtue of his simplicity of faith, we say thrice daily, "*Elokei Yaakov* – The L-rd of Jacob.*" Elokei* refers to the attribute of strict justice. When we say, *"Elokei Yaakov,"* we refer to the fact that Jacob accepted all of Hashem's judgments completely and lovingly. Even though he did not necessarily understand what Hashem was doing at the time, he nonetheless believed it was all for the good.

That's not all. When Jacob arrived at the home of Laban his uncle, he was penniless, yet worked for him for nothing. When Laban offered to pay him, Jacob asked for the hand of Rachel, Laban's daughter. "No problem," answered Laban, "work another seven years to pay me for her."

Just think – if Jacob would have come to Padam Aram with the money that Eliphaz took, he could have married Rachel that same day! But now, as a pauper, he had to work for seven years in order to marry her. Did he question Hashem? Absolutely not! He accepted his lot lovingly and with emuna.

What Would Have Happened If...

Our forefather Jacob certainly did not know at the time of his test what good would blossom from everything that was happening to him. He simply clung to his emuna. Only after the fact are we able to see the positive that came from his troubles. Let's look at several that were revealed:

If Jacob would have come with all his money, and would have married Rachel immediately, he would have returned home right away. Esau, who still thirsted for revenge in losing his birthright to Jacob, would have killed him on the spot. Even if Jacob would have been saved from Esau, he would not have had children because Rachel was barren. Rachel merited children only by virtue of not embarrassing her sister Leah when her father Laban deceived Jacob by substituting Leah for Rachel under the wedding canopy. In addition, had Jacob not married Leah, he wouldn't have had eight of his twelve sons – the six that were born from

Leah and the two that were born from Leah's maidservant Zilpah.

It's easy to see in retrospect that Hashem did everything for the very best: Eliphaz took Jacob's money so that Jacob would be forced to work for Rachel; Rachel and Leah were switched under the wedding canopy so that Jacob would end up marrying both; Jacob left Laban's house only after many years, giving time for Esau's anger to abate; and Jacob ultimately had twelve sons.

Hashem's promise to Jacob when He said, "And I will guard you wherever you go," was not merely protective lip service according to our sorely limited intelligence. Hashem did everything for Jacob's ultimate benefit, despite the seemingly bad occurrences at the time.

First Emuna, Then Understanding

There will always be a limit to the extent we can understand Hashem's actions. But where understanding leaves off, emuna must begin. Someone who thinks or hopes to understand Hashem will not attain emuna.

Not even Moses could understand Hashem. When Moses asked Hashem to show him the secret of how He works, Hashem answered him, "You cannot see My Face." In other words, you can never understand how I work on an a priori basis. You'll only be able to understand what I do in retrospect. This is the intrinsic meaning of what Hashem says, "You can see Me from the back, but my face cannot be seen" (Exodus, 33:23).

Never forget that at the time of a test, a person cannot really know or understand that all is for the good! If he understood clearly that it is really good, it would not be a test. Every test of emuna occurs only when a person's intellect perceives a situation as bad. The level of knowing from the outset that everything is good is one that no human can attain, because understanding the situation with such clarity nullifies free choice.

Therefore, it doesn't matter who a person is - whether a simple shoe shiner or our forefather Jacob – no person in this material world with tests of faith right and left can know from the outset that everything is for the good. Even if the person is a Moses or a Rabbi Akiva! For every person, a trying situation appears to be bad at the time of the challenge. We cope by strengthening our emuna - even without understanding - that it's all for the good.

During a difficult challenge, don't try to understand what's happening to you, for you won't draw strength and encouragement, only frustration. When a situation looks completely despondent from a logical perspective, emuna will enable you not only to cope, but attain tremendous personal growth as well.

What's Good about It?

Let's refer back to our forefather Jacob. Was his life easy from a logical standpoint? Was arriving bereft of any worldly possessions to the house of Laban a good thing? What could be the advantage of having swindler Laban for a father-in-law? According to intellect, there would seem to be no apparent good in Jacob's situation.

Through eyes of emuna, however, everything is good! We don't necessarily understand how it's all for the good, but we believe that it's all good.

Don't think that great prophets and tzaddikim on higher spiritual levels have an easy time coping with their tribulations. They suffer excruciating tests of faith in accordance to their lofty spiritual level; they also cannot see that their suffering is beneficial. Indeed, with their mighty intellect, it would seem that all is NOT good! But they have the emuna that everything is for the very best.

Sometimes a person tries to convince himself that the tribulation at hand is all for the good. But then his wife, parents or neighbors convince him in unison that his ideas are skewed. With a lack of genuine and steadfast emuna, he loses resolve, becomes confused, and begins to question everything.

A person must first understand that he will not be able to see from the outset how his tribulations are good - otherwise they wouldn't be tribulations. For example, an Olympic boxer understands that he'll be hit during training; he doesn't complain when the coach catches him off guard and punches him, since he knows this is part of becoming a champion. But if a person walking down the street gets punched for no apparent reason, he won't be able to know how and why this is for his ultimate benefit. That's where complete emuna steps in.

Complete emuna in Hashem means that we believe - without any doubt - that He directs and observes each of us individually with exacting precision, and He sees what we don't see. In short, complete emuna gives us the peace of mind that Hashem is doing everything for our ultimate good, regardless of the fact that this is not revealed to us at the time.

Therefore, a person should tell himself "I understand that my suffering is seemingly very bad. I even feel tremendous pain. My tribulations seem unbearable, but I believe that they're all for the best, despite the fact that I don't see how…"

I Don't Understand a Thing...

This is a song we have been singing at our Yeshiva for years now: "I don't understand a thing, I don't understand a thing, just believe, just believe, that all is for the good." The intellectual understanding of the difficulty is what we refer to by, "I don't understand a thing." When it seems really bad, "I don't understand a thing." However, I can believe that it is for the good.

Whenever one encounters a test of faith, he should not expect to understand how even the smallest detail of the test is for his good. He should rely on his emuna only. In this way, he'll be able to give thanks to Hashem in any situation. Gratitude mitigates all harsh judgments and invokes miraculous salvations, as we've already learned.

This Too is for the Good

The Gemara (Tractate Taanit, 21a) tells the famous story of Nachum Ish Gam Zu. The leaders of Israel sent him to Rome with a jewel-filled treasure chest in order to appease Caesar, with the hope that Caesar would rescind the many harsh decrees that he dealt the Jewish people. We hereby take the liberty of dramatizing the Gemara's telegraphic account in order to enable us to feel the immense challenge that Nachum faced.

Nachum lived in a period of turmoil, when the Jewish people suffered at the hands of a vicious conqueror. Rome persecuted Israel terribly. The Jewish leaders did what they could to placate the tyrannical Caesar, who implored their fellow Jews to give as much as they possibly could for this important cause, gathering every last cent from a nation that was already downtrodden from poverty and Roman taxation. They finally amassed enough money to buy precious stones, which were placed in a beautiful box. They asked, "Who will go on this important mission?" One person answered, "Nachum Ish Gam Zu, he should go, because he is a righteous man who is experienced in miracles."

The first lesson we learn is that whoever believes that everything is for the good is well-experienced in miracles. Such a person sees miracles wherever he goes...

Nachum Ish Gam Zu set out on his long journey to Rome, with the treasure chest filled with jewels. Evening fell, and Nachum entered an inn to rest. In the morning he arose, opened up the treasure chest, and what did he see? Instead of shiny, precious stones, he found sand mixed with rocks, straw, and dirt.

What did Nachum say? "This, too, is for the good."

At first glance, such a reaction seems crazy. "This too is for the good"?!? Where is the good? The poor Jews worked so hard to scrounge together enough money in order to purchase this precious treasure, their hopes pinned on this crucial mission to ease the yoke of harsh decrees.

Just about any other person would have felt guilty. He would think, "I didn't guard the treasure properly!" He would look for a place to 'bury' himself. Who knows how such a person would persecute himself for such a mistake. But here we learn another important lesson in emuna: Even if trouble comes to a person because of his own mistake – after the fact, he should know that it was Hashem's Will.

We see that Nachum was a man of emuna and that he believed everything is for the good. But what was to be done with the treasure lost - go home? That's not what he did. He continued on his way to Caesar with the chest filled with sand and pebbles. As Nachum Ish Gam Zu was a man of pure emuna, he knew that it was better to go as Hashem willed rather than with the precious stones that had been there previously.

Nachum was a holy Tanna, a Mishnaic sage! He was far from stupid! But he put his logic aside and continued his journey to Rome girded with the emuna that whatever Hashem does is certainly good. Intellectually, it was obviously preferable to go to Rome with precious stones, but he reasoned "If the Creator did this, then surely it is for the good. I don't understand what the Creator did here, but I believe…"

Nachum Ish Gam Zu arrived at the entrance to Caesar's palace. The guards announced that an ambassador for the Jews had arrived with a gift for Caesar. They escorted him in with honor before Caesar who sat among his officers and advisors. With complete confidence, Nachum presented Caesar with the gift from the Jews. Caesar opened the chest, and saw that it was filled with sand, dirt and straw. Understandably, he immediately became enraged, and screamed, "Insolents! Now I will kill all the Jews! First, take this man out to be executed."

Nachum Ish Gam Zu calmly said, "This too is for the good!"

Astonishing! What?!? This too is good, that Caesar and the Romans should kill all the Jews, starting with him?

Despite Caesar's rants, not a hair on a Jewish head can fall without Hashem willing it so. Only Hashem decides who lives and who dies. Therefore, Nachum could reply with no fear, "This too is for the good." Even if Hashem did decide that it should happen, then He knows what He is doing, and everything He does is for the good. Consequently, there is no bad in the world, none at all!

Imagine that Nachum lacked the complete and steadfast emuna that everything is for the good. He has now arrived at a predicament where he might fear that others will die because of him. Had he succumbed to the slightest measure of self-blame or self-persecution, all would truly have been lost. But Nachum was not worried or upset in the slightest. His trust in Hashem was complete.

Nachum Ish Gam Zu lived his emuna: There is no bad in this world and there is nothing but Hashem. Nachum saw Hashem only! Let Caesar threaten! He is powerless without Hashem. "If Hashem wants me killed, then that's fine with me! But if Hashem wills for me to live, then nothing Caesar can do will hurt me. Hashem could just as easily take Caesar's soul away."

Know Your Place

Why can't we all be on Nachum's level? Why can't we emulate him and declare with confidence, "This, too, is for the good"?

Either we attribute power to people like Caesar and mistakenly think that they control our lives rather than realizing that the high and mighty are merely marionettes in Hashem's hands; or we want to understand Hashem. We think we know more than Hashem, or can do a better job than He in running the world. That's why we lack Nachum's pure and simple emuna that everything is for the best.

We should really stop and reprimand ourselves. "Hey, how about a little respect here… a little thought! Do you really think that you are capable of understanding Hashem? Do you understand the pilot's skills on your coast-to-coast flight? Do you understand what the power company technician is doing to restore the electricity after a power failure? You don't even understand what they're doing, so how do you expect to understand Hashem?"

Aha, you have grievances against Hashem! Why did Hashem make the Holocaust? Why does Hashem allow babies to be killed? Do you have additional questions? Would you want to change places with the Creator? Perhaps you'd prefer to elect G-d in a democratic election? Your questions are statements that you understand more than the Creator of the world, that you have more compassion than He does, and that if you were responsible for the world, you'd behave differently.

The fact is that those who question Hashem lose their emuna. Life without emuna in this world is torture, to say the least.

Our inflated egos bring us to doubt Hashem. If we had a bit of humility, we'd ask ourselves, "Can I understand the Creator? Do I know what every soul came here to correct? Do I know why every soul came to this world? Where do I get off thinking that I should know what Hashem does? I don't even understand what my employer is doing."

A person should be embarrassed to question Hashem's actions. Hashem doesn't have to give an accounting to humans. Should you like to believe? Please feel free. Do you prefer not to believe? The loss will be yours alone.

Secret Weapons

Let's return to Nachum. When he saw how Caesar became enraged and decided to take revenge against the Jews, starting with himself, he said, "This, too, is for the good." Once Nachum passed this grueling test of his emuna, Elijah the Prophet appeared, disguised as one of the Caesar's officers. He said to Caesar, "Why are you upset by this Jew?"

Caesar answered, "Because he brought me sand and stones!"

Elijah the Prophet remarked, "I read in some book that Abraham, the father of the Jewish People, threw sand and straw at his enemies, and miraculously it all turned into arrows and daggers, and destroyed them all."

Caesar said to Elijah, "Are you sane?"

Eliyahu answered, "Let's give it a try."

Caesar sent a lone horseman to an enemy city that he had not succeeded in conquering, carrying some of the sand and straw from the Jews. After a short time, the horseman returned and told the Caesar his amazing story: "Listen here! I alone conquered the city! The sand turned to arrows and the straw to swords, and killed all of them! Miraculous!"

Caesar mumbled to himself, "These Jews are dangerous. They have serious weapons. Let's not instigate trouble with them." Caesar then commanded that several boxes be filled with diamonds from his treasury, and he sent Nachum Ish Gam Zu back to Eretz Yisrael with them in a kingly chariot and an envoy of soldiers to guard him on the way.

Hashem Decides

What would have happened had Nachum Ish Gam Zu come to the Caesar with the treasure chest of jewels as originally planned? The Jews would have not received a thing! At most, Nachum would have received a thank you from Caesar; he already had entire coffers full of jewels, so the gift from the Jews wouldn't have been remarkable at all. Consequently, Caesar would not have done a thing for the Jewish people other than grant them a short respite until his next insane period of harsh decrees. Hashem had a better plan, one which would provide the needed salvation for the Jews, but it could only be implemented by Nachum Ish Gam Zu's steadfast emuna!

We now appreciate how Nachum thought that the sand and straw that Hashem put in the strong box were superior to the precious stones that humans put there. He made a simple calculation: If the Sages of Israel filled the trunk with precious stones, and Hashem decided to override them by replacing the gems with sand and straw, that must be for the best! And indeed it was, because only through the sand and straw did Caesar understand the spiritual powers of the nation of Israel.

We now know the end of the story, but at the time of this test, would we have said, Gam Zu L'Tovah, "This, too, is for the good"? Would we have continued on the mission? It's highly doubtful.

Nachum's emuna was unshakable. Even when the jewels were stolen, he didn't focus on the thieves and allow worry and depression to immobilize him. He knew that Hashem was doing everything for the best. Nor did he persecute himself for not sufficiently guarding the treasure and so forth. He didn't blame anyone else either. He cast his eyes toward Hashem only - this is emuna!

Emuna During a Challenge

Generally, during a challenge or test, a person cannot understand how it can possibly be all for the good. This is crucial, for if a person doesn't develop emuna, then even the smallest test will bring him to a state of anxiety and depression.

If a person would know at the time of a challenge that it was for the good, then it wouldn't be a challenge at all. The best way to withstand this test is to say to oneself, "I don't understand what the Almighty is doing but I believe that it's all for the best."

Everyone Says Thanks

The foundation of gratefulness is the precise faith in the Creator that He's doing everything for our good despite the fact that it seems otherwise. If we were to thank G-d for it all, the seemingly bad and especially the good, we'd never feel like we're suffering.

Rebbe Natan of Breslev teaches us this seminal idea by explaining that gratitude rectifies the sin that triggered the suffering in the first place.

What was the sin? Failing to give thanks…

One's failure to express gratitude for his many blessings invokes severe judgments. A sense of entitlement makes a person feel like he deserves everything; such people are spoiled, never satisfied and usually unbearable. Hashem doesn't want us to be like that. He wants us to understand that nothing should be taken for granted, nothing is owed to us, and everything comes to us by way of Divine Providence and loving-kindness. Suffering reminds us how totally we depend on Hashem; we praise Him for the wake-up call, and again when we're saved from a difficult predicament.

Sincere Thanks

Someone once claimed, "I say 'thank you' to G-d repeatedly for my problem, but I see no salvation!"

I responded, "You say thanks because you heard you are supposed to say thanks, but you don't say it because you believe that it's all for the good. Therefore, you are not helped. You should know that as long as you don't believe that it's all for the good, your thanks are not sincere and won't bring true salvation. Even if you say thank you a thousand times! Perhaps it would help mitigate the harsh judgments a bit, because after all, you are saying thanks and not complaining. Once your thanks are sincere and reinforced with the faith that everything is for the best, just wait and see what happens!"

Giving thanks reinforced with emuna is sincere gratitude. Telling Hashem, "I am happy with what You do, and I thank You with all my heart," unlocks the gates of salvation by invoking phenomenal Divine compassion.

When a person harbors the feeling that what Hashem has done is detrimental and only says thanks in order to hasten salvation, then in reality he is not being honest. According to his understanding, he really should be crying and complaining. Dishonesty can't bring salvation; only truth and sincerity can. That's why we must strengthen our emuna to the level where we truly believe that Hashem is doing everything for our ultimate benefit. Then gratitude comes easy. **True gratitude is when our desire to get close to Hashem is even greater than our desire for salvation.**

A person's ultimate goal should be maximum proximity to Hashem. As elaborated in The Garden of Emuna, emuna is divided into three levels:

1. Everything comes from Hashem.

2. Everything is for the good.

3. Everything has a purpose.

As a rule, the Gemara states that there are no tribulations without prior transgressions. Therefore, tribulations are an indication that a person has something to correct.

When a person realizes that life's challenges and tribulations are a golden opportunity for self-assessment and rectifying misdeeds, thus enabling him to get closer to Hashem, he'll certainly be grateful. But when his objective in saying thanks is only to be saved, then the thanks is nothing more than lip service. Such token gratitude doesn't bring him reprieve.

By failing to come closer to Hashem in a trying situation - even if he or she prays profusely – a person misses the entire point of the tribulation in the first place. Only when a person begins to come closer to Hashem because of the tribulation and thanks Hashem sincerely, will the suffering cease.

The prophet Jeremiah said, "It's a time of trouble for Jacob, and from it he will be saved." When we look at our times of trouble through eyes of emuna and gratitude, we are surely saved.

True Light

Rebbe Nachman of Breslev teaches that truth pierces the darkness of a difficult situation. Since there is no truth like genuine gratitude to G-d, a person's gratefulness enables him to virtually escape from darkness.

To paraphrase King David in Psalm 145, Hashem is close to those who call out to Him in truth. This is the case with regard to prayer requests and expressions of gratitude alike.

Day-To-Day Wonders

Expressing gratitude should be a vital part of our lives - from the milestone events to the tiniest mundane occurrences. For example, a student of mine told me that one day in the late morning, he was at home and his son returned from school in tears. No one enjoys having a crying child return from school in the middle of the day, but emuna teaches us that whatever Hashem does, He does for the good.

This student, having heard several of my classes on gratitude, began to thank Hashem. He did some on-the-spot self-assessment to search for what Hashem wanted from him, and only then did he begin to ask his son questions. His son told him that another child was bullying him, and he began to cry and ran home. His father explained to him gently and softly the emuna perspective, and said the following:

"Who frightens you, my son? That bully? You know that everything comes from Hashem, so He made the bully bother you. And you also know that everything Hashem does - He does for the good. So it seems that Hashem loves your prayers and He wants you to pray to Him. So from this day on, pray to Him that He should guard you and that the bully should leave you alone. You must strengthen yourself with emuna." After that, they prayed a bit together, and his son returned to school.

As a result of a trying situation, the child learned a lesson in emuna and he learned how to pray better. Even though his parents taught him how to pray, it's no comparison to his own heartfelt prayers from experience, despite his tender age.

After the fact, things worked out for the best. But at that moment when the parent gave thanks, he didn't know how it would be for the good. Rationally speaking, the situation didn't look good at all; his son ran home from school without permission, crying. At that moment in time, the father could not fathom what Hashem was doing, but he prayed with all his heart with complete trust in Hashem. Only then did he see a positive outcome.

Our takeoff point in dealing with any crisis should be emuna. First, we must wholeheartedly thank Hashem; later, Hashem will open our eyes and show us how the situation was for our ultimate benefit. There are situations where we quickly see the ultimate good, but there are also situations that require a much longer period of time before we understand how everything is for the best. Our forefather Jacob waited a long time to see the good that came out of what happened with Eliphaz and Lavan, as we learned earlier. However, Nachum Ish Gam Zu knew in just a few days how what seemed so terrible turned out for the very best. So in every occurrence, we must look for the inherent good. Emuna keeps us going with a smile on our face until we find that inherent good. Just because we don't see it certainly doesn't mean that it's not there.

Words of Comfort

On Lag B'Omer in 5769 (May 2009), a terrible accident occurred on the way back from Meron, Rabbi Shimon bar Yochai's gravesite in the Upper Galilee. I was at funerals until 2:30 am for five holy martyrs, two adults and three children. I awoke the next morning with a terrible discomfort in my heart, which I felt I had no control over. I strained to encourage myself after this wrenching tragedy.

I reminded myself over and over that everything Hashem does, He does for the good. There is no evil in this world, and I don't know or understand anything! I only have emuna that everything is for the good. My own teachings echoed in my heart, and then my emuna and happiness returned to me. These thoughts are what revitalized me.

Then I wondered: What would a person do without emuna? How could he survive? We all know stories of people who are completely broken after going through a trauma, even one that is not so tragic. This propelled me to be even stronger in my faith that everything is for the ultimate good.

We are human and we feel pain when we suffer. This is an inescapable fact. We won't succeed by suppressing our true feelings. We don't doubt the pain – instead, we encourage ourselves that it's all for the best and for a good reason, irrespective of whether we comprehend how or not. Emuna is like a spiritual Aikido – it lets us channel our pain into something worthwhile; namely, getting closer to Hashem.

Consoling the Comforters

I once went to console a very young widow. I came to comfort, and it was I who came out consoled and strengthened. The widow told me that her husband, during his last months, discovered a great treasure: The books **The Garden of Emuna**, **In Forest Fields**, and **The Garden of Peace**. She explained that in his last months of life, her husband would read and learn these books with a passion, as well as listen to many of my CDs about emuna and gratitude. Despite his terminal illness, he would smile and express his gratitude all day long, both to G-d and to me. Living with him was a privilege, like living with an angel. Before he died, he succeeded in learning the truth; he was neither afraid nor sad in any way.

The widow said to me, "Rabbi, I say thanks for everything. If it would be appropriate, I would even dance and rejoice.

My husband so prepared me, and I really saw it as his will that I should give thanks for everything. So thank you! I give thanks to Hashem! I accept everything with emuna. I understand nothing – Hashem knows what He is doing – and what He does is only good."

This young widow touched on the ultimate truth. If she would cry and mourn – would her husband return from the grave? Sure she feels pain! But, rather than being miserable, asking questions and denying Hashem, G-d forbid, she was illuminating herself, her family, and the entire world with the light of emuna.

This young widow must move forward with her life and continue raising her orphans. How effective would she be if she were to mourn excessively and fall into self-pity? Of course she's allowed to cry from longing, but not from sadness and depression. Emuna emphasizes that whatever Hashem does is good. If a person has more pain than appropriate, it's a statement that he believes and feels that his situation is not good. So every person must remember - Hashem is good! There is no bad in this world. What we call bad or evil is denial of Hashem.

The Torah allows a person to mourn and acknowledge pain. But we're not allowed to mourn more than what the Code of Jewish Law prescribes, because excessive mourning is a statement that a person does not accept Divine judgment.

Guarding our Soul

In another instance, I made a condolence call to the widow of a young rabbinical student who became religious through my influence, and again I ended up being the one who was consoled. At the funeral hall, she was standing near the deceased and giving thanks to Hashem with all her heart. She uttered nothing but words of gratitude and emuna; everyone standing there was in awe of the young woman's strength of faith and character.

Had she wailed, no one could have faulted her. Indeed, the cries of a widow are readily accepted in Heaven. But there's always the danger that sorrow devastates a mourner with the venom of despair and self-pity. Those who experience intense grief sometimes perceive that their lives have terminated, as if there is no longer anything to live for, Heaven forbid. This of course is the Evil Inclination speaking, all too ready to attack any emotional front that's not fully fortified with emuna.

The *shiva* house, the house of the deceased where the prescribed 7-day mourning period was taking place, amazed me. The children had teary eyes, but they were smiling because they saw that their mother was smiling. Had I not seen it with my own eyes, I would have never thought such a thing was possible. But when I noticed it, I thought to myself, "What would have been their lot if their mother was uncontrollably sobbing, screaming, and demanding answers from Hashem?"

If the orphans had heard questions or complaints, the intensity of their pain would have been magnified. How could they grow up, thinking that Hashem is so cruel for making Mommy so sad? They too would have questions that would jolt their faith: Why did this happen to us? Why were we left as orphans? Why was our righteous father taken from us?

What a tremendous gift that the mother learned about emuna and was able to choose the path of thankfulness and gratitude. She spared herself from bitterness and excessive pain, and she preserved the emotional health of her children.

Because she so honestly conveyed the message "Daddy is always with us. He is always praying for us," they were able to accept everything with emuna.

Her emuna had a profound influence not only on her children, but on her in-laws as well. Indeed, all of the relatives derived strength from the widow's unwavering emuna.

Overcoming

Everything is for the good. It's been said numerous times in this book already. And it is not some trite expression – it's the spiritual reality of things. If a person conquers his Evil Inclination, and lives this truth, then he will live a good life no matter what happens to him. If he does not believe that everything is for the good, then he'll complain and ask questions, and end up a heretic with no solutions and no comfort for his pain.

Specifically, the test of widowhood (which should not befall anyone) is an excruciating one, especially for a young woman with small children. But, with emuna, she was able to comfort those who came to comfort her. This is the awesome power of emuna.

The widow learned about emuna from our books and CDs. She was able to accept stern judgment with emuna, joy and thanks. She acquired a lofty level of spiritual awareness that enabled her to pass a grueling test of faith heroically and most admirably.

Living the Life

Life is full of day-to-day challenges. Emuna is the difference between a life of bitterness and disgruntlement and one of beauty and optimism. This is especially true in matters of debt and finance.

If a person in debt does not accept his situation with emuna, he experiences purgatory in his own home – constant guilt, frustration, anxiety, and anger with himself and those around him. If he accepts his lot with gratefulness, his wife and children won't even realize that there is a problem. They won't construe that anything is lacking if he still smiles and is cheerful.

The same goes for every trying situation in life: A rebellious child, difficulty finding a soul-mate, divorce, moving house, renovations, or a medical problem, among many others. A person can emerge strengthened or broken, reinforced or destroyed. The tests of life can substantially fortify a person if he accepts them with emuna. If he realizes that Hashem only does everything for the best, then he can always be encouraged no matter what happens to him. But if a person does not have emuna in Hashem, and he harbors feelings that Hashem wants to torment him for no reason, then he is devastated by whatever happens to him. Everything depends upon the person's emuna.

Consequently, the difference between a person with emuna who accepts everything with joy and gratefulness, and one disgruntled with no emuna, is the difference between paradise and purgatory. That's why learning and internalizing the principles of emuna are so vital to attaining happiness and peace of mind.

Endless Joy

Who doesn't prefer paradise to purgatory? Like many things in life, the greater the rewards, the greater the obstacles. Many people have difficulty learning emuna and expressing gratitude, especially in trying times. They refuse to subjugate their own desires and accept what Hashem wants instead.

According to a person's thinking, what he wants is the best for him. He thinks that he can run the world – and his life in particular – better than Hashem can. Some agree with Hashem's overall scheme, but take exception when it comes to the way Hashem runs their own personal affairs.

For example, suppose a young man is having a hard time finding a spouse. Hashem's desire has been that he remains single until now. This has surely been the best for that person. But, according to his thinking, he was supposed to have found his mate a long time ago.

Such a person has difficulty thanking Hashem. Why? He can't seem to let go of his expectations in favor of Hashem's will.

Few deny Hashem knowingly; however, by not accepting His will, they deny Hashem unwittingly. They fool themselves by thinking, "It's true that what Hashem does is the best - I am not denying that, Heaven forbid. But my situation is different!" One should never think that any situation transcends the boundaries of Hashem's righteous rule. There are no exceptions.

Suppose a person intended to travel to a certain destination, and on the way, he was in involved in a car accident. Thank G-d he was only lightly injured, but his plans were spoiled. He wanted a certain result, but Hashem had different plans. In such a case, he should discard his own expectations and embrace Hashem's will, with the emuna that Hashem only wants the very best for him. It's a good idea to say something like, "Master of the world, I wanted it to be one way, but I see that Your will is different. I accept Your will, and thank You for the change in plans, for it is surely – as always - the absolute best for me."

When a person truly gives thanks with all his heart for everything that happened until this moment, then his prayers become imbued with the light of emuna. In the case of the young man who has not yet found his soul mate, once he accepts with love the way Hashem has directed his life until now, can he then ask humbly for his soul mate: "Master of the world! Please send me my life partner, since I can't fulfill Your commandments without her. May it be Your will that I get married soon…"

Genuine emuna means total acceptance of Hashem's will, whatever it might be. We must nullify our will for His. The greater the emuna, the more effective our prayers will be.

Perception

When a person endures frightening circumstances or receives harsh tidings, it scares her and she thinks, "How can I say this is for the good? How can I contradict the reality? Am I the town idiot?" Such an attitude is according to her perception and intellect, both of which are far from objective.

When a person sees what appears to be the worst situation in the world, she should say to herself, "True, the circumstances appear to be awful. But emuna says that everything that Hashem does is good and for the good. Since my life revolves around emuna, I'll thank Hashem for this too. Even though I don't understand anything, I just believe that everything is for the good."

Emuna must precede intellect. The intellect says that the situation is catastrophic; emuna says otherwise, that everything is for the best! We call the Evil Inclination "evil" because it convinces us that there is "evil."

If you're not yet on the level where you can thank Hashem for every situation, don't feel guilty and certainly don't castigate yourself. Simply appeal to Hashem for assistance in acquiring and strengthening your emuna, understanding that emuna – like everything else – requires extensive prayer.

Learning to Give Thanks

One of my married students once approached me and told me that his wife was pregnant; two months before her due date, she went in for tests. The doctors told her that she must have the baby via caesarean section, and scared her by telling her all sorts of theories and possibilities of potential dangers and so forth, until she became deeply depressed and suffered from acute anxiety. She stopped eating and drinking, and couldn't sleep; she just cried and cried. But Hashem had mercy on her: Someone gave her our CD lesson, **Stop Crying**. She learned to say thank-you for everything, even the seemingly bad. And so she began to give thanks to Hashem.

The expectant mother said: "Hashem, from what do I fear? That I should have a c-section? Everything You do is for the good, so whatever will be is good, even if I need a c-section. I thank You – thank You so much, Hashem! I know nothing except that whatever You do with me is good. Thank You for everything You do for me." She continued thanking and thanking and thanking. Every thought that entered her head to frighten her, she said, "Thanks. If Hashem wants it to be that way, it's good. Thank You, thank You, thank You!"

She continued to give thanks, dancing and rejoicing all the rest of her pregnancy up to the birth – and she experienced miracles. The birth experience went well, and even after the birth, when most women experience pain and contractions, she did not feel a thing. No pain whatsoever!

In other instances, we have witnessed how people have overcome terminal illnesses by thanking Hashem. Thanking Hashem in trying circumstances is certainly not "natural"; Hashem responds in like manner by performing miracles for those who thank Him.

Speedily in Our Days

Spiritual awareness can hasten the redemption, for in the time of the redemption, knowledge will increase (Isaiah, 11:9): "For the land will fill with the awareness of Hashem, like the waters cover the oceans." Every person will know that Hashem is good, and that there is no evil in the world. Therefore, the more we get to know Hashem, the quicker we hasten the ultimate Redemption!

Rebbe Nachman teaches (Likutei Moharan, I:21), "All pain, suffering and the Exile is proportionate to one's lack of spiritual awareness." A person has problems because he lacks emuna. His lack of spiritual awareness is like exile to the soul. Contrastingly, the more one attains spiritual awareness, the more one attains a level of personal redemption - ending the exile of the soul.

Why Complain?

Despite these teachings, there will still be those who continue to complain. They feel justified in being sad and depressed. Many try to convince me, as if they were saying: "Listen, Rabbi, listen to my pain, and give me permission to be sad, to give up hope, to be confused, and to not pray and learn. Look at this trauma, at this big problem – certainly you have to agree with me that the right way to deal with it is only sadness and giving up and depression and confusion. I am telling you about such problems, and you want me to say thanks? Perhaps I can be quiet a little, but to say thanks!?!"

According to such people, their problem is a justifiable reason to sever relations with Hashem, Heaven forbid. Nothing could be more self-damaging - the bigger the problem, the more one needs Hashem.

Sadness

Sadness is tantamount to self-destruction, as Rebbe Nachman teaches in **Sefer Hamiddot**:

"Through sadness, a person becomes weak."

"Through sadness come fires."

"Sadness is a sign that some sickness is coming."

"Because of sadness, Hashem is not with a person."

"Due to sadness, a person doesn't attain his potential."

"Through sadness a person is embarrassed."

"Sadness is in the heart of a person who feels his own evil."

"A person should guard himself from sadness so that he should not become a mourner," G-d forbid.

And finally – "Because of a person being sad, the Heavens consider sending bad to that person!"

Gratitude eradicates troubles. The opposite is also true, since sadness invokes troubles. By choosing sadness, life is purgatory; by choosing the path of gratitude, life is paradise. If you don't say thanks, your troubles will multiply. If you give thanks, then all your troubles will be nullified.

Chapter Four:
Thanking Hashem

A Labor of Gratitude

Feeling grateful to Hashem is indeed our most important task. We build a steadfast connection by way of our gratitude to Him. Therefore, as long as our gratitude to Hashem is deficient, our connection to Hashem remains weak and incomplete.

Our gratitude opens the upper gates of Heaven and enables us to be judged favorably. Thankfulness cancels all accusations.

The Ramban explains that gratitude is essentially the purpose of man's creation, and is the prime expression of emuna. It is the recognition of all the good Hashem has bestowed upon a person every moment of his life. The grateful individual does not take things at face value. He perceives that even the seemingly undesirable things in life are actually a result of Divine Providence and for the best, whether or not he comprehends it all.

Through gratitude a person attains spiritual awareness - the cognizance that there is no real difference between stern judgment and mercy, since Hashem does everything for a person's ultimate good. Expression of our gratitude must consequently be the main focus of all our prayers. It should precede everything else that may constitute our prayers, such as confession, repentance, special requests and pleas. Before everything else, one must convey his gratitude.

Thankful for What We're Lacking

As strange as it may sound, we must also thank Hashem for what we do not have. Why? It's natural and easy to thank Hashem for our blessings, and all the good things He gives us. But the more profound aspect of gratitude is to thank Hashem for those things in our life that seem to be negative. When we espouse perfect faith, we recognize that if Hashem has decided to withhold something from us that we want very much, this too is for the very best.

Once a person thanks Hashem for these seemingly negative challenges as well, he'll begin to see amazing salvations to his problems - the very same problems that could have never been solved through crying and whining.

For example, a person without livelihood will likely pray by complaining to Hashem about his desperate situation. Such an individual will usually continue to suffer in poverty. Yet, if the same person would sincerely thank Hashem for these financial difficulties, realizing that they are a soul correction and a substitute for something much worse, he'd soon see relief. This is true in other situations such as illness, inability to find a soul mate, or childlessness. Whereas whining delays salvation, thanking Hashem for the very problem unlocks salvation's gates.

The Purpose of Good

Rebbe Nachman of Breslev teaches that both one's individual redemption and the redemption of the world at large depend upon our gratitude. His prime disciple Rebbe Natan explains in **Likutei Halachot**: "If everyone would follow the instruction of the true tzaddikim and believe that everything Hashem does is for the best, and always thank and praise Him, both for the things that we perceive as good as well as for everything that we perceive as not good... then surely all the tribulations and all the exiles would come to an immediate end and we would already be welcoming the complete and final redemption!"

Rebbe Natan writes very clearly that all our trials and tribulations are nullified through expressing our gratitude to Hashem. Furthermore, he explains that not only our own person tribulations cease through our thankfulness, but the Diaspora and exile are terminated and the final redemption can arrive! This is an awesome revelation that deserves our close attention.

The Perfect Remedy

Many years ago a woman came to me for guidance because she was childless. She told me she had done everything possible – prayer, repentance, giving charity, undergoing medical treatments, and making dietary changes, among other schemes. She told me that she and her husband were discouraged and close to desperation. Would their salvation ever come? Would they never merit holding their own child?

I told this woman she must abandon all these 'remedies.' She must even stop praying for children. Instead, I instructed her to devote an hour each day to personal prayer, thanking Hashem. "Say thank you!" I advised her. "Tell Hashem, 'Thank you that until now You have not given me children, because surely it is for the best and surely this is the way for me to attain my soul correction.'"

I also told her to thank Hashem for every child born to a friend and to work hard to accept all this favorably. "Feel genuine joy when you hear of another woman who has given birth," I instructed her. I then told her that every time she succeeds in feeling joy, she should add her own personal request: "Master of the Universe, may it be Your desire that I have children." I then blessed her that she soon has her own children.

The woman replied, "In what way is your advice better than anything I have already done? After all, I have prayed, cried, pleaded, repented…"

I responded, "The difference between what you have done so far and what I have instructed you to do is to express gratitude! Through thankfulness, you will attain emuna. Gratitude is an expression of true faith that everything is for the good and precisely according to Hashem's will with no mistakes. Expressing gratitude reflects your emuna - you trust that everything is in the Hashem's hands and the reason you have not yet had children is because this is Hashem's will."

Childless women fall into despair because they believe that, according to the laws of nature, they will not be able to bear children. In this respect, despair signifies that a person is depending upon circumstance and nature rather than on Hashem. Such a person blames external causes and is usually angry at Hashem, whining and weeping out of ingratitude.

Thankfulness repents for whining, despair and complaining. Only through gratitude can a person attain complete emuna.

Awesome Joy

All the tribulations a person must endure during his life are for his eternal benefit, and if one ponders the true purpose of these trials, one can in fact find great joy in them. Rebbe Nachman writes (Likutei Moharan, I:65): "Even the woes and tribulations a person must suffer, if one contemplates them, he will see that they are not bad at all but rather for his benefit, for they are given to him intentionally by Hashem for his own good, in order to remind him to do teshuva, and to repent for his sins; all of his suffering is only for his good, for they are delivered by Hashem and Hashem is all good. Therefore, if a person contemplates the trials and tribulations he is facing, he will see that the true purpose of this suffering is for his benefit, and he will thereupon realize that all this suffering is truly entirely good and he will be filled with joy to see that in truth there is no bad in the world and everything is good."

No one wants to suffer. But, if we do encounter suffering in our lives, then Rebbe Nachman explains that it is all for our ultimate benefit. The purpose of tribulations is to bring us closer to Hashem. King David said, "But as for me, the nearness of G-d is my good" (Psalms, 73).

One who understands that suffering is for his eternal benefit avoids sadness and despair; indeed, he'll be able to praise Hashem sincerely and pray in earnest.

Someone who does not seek closeness to Hashem won't joyfully accept anything that he perceives as being "bad." However, a person who longs to be close with Hashem realizes that everything is a result of Divine Providence and everything is intended for his eternal benefit.

Whining – The Source of all Evil

A couple came to seek my advice after the husband had been in an accident. Both the husband and wife complained how difficult their lives were, and cried about how bitter their lives had become. Obviously, their complaints could be readily understood. After all, life is easier without problems. Since I was familiar with this couple, I knew their whining was truly exaggerated because in truth, they also had a great deal for which to be grateful.

"Tell me," I asked them, "With thanks to Hashem, have you not been married for a number of years already? How many men and women do not succeed in finding a spouse? And, thank G-d, you live in marital bliss – how many couples lack such peace between them? And, thank G-d, you have been blessed with children – how many people remain childless? You have been blessed with many other spiritual and material merits, thank G-d." And so I sat with this couple, and showed them that they truly had very many blessed things in their lives.

I also told them, "If you would feel true gratitude for everything Hashem has given you, you would not come to me with your whining. Even though it is true that you have suffered tribulations, you would not whine, since you would continue to recognize all the good in your lives. Precisely when things seem to be difficult, we must say, 'thank G-d.' If one has true faith that everything is from Hashem and Hashem is all good, then you would be able to thank Hashem even for life's difficult trials. Such praise to Hashem mitigates all harsh judgments. Your whining only makes life more difficult for you."

Can we say that those who are happy in life never face difficulties, trials or tribulations? Of course not! They remain happy despite life's challenges because they constantly express their gratitude to Hashem. They are happy with their lot, no matter what that may be!

On the other hand, there are those who feel that their lives are pure torture, not because they suffer more than others, but because they don't know how to be grateful. Faith means believing that Hashem is good and being constantly thankful for everything that He gives us. A person's attitude – not the events in one's life - determines whether a person is happy or sad. A happy person accepts anything that comes his way with faith and sincere gratitude. He is appreciative and aware of the miracles in his life. The sad person feels shortchanged all the time, whining and crying about his misfortune. His feeling that life is bad only invokes more harsh judgments from Above.

Without Complaint

An elderly bachelor came to speak to me, full of complaints for the hardships he has endured and for the fact that he has remained a bachelor all these years. I told him, "First thank Hashem that you have yet to marry. Then, and only then, can I help you."

He replied, "What?!? How can I be thankful that I have not married? It's so painful for me that I have remained a bachelor all these years!"

I continued, "If Hashem has not let you marry until now, you must understand that it is for your own good. So thank Him! So long as you continue believing Hashem has done you an injustice, you can't smile. Therefore, say 'thank You.' Thank Hashem and pray with the true belief that if you have not yet married, it is for your own benefit. Hashem makes no mistakes. Through gratitude you will find the faith that not marrying up until now is part of your soul correction and for your true benefit. If you listen to this advice, you will witness salvation!"

A person who truly believes that there is no bad in this world ascends to a level of Divine loving-kindness, where there is no judgment and prayers are answered completely.

A Good Trait

Why is gratitude so much loftier than its counterpart – senseless whining? Whining and complaining extinguish Divine compassion. Why? Whining is a denial that everything comes from Hashem and that everything Hashem does is good. In that respect, whining is tantamount to heresy, and consequently invokes the harshest judgments and endless punishments, as we witness with the sin of the spies.

Just as whining and complaining bring about harsh judgments, in contrast, our gratitude mitigates severe judgment and arouses endless blessings.

Practically speaking, if a person is enduring some sort of tribulation, or lacks something that is critically important to him, the best action he can take is to give thanks for that which he lacks.

As long as a person is incapable of thanking Hashem for his circumstances no matter what they may be, his emuna is incomplete. If he cannot thank Hashem, then he lacks the realization that his suffering and tribulations are for his eternal good. Therefore, he must be careful to not whine and complain, but rather to pray to Hashem, asking for the strength and faith that will enable him to truly thank Hashem for everything.

Gateways to Happiness

Most people assume that true prayer requires praying with tears streaming down their faces. People are concerned that if they don't succeed in crying, their prayers aren't sincere enough. True, the Gemara teaches us that the gates of tears are never locked. However, Rebbe Natan of Breslev teaches that prayer with joy surpasses prayer with tears. "Prayer is an aspect of joy, since one must pray in joy, as it is written, 'Worship the L-rd with gladness'" (Psalms, 100).

When our sages spoke of praying with tears, the intention was that a person should be roused to cry not from commonplace sadness, but rather from ecstasy - from his sense of joy, as well as from his yearning to grow closer to Hashem.

Imagine that a son approaches his father and tearfully pleads for something. Invariably, the father's mercy will be roused and he will fulfill his son's request. Now, let's imagine a son who is always joyful, and is always praising and thanking his father. The son asks nothing of his father. The father will be deeply gratified by the son's words of gratitude and praise, and will constantly want to give his son more on his own accord.

The son who comes before his father in tears inspires his father's mercy and receives whatever it is that he requests. Yet the son who is constantly praising his father and thanking him joyfully inspires his father's attribute of love. Consequently, the father will always give to such a son generously.

Crying may arouse the attribute of mercy and result in receiving the specific thing for which one is crying. At the same time, joy and thankfulness arouse love and desire, attributes much more powerful than mercy. Joy and gratitude invoke Divine abundance.

Try a Smile!

If, while praying with joy, one is inspired to tears of longing or a broken heart, this is surely for the good, so long as he is careful not to slip into tears of complaint and self-pity.

Happiness and emuna are closely related. We pray best when we are inspired to experience joy.

A Big Favor

A woman suffering from very unattractive sores on her face came to me for advice, and told me that she planned to do a six-hour personal-prayer session to invoke a heavenly cure. I told her that she can do personal prayer as long as she desires, but she must be careful to begin her prayer session by thanking Hashem for these hideous sores, which are surely for her advantage. These sores were bringing her to a lofty level of prayer and a deep relationship with Hashem. Once she expressed her gratitude, she could ask Hashem to clarify for her what she must correct. Only then could she finally pray for a true remedy and complete cure.

Always remember that faith means believing that everything is for the good; therefore, we should undoubtedly thank Hashem for everything we lack and suffer. Our problems and tribulations are what bring us closer to Hashem and arouse in us the desire to pray and open the depths of our hearts to Hashem. As such, they are an immensely big favor from Above.

A Wondrous Gift

A personal experience of my own illustrates how serious troubles can actually be a great gift. Approximately thirty years ago, I fell into enormous debt. I do not mean a few thousand dollars; I was in debt for many tens of thousands of dollars. There was no practical way for me to get myself out of this crushing debt. I would have had to work day and night only to repay the monthly interest on my loans, so how could I possibly ever return all the money I owed?

Since the Gemara teaches that there are no tribulations without prior transgression, I realized that there is a spiritual reason for my predicament and why I had fallen into debt.

I looked at my monetary deficit as if it was a tree with many branches. No matter how great an effort I would make to remove one of its branches, another one would inevitably grow in its stead. I came to the understanding that the only true solution was to deal with the root of the problem, which can be done only through prayer and teshuva. My teacher and spiritual mentor, Rav Eliezer Berland Shlit'a, who had endured his own battle with severe debt, encouraged me and emphasized that the financial woes he had suffered had brought him closer to Hashem than anything else.

Another friend also encouraged me during this difficult time. He told me of a time he was indebted to a certain rabbi. This rabbi told him that according to Jewish law, he must leave yeshiva to work and pay off the debt. My friend, who had a very sweet and innocent soul, opted for personal prayer. He opened his heart to Hashem, telling Him that although the rabbi had instructed him to seek employment, he would like to make a Divine deal. Instead of working odd jobs, which would inevitably lead him to spend much time away from Torah studying and praying, he would go to work for Hashem. In lieu of working odd jobs for eight hours a day, he'd do personal prayer for eight hours each day! He diligently prayed for eight hours a day and he soon found himself out of debt.

True, this friend was in debt for a minimal sum - much smaller than my own - but the story encouraged me. I thought that I too would go to work for Hashem! When others would tell me to get a job or go collect charity, I would not argue with them. After all, I was indeed listening to their advice – I got a job with Hashem, and I went to collect charity… from Hashem!

It was clear to me that only Hashem could solve my problem: No "natural" means - no salary or charity - could cover the exorbitant sum of my debt.

Double Earnings

So, I devoted hours to personal prayer, concentrating on my financial situation. I began by thanking Hashem for putting me in debt, a "gift" since it led me to become closer to Him. My personal suffering was a cloud with a silver lining for two reasons:

First, the severity of my financial woes stimulated me to pray from the depths of my soul for hours on end. Without such a tribulation, I would not have been inspired to such heartfelt and lengthy prayer. My personal prayer session was no longer a habitual rambling list of requests, but rather a sincere call to Hashem. The difference between how I used to practice personal prayer and the way I was now praying was immense.

Second, I noticed that in every personal prayer session, Hashem would reveal to me another point that I had to rectify. As such, my financial problems were a catalyst for teshuva, character improvement, and getting closer to Hashem.

I became much more spiritual as a result of my prayer and teshuva. Nothing generates more joy than the feeling of increased proximity to Hashem. I consequently found myself initiating each new personal prayer session by profusely thanking Hashem for my debt.

Those who were familiar with my financial struggles could not understand my joy. They thought perhaps I had gone mad, since after all - with such debt - how could a person be happy?

My happiness and inner calm came from my complete faith in Hashem's Divine Providence. I fully believed that the debt was for my true benefit.

I encouraged my wife to have faith that we would eventually see the light at the end of the dark tunnel of this tough test. I explained to her that if we deal with our woes with emuna, then when we do eventually succeed in overcoming the debt, we will have acquired a level of faith in Hashem that will serve us well for the rest of our lives.

And so I continued praying. Meanwhile, I witnessed endless salvations and miracles. Within a year of such concentrated personal prayer, all my financial problems were brought to an end!

My debt had in fact brought me to a level of closeness with Hashem that I had not previously known. I felt blessed with the wondrous gift of emuna that accompanies me to this day, a gift that I have merited and pray I use for the benefit of people everywhere.

Boomerang

Any self-pity or disgruntlement that one feels as a result of harsh judgments is a dangerous boomerang. While a person languishes in misery, the Heavenly Court is asking, "Why isn't he repenting? He is in debt, and instead of being inspired to do teshuva, he attributes his financial trouble to fate and random circumstance." This only leads to more severe judgments.

A person's harsh "wake-up calls" are rendered superfluous upon repenting for his sins. As stern judgments fade away, a person no longer feels saddened or sorrowful. If a person chooses to do teshuva daily, he will not feel sad even if he has not yet rectified all his transgressions - even if he is still suffering severe physical hardships. His faith will illuminate his soul and he'll feel nothing but joy.

It Could Have Been Different

If I had lost faith as a result of the debt I had accumulated, or if I had blamed my wife or others for the financial woes I was encountering, I would have surely fallen into deep depression. I would have tortured myself, become anxious and guilt-ridden, angry, and obsessed with self-pity. I would have expected everyone around me to feel sorry for me, and would have ignored my personal responsibility for my predicament. As such, I would have brought nothing but bitterness to my surroundings. Surely my debt would not have been resolved so quickly and perhaps I would have remained forever in enormous debt.

Who knows what trouble I would have encountered had I succumbed to despair and depression? Who knows the guilty feelings my family and acquaintances would have suffered had I chosen to blame them instead of taking responsibility myself? Most of all, I would have never acquired the splendid gifts of faith and trust in Hashem that I received. I would have never composed the books I have written, especially the international best-seller, **The Garden of Emuna**. I would have never been able to help others get close to Hashem, and I would have never succeeded in establishing a yeshiva. I would have never been able to guide others on how to successfully survive and grow spiritually as a result of the financial crises from which they suffer.

Without emuna, I could never have survived this tribulation. The power of emuna, especially in such time of stress, inspired me to help others benefit from my experience.

Wake-Up Call

In light of everything we've learned until now, thanking Hashem should be our initial move in any challenging situation. Only after we realize that the difficulty at hand is for the very best, and most likely a wake-up call to bring us closer to Hashem, should we begin to ask Hashem for salvation. Our prayers will consequently be optimistic and full of emuna, rather than full of complaints and self-pity. Positive-oriented prayers have a much greater chance of being answered.

A yeshiva student once told me that he had difficulty waking up each morning; even if he set several alarm clocks and placed them right next to his bed, he couldn't wake up. His wife would shake him but he'd keep on sleeping. He'd finally get up around midday, angry and frustrated that he slept his life away once more. Waking up in such a bad mood, the rest of his waking hours were tainted with doom and frustration.

The wife, so upset at seeing her husband decay in bed, left the house each day in bad spirits, and had already threatened to file for divorce.

The student sought my advice. "How can I be happy," he asked, "if others constantly humiliate me about my sleeping habits, when my wife is threatening me with divorce, and when Hashem is also angry at me for missing my morning prayers?"

I instructed this young man that he must use this problem as a crow-bar to pry his heart open to Hashem in lengthy personal prayer. From the 60 minutes a day of personal prayer that I prescribed for him, I told him to devote at least 30 minutes to asking Hashem to help him wake up in the morning.

But most importantly, I told him to maintain his happiness, reminding him of Hashem's infinite love and patience for every one of us. Rather than wasting energy on despair, he should channel his power into personal prayer, the only viable solution.

Here too, I instructed the young man to be grateful for the problem, since it is a catalyst for prayer, teshuva, and getting closer to Hashem. Again, after thanking Hashem profusely for this obsessive desire to sleep, he could now ask Hashem to help him wake up on time in the morning. In this way, he'd develop true faith and a nearness to Hashem that he could not achieve otherwise.

Why Negativity?

Try making a list of all the things that you find difficult, or that sadden you, worry you, or arouse negative emotions within you. Now try thanking Hashem for these things too.

Our negativity is simply the result of weak emuna. Thankfulness for the seemingly negative aspects of life helps us build true faith; namely, to believe and ultimately realize that everything, no matter how we perceive it, comes from Hashem and is for our complete benefit. Our gratitude for life's less desirable moments and the tribulations that we suffer builds both our personal prayer and our lives.

Many people complain that they have difficulty speaking to Hashem in personal prayer. That's understandable because in order to speak to Him, one must believe in Him. To ask Hashem for anything, we must first build our emuna. Once a person believes that everything is from Hashem and that everything Hashem does is for our benefit, he finds peace of mind. Only after he sees the good in his suffering can he begin to speak to Hashem with optimism and positivity. Thanking Hashem for life's difficulties invokes Divine mercy and opens up the gates of salvation.

Rebbe Nachman stresses (Likutei Moharan, II:24): "We must use all our strength to overcome whatever we face, and always be happy. It is human nature to sink into sadness because of our suffering, and therefore a person must utilize all his strength to be happy, and bring himself to be joyous even if it necessitates making jokes and so forth. A broken heart is also good, but only for an hour a day to pour his heart out to Hashem. One can be broken-hearted during that one hour, but he must be joyful the rest of the day. For such broken-heartedness can lead to gloominess faster than joking can lead one to tomfoolery. Therefore, a person must always be happy, and allow himself to be broken-hearted only during the specifically designated hour of personal prayer.

The Circle of Joy

"They shall achieve gladness and joy, and sadness and sighing shall flee" (Isaiah, 35:10). Rebbe Nachman explains (Likutei Moharan, II:23) that a person must forcefully uplift negative emotions and turn them into joy. He uses the parable of a depressed person standing morosely on the sidelines of a group of joyful dancers. One of these cheerful dancers grabs this sad individual and pulls him into the circle. The sad person finds himself partaking in the joy until he is truly happy.

Frequently, we begin personal prayer preoccupied with some pressing problem. Sometimes we can't see the light whatsoever. It may seem impossible to initiate words of gratitude. We might be so upset that we just can't thank Hashem for the good things in our lives, let alone the difficulties and suffering.

Our first task is to rid ourselves of even the slightest bit of sadness and anxiety. How? We pull it all into the circle of joy…

Joy doesn't mean that we ignore our pain and sadness, pretending that they don't exist. This solves nothing, since the problems are still there. We simply make our pain or problem the second item on our personal-prayer agenda, rather than the first.

Personal prayer should always begin with rejoicing in the positive points of our lives and thanking Hashem for them. Voila! The circle of joy appears. Reminding ourselves of our good points and thanking Hashem for them uplifts our spirits and enables us to realize that the problem at hand will also turn out for the best. We use the opportunity to assess ourselves, draw proper conclusions and do teshuva, and then implement the changes that we deem necessary. Once we see the worthwhile role our troubles played as wake-up calls, we can sincerely thank Hashem for them too.

The entire purpose of our tribulations is to trigger the aforementioned process of self-assessment, teshuva, and self-improvement. Once we've done this, the problems eventually become superfluous. What's more, our requests for Divine assistance are so much more positive and so much more cogent than the whining and complaining of a person that approaches Hashem with a negative attitude.

Let's never forget that life's trying times are all for our benefit, as the prophet says, "It is a time of trouble unto Jacob, but out of it shall he be saved" (Jeremiah, 30:7).

Don't Fake It

Beginning personal prayers by expressing gratefulness to Hashem for everything, including our suffering and deprivation, is vital in order to guard us from self-persecution, depression and despair while we're engaged in teshuva and self-assessment.

Rebbe Nachman says that a depressed or harshly self-critical person will find it impossible to open his heart to Hashem. Sadness signifies a lack of faith in Hashem; hence, if a person can't seem to overcome the sadness, he shouldn't "fake it." Honesty is so important - we shouldn't lie to ourselves and we certainly shouldn't lie to Hashem. A person who suffers from a less-than-positive mood should candidly tell Hashem what's bothering him and what hurts. He should lay his worries and anxieties out there openly on the personal-prayer table, but without crying and complaining. There's a tremendous difference between telling Hashem what hurts us and complaining about the pain.

Now that we've unloaded the weight of our problems from our hearts, we can thank Hashem for the good points and assess ourselves in light of the problems. This will enable us to genuinely express our gratitude for these very same problems that made us feel anxious and sad in the first place.

Praying for salvation is almost futile as long as we're not sincerely thankful for our deprivations and tribulations. We must ask Hashem to give us the faith that all everything is for our own good and strive to feel grateful in our hearts for whatever difficulties we encounter.

The Evil Inclination ... Great!

Emuna enables us to taste the sweetness of this world. Emuna is the only answer to life's riddles and difficulties. With emuna – everything is good! Even the Evil Inclination is a good thing when one looks at life through eyes of emuna.

A person with emuna – with pure and complete faith - will ask Hashem to guide him throughout life. With the cognizance that Hashem is guiding him, he sees everything that he encounters, even suffering, as an opportunity to grow closer to Hashem!

Try appealing to Hashem in this manner: "Beloved Father in Heaven, You created me and You know what's best for me, what my mission in life is, and what I need to rectify. So please, guide me! Teach me! Please show me what I should do. Lead me down the proper path and help me do Your will. This is my choice!" Our sages teach us that when we make Hashem's will our will, He makes our will His own.

The faith that everything is for the best devastates the Evil Inclination. The Evil Inclination attempts to destroy an individual by injecting him with the venom of self-persecution and despair. The Evil Inclination's strategy is built on a person's thoughts of heresy - in other words, that there is bad in the world. Once a person doubts Hashem, the Evil Inclination goes in for the kill, telling a person,

"Things are hopeless! Catastrophic! You're doomed!" The Evil Inclination convinces the person that there is no hope to survive or overcome his current challenge and suffering.

The greatest problem we face today is despair. If a person would begin to smile and be a bit cheerful, all his problems would be solved! Emuna gives a person the understanding that everything is for his own good; even the obstacles he faces in spiritual ascent are for his eternal benefit.

For example, if a person finds that there are obstacles in his path of getting closer to Hashem, he should have faith that these obstacles are for his own good. Hashem wants him to first prepare himself for subsequent spiritual ascent. Without proper preparation, spiritual ascent is liable to trigger arrogance. Conceit is a barrier to Divine light, causing a person to be distanced from Hashem. Hashem consequently protects a person from arrogance and complacency by giving him difficulties. These hardships are good for a person since they necessitate lengthy personal prayer. One should, therefore, thank Hashem for these obstacles, understanding they have indeed been created for his benefit.

Our outlook should be that Hashem gives us only what is good for us; no matter what the situation, good or seemingly otherwise, we must be grateful. When we are truly grateful, the Evil Inclination cannot weaken us. The Evil Inclination's ploys to pull a person into the self-persecution mode are ridiculously ineffective against a person who views life through the rosy lenses of emuna.

A person must remind himself that Hashem is responsible for his failures, as well as his successes. Know the Hebrew expression, *Ein Od Milvado* – there is nothing but Hashem! Everything comes from Hashem!

Depression, as well as thoughts of despair, is heretic in nature. Without G-d's help we surely cannot overcome the Evil Inclination. Indeed, we must never think we can overcome the Evil Inclination on our own, without Hashem's help, and without prayer. Failing to understand this concept means that Hashem did not help us understand, and we should be grateful for this too. With emuna, we know that every failure is a gift from Hashem and all for the best. In that respect, all failures are gold-mine opportunities and gifts from Hashem – for this we should be grateful.

Sure, everyone wants to succeed. But if we do have a setback, know that this is also from Hashem and for our ultimate benefit. Setbacks are good for humility and stimulating a stronger second effort. Therefore, we must thank Hashem for them as well.

Nothing will be beneficial for us in the long run if we don't pray for what we want or need. We should begin our prayers by thanking Hashem for our failures; through them, we learn that we are nothing without His help.

Disarming the Evil Inclination

The root of conceit is dissatisfaction and whining when a person thinks he deserves more. Humble people are grateful people, since they believe that they deserve nothing. In that respect, they are very close to truth, are satisfied with their lot in life, and are honest. The arrogant are just the opposite.

Discontent is a statement that we are displeased with Hashem's will. A person who is displeased with what life has in store for him is, in effect, displeased with Hashem. It suggests that the person wants Hashem to do his will, rather than him doing Hashem's will.

On the other hand, when a person is grateful for everything Hashem does, he neutralizes and rectifies all his negative character traits, such as hatred, envy, and anger. He becomes truly happy with his lot, and is spared of such Evil Inclinations as greed, thievery, and even murder. Emuna and gratitude form a virtual bomb squad that dismantles the Evil Inclination's destructive potential.

A person who is happy with his lot in life has no motivation to do evil things, since he feels no deprivation that could possibly lead him to desire to do something damaging to another person. He accepts everything with true faith. Even if he has no money, he won't steal, since he believes that if Hashem wants him to be without a penny in his pocket, this too is for the best. He doesn't envy others because he is genuinely content with what he has, no matter how much or how little. He knows that whatever his lot may be, it's the best for him. His absolute faith in Hashem disarms his Evil Inclination.

Emuna neutralizes self-centeredness and arrogance as well. Knowing that everything is from Hashem, a person is no longer plagued by a sense of entitlement.

Happy with One's Spiritual Lot

A person should be happy with his spiritual lot in life too. Sure, we all long to reach a point where we'll never fail or sin again and only ascend higher and higher. This is certainly a desirable goal; yet, we can attain higher spiritual levels only if such success is G-d's will! In the meanwhile, we must be content with the level we're currently holding, keep making our best effort, and wait patiently until Hashem decides to bring us closer to Him.

Surely Hashem wants us to rectify our character traits, immerse ourselves in Torah, be modest and humble, grow spiritually, and make the right decisions. But, if He were to give us a higher spiritual level than we're capable of handling ("excessive light" in kabbalistic terms), we'd either go insane, die, or become a heretic, Heaven forbid. We must wait patiently and lovingly accept our current spiritual level, no matter how distant it may be from our goals. Only by being genuinely grateful for our present limited spiritual level can we eventually ascend. Measured, gradual growth prevents a person from ending up in a mental institution or becoming a heretic, G-d forbid.

Many newly-observant people have meteoric spiritual rises followed by catastrophic falls. It's readily understood that a fat person who never exercises is at high risk for a heart attack if he tries to run a marathon. Just as physical prowess must be built slowly, gradually, and cautiously, so should spiritual prowess.

One must be grateful for his current level, and pray for future ascent when it is Hashem's will. Spiritual growth consists of endless ascents and falls, all sorts of obstacles and barriers, and even misdeeds and transgressions. The path to Hashem is long and trying, demanding effort and much hard work. This is neither the path of instant gratification nor least resistance. It is not a road to fantasy land that can be traveled speedily and effortlessly without a struggle. But don't be discouraged; the mere desire to get closer to Hashem opens doors of Divine compassion and assistance.

We should subsequently be grateful for what we have spiritually, just as we are with what we have materially. Rebbe Natan teaches that we should express our thankfulness for what we have, yet pray for what we aspire.

Focus on the True Purpose

We can especially thank Hashem for what we have when we realize that everything He gives us is intended to help us find and fulfill our true purpose. Disgruntlement with our lot in life means that we're not devoted solely to the main purpose of our existence - growing closer to Hashem.

People tend to focus on worldly success, thinking in terms of wealth and material gain while yearning to satisfy animalistic desires. They demand that things go smoothly, seeking instant gratification in the most convenient and effortless manner. They're inevitably dissatisfied any time life goes against their wishes.

In contrast, a person devoted to fulfilling his true purpose on earth will always be happy and grateful. He understands that whatever he encounters teaches him something about how to grow closer to Hashem. Such a person will surely thank Hashem for everything and will appreciate whatever failures and hardships he must face. He trusts that Hashem knows exactly what is best for him and what's most conducive for the fulfillment of his true purpose - to grow closer to Hashem.

Hashem performs miracles to create the circumstances that help us attain our *tikkun* - the complete rectification of our soul.

The Light at the End of the Tunnel

Whenever we experience difficult times, we can be encouraged by the knowledge that Hashem always creates the remedy before He sends the infirmity. In other words, no matter how difficult the tribulation may appear to be, Hashem has already prepared the solution and salvation.

Avoiding despair in trying situations is a challenge. Feelings of futility and hopelessness lead to despair. Without faith, a person can succumb to the feeling that there's no solution or salvation to his problem.

We might not see where our salvation will come from, but that's inconsequential. Everything is from Hashem, and Hashem is not limited like our human powers of reasoning. He surely has a solution! Therefore, during life's dark and frightening moments, a person need not attempt to conjecture where his salvation will come from.

One should rather do what he can do; first, to thank Hashem for this suffering which surely is for his ultimate good, since it triggers self-assessment and subsequent repentance. Second, he should turn to Hashem in personal prayer: "Father in Heaven! You can transform the very worst tribulation into the greatest possible good. Help me use this opportunity to rectify what You want me to rectify and get closer to You. Help me accept everything with full faith, gratitude, and happiness." With such an attitude, it won't be long until everything turns around for the very best, in the revealed sense as well.

In difficult times, it's vital to cling to the faith that everything Hashem does is for our own good. We don't always understand why we must undergo pain and anguish. Still, our faith in Hashem should become even stronger during tests and trials. At any given moment, He can turn the most devastating predicament into a blessing, as it is He who creates the remedy for any affliction! No matter what ails a person, he has much more reason to smile rather than cry.

Sadness is self-defeating. Rebbe Nachman says that when a person is mired in sadness, Hashem is not with him. But when a person expresses his gratitude to Hashem, all the gates for his salvation suddenly swing open.

Once he has thanked Hashem, a person can then speak freely about the problem he is facing, with a genuine desire to understand the message that Hashem is conveying through this difficulty. He must speak with a sincere smile on his face and with faith, for if he begins to complain, Hashem will turn away. After all, did Hashem create the world so that His creations can whine? Hashem created the world for His creations to smile, believe in Him, and trust that everything He does is for the good!

Sometimes, after people pray it appears that they only receive more tribulations. That's the result of whining and complaining. Thanking Hashem profusely and frequently prevents further tribulations. By expressing gratitude, a person feels more joy and dispels the sadness that enables complaining or whining to sneak into his prayers.

Restoring Emuna

An important part of our daily personal prayer is thanking Hashem not only for our blessings, but for our less desirable moments in life too. Thanking Hashem is conducive to miraculous deliverance.

An hour a day is the minimum one should devote to personal prayer. At least a third of this hour should be devoted to expressing our gratitude to Hashem. This daily hour builds the spiritual vessels necessary for receiving the light of emuna. The book **In Forest Fields** explains the art and practice of daily personal prayer in greater detail.

We are all constantly challenged with difficult situations. Consequently, even a spiritually strong person can lose his faith if he does not practice this daily hour of personal prayer.

A daily hour of personal prayer has the power to restore a person's emuna, even if it has been significantly weakened. No matter what difficulties one experiences, an hour of intimate conversation with Hashem restores a person's faith and revitalizes his soul. It thereby enables a person to be happy with his lot, and attain true gratitude for his tribulation.

To effect genuine personal growth, we need profuse personal prayer - the more the better. We should speak our personal prayers in our most natural and comfortable language, even with our own local slang and jargon. Hashem understands a Texas drawl or Harlem street-talk just as well as He understands Oxford English. He certainly understands the Hebrew, Yiddish or Spanish expressions that we pepper our personal prayers with too.

People ask, what should we pray for? Nothing should be taken for granted. We pray for the health and sustenance of every limb and organ in our body. We pray for our loved ones. We pray to internalize what we have studied, so that the teachings become second nature to us. We pray for true faith. We speak to Hashem about anything that we harbor in our hearts, since everything that comes from our hearts belongs to the realm of prayer. The list is endless; when one sincerely contemplates the concept of personal prayer, an hour a day is sorely inadequate. But, we do our best to do what we can.

Through personal prayer, a person connects to Hashem. Let's be realistic. We frequently forget Hashem during the day. People attribute success to themselves. They also persecute themselves in times of failure. Those who don't persecute themselves blame others; a spouse, a parent, or a loyal friend. Such people have indeed forgotten that success and failure come from Hashem. They react without emuna because they forget about Hashem, or else never knew about Him in the first place. Personal prayer rectifies this spiritual amnesia through an intimate hour of one-on-one time with Hashem.

The more one engages in talking to Hashem, the more one remembers Hashem.

Putting an End to the Race

A person with faith lives a life that is heaven on earth. To attain such a level, one must practice this hour of daily personal prayer; without it, he won't attain the type of tangible emuna that everything he experiences is for his best. Emuna puts an end to the arrogance that comes from success and the self-persecution or blame game that result from setbacks.

Proper Self-Assessment

People are shocked to find out that even our sins come from Hashem. But wait a moment – Hashem surely doesn't want us to transgress His Torah. So why does He allow us to sin?

Sometimes a person is complacent, thinking that he has nothing to correct. Others feel that they can get by without learning emuna and manage with spiritual mediocrity. Still others may have failed to learn certain laws properly. Hashem will let these people sin so that they will have to make teshuva, learn emuna, and seek Hashem.

The first step to true teshuva is confessing one's sins, and tell Hashem anything he or she has done which violates the

Torah. The second step is to truly regret this sin, and tell Hashem about any regrets about having disappointed Him by failing to observe His Torah. These sins are acknowledged because they distanced the person from Hashem. The third step to teshuva is to ask Hashem for His forgiveness.

Hence, the first three steps are confession, remorse, and apology.

Following these three steps, a person who has sinned must ask Hashem to show him why he in fact failed to overcome his Evil Inclination. "Master of the Universe! Why did I fail? Why did You not help me? What did You want me to learn from this?" Usually what Hashem wanted is for the person to be roused to pray for the particular matter in question - to pray to be able to overcome his Evil Inclination both regarding this particular transgression and his overall observance of Hashem's commandments.

For example, someone came to seek my advice because he had been looking at immodest sights in breach of personal holiness. I told him that he must do teshuva – confess, express remorse, and ask forgiveness. I also reminded him that beyond the various stages of teshuva, he should ask Hashem why He did not help him guard his eyes. By realizing that Hashem did not help him, he'll now pray more and try harder in this particular area.

Failure that initiates a process of self-assessment and subsequent teshuva is an amazing impetus to get closer to Hashem. A person should contemplate everything in this life within this context; if he has failed, rather than blame himself and succumb to depression, he should first seize the opportunity to get closer to Hashem through the three steps of teshuva - confession, remorse, and apology – and the fourth step of asking Hashem's guidance in helping him strengthen and rectify whatever weakness led to the misdeed. Finally, one must resolve to do better from this moment on, while appealing to Hashem for help in avoiding future sin.

If a person says "I obligate myself to guard my eyes always," he is merely deluding himself. He will surely fail to guard his eyes once again the very next time he encounters temptation. Instead, he must pray to Hashem, "Father in Heaven, I obligate myself to pray daily for Your help with guarding my eyes." This is a worthwhile resolution that he can surely keep.

Proper self-assessment and daily personal prayer turn setbacks into triumphs by bringing a person so much closer to Hashem.

The True Path

Expressing gratitude is the most important part of our personal prayer. Precisely because of its importance, it is not a simple task. Prayer through whining, crying and begging appears to us to be the natural way to go, but it's a path of least resistance. The Evil Inclination is happy when we cry and complain, and it certainly won't try to stop us.

Effective prayer is the result of a grateful attitude, even in the face of apparent calamity. Such emuna-filled prayer brings Hashem enormous gratification and is readily heard and accepted. The Evil Inclination will try to interfere with such prayers, but we can strengthen our resolve by realizing that nothing of true value comes easily.

Gratitude Redeems

The Evil Inclination will try anything to hamper our words of gratitude. A person must be strong and determined in devoting adequate time to thanking Hashem. He might face huge obstacles; he might even feel like breaking down in tears because of the difficult challenges he faces. However, he must strengthen himself with the trust that by virtue of his uncompromising and unconditional gratitude to Hashem, his troubles will disappear.

How does gratitude bring an end to suffering? Tribulations begin as a consequence of ingratitude in the first place! Rebbe Natan explains that our troubles result from a lack of emuna and the suspicion that Hashem has mistreated us or hasn't been fair with us, Heaven forbid. Such an erroneous presumption leads to Divine concealment and stern judgments, which manifest themselves as additional troubles.

If we accept everything with gratitude, we will understand Hashem's message to us from the outset. We then will be spontaneously inspired to strengthen our sense of gratitude and do teshuva, and our troubles will dissipate rather than increase.

Don't worry if you haven't sufficiently expressed your gratitude to Hashem until now. Rebbe Natan teaches that anyone can declare a new beginning, anytime. So, from this day forward, start thanking Hashem. Get used to looking at how everything is for the good; not only will it spare you from untold grief but it will help you express gratitude and praise to Hashem for everything in your life.

Gratitude mitigates harsh judgments and invokes salvations. I've compiled some practical guidelines to help you incorporate gratitude in your personal prayer, invoking Divine compassion:

A 3-Point Strategy for Dealing with Tribulations in Personal Prayer

Point One: For about 30 minutes – the first half of your next personal prayer session - forget momentarily about your troubles, and only thank Hashem for the good things in your life.

You're probably raising an eyebrow. Why should we forget our troubles if the whole purpose of our personal prayer session is to invoke Divine deliverance? Aren't we better advised to beg Hashem to redeem us from our tribulations? If we begin our personal prayer session with pain and anguish, we're liable to fall into a mode of self-pity, replete with unnecessary tears. Our whining will only bring more trouble, rather than salvation. We must always keep in mind that unwarranted crying results in the most difficult of tribulations.

Everyone enjoys endless kindness and salvations from Hashem. The Evil Inclination blinds a person, however, by showing him an inflated view of life's current difficulty – the "black spot" - and by underplaying and concealing all of life's many good points. The ungrateful individual falls prey to the Evil Inclination's ploy, becoming totally disgruntled when anything in life goes awry.

A person's lack of gratitude enables this "black spot" to distort his perception, masking the endless beauty and good in his life. So practically speaking, the person himself intensifies his own suffering by solely focusing on the "black spot."

Therefore, the first thing we must do is put the current tribulation out of mind, so that it cannot blind us to life's wonderful side. By disregarding our present trouble, we can remember our many blessings such as our beating heart, our working lungs, our seeing eyes, and our daily bread.

Another advantage to momentarily snuffing out suffering is that it enables a person to focus on his own good points. He can then remember how many times Hashem saved him from difficult situations and peril. He can begin to thank Hashem for his truly beautiful life.

If at this point, the Evil Inclination wants to block out the bright lights in your life and tell you that everything is black, just tell it that black is beautiful!

We are suggesting that you put aside the current difficulty for only half an hour. You may find that it will be a welcome break from misery.

Point Two: After thanking Hashem and truly feeling content with your lot, examine the current tribulation. Seek out the intrinsic good in what you are facing and thank Hashem for this problem.

After thanking Hashem profusely for the good, one can now examine the "black spot" with true faith. He can start by asking Hashem to help him understand the silver lining within the current dark cloud. Through honest contemplation, he will surely discover that Hashem is giving him the present tribulation for his ultimate benefit. Through life's difficulties, Hashem leads a person to his true purpose in life.

A young man came to my yeshiva, not with a desire to learn but rather to use it as a place of refuge from his personal problems. One day he approached me, complaining that these problems were causing him great distress. I reminded him that were it not for these problems, he would have never dreamed of attending a yeshiva and studying Torah;

therefore, he should recognize that these difficult problems were in fact his salvation, and thank Hashem profusely for them. It turned out the young man completely remade himself as a yeshiva student, all thanks to the severe problems that were the catalyst for his seeking an asylum in the first place.

Point Three: Having expressed your gratitude and discovering the reason you have been given this trial, now do teshuva and pray for deliverance.

When someone restores his faith and understands that the "black spot" is for his own benefit, serving as the seed for future redemption, he can move on to the third stage – seeking to grasp why this has happened to him, for what he must do teshuva, and - finally - to pray for salvation.

As I composed this chapter, I was tempted to omit this third stage altogether. From experience I know that most people want to concentrate on praying for salvation, and will either skip or shorten the first two stages so that they can get on with what they really want to do: Pray for an end to their tribulation. Even if they carry out the first two stages, they inevitably will not be truly putting their current suffering out of mind. And without genuine gratitude for what they are suffering, they will end up spilling unwarranted tears.

For those who are not absolutely certain that they will not end up whining and crying needlessly, please forego this third step. Concentrate intensely on the first two steps in the meantime.

The Hall of Gratitude

A female student of mine told me she was keeping a gratitude journal. She promised Hashem that she will try to recognize and record every good thing that happens to her and thank Him for each of these blessings. Indeed, she received wonderful Divine "gifts" of salvation, all because she knew how to be sincerely grateful.

A yeshiva student told me of a calamity that had befallen him. He was in debt and had no possible solution for his financial crisis. He went out to a field to pray to Hashem, and on his way he met an important and well-known Jerusalem rabbi. The rabbi asked him how he was doing, and the yeshiva student admitted that he was in serious trouble because of an enormous debt. The rabbi asked, "And you are going to cry over this debt while in the field?"

The yeshiva student replied, "Of course! That is why I have come to the field."

The rabbi asked further, "How long have you already been coming to the field to cry over your predicament?" The yeshiva student told him that he had been doing so for quite a while. The rabbi then asked, "And have you seen any salvations from your crying?" The yeshiva student shook his head. The rabbi recommended that instead of crying, he spend his hour of *hitbodedut* praising Hashem and thanking him for this debt.

The student heeded the words of the rabbi, and for two consecutive weeks devoted his daily hour of personal prayer in the field to thanking Hashem for this overwhelming debt. At the end of the two weeks, someone gifted to him an amount covering nearly all the money he needed to pay back the debt.

Three Chambers

A tzaddik once had a vision in which he visited the upper worlds. He entered a great hall, amazed at the hustle and bustle, with tens of thousands of angels rushing to and fro.

When the tzaddik asked which chamber he had entered, he was told that it was the hall of the prayers of those praying for salvation. The tzaddik then moved on to a second great hall that was also filled with tens of thousands of angels rushing around. He inquired about this chamber and was told, "This is the chamber of the prayers that have been answered; we are delivering the salvations."

The tzaddik then entered a third chamber. Here there were only a few angels, with seemingly not much to do at all. When he inquired about this particular hall, he was told that he was in the chamber of thanks from those who had received salvation for what they had prayed. "This should have been the busiest room of all," the attending angel said. "But unfortunately, you can see that it is not…"

Follow-up with Teshuva

Thankfulness does not exempt a person from repenting when needed. Every person must do teshuva, since without teshuva, a person doesn't rectify the root cause of his tribulations. Without teshuva, suffering is prolonged. So, once a person has thanked Hashem for his tribulations, he must do teshuva. This will surely mitigate any stern judgment set against him. He'll then have even more reason to thank Hashem!

As long as a person's teshuva is incomplete, he won't be capable of seeing how everything is truly good. He'll have difficulty thanking Hashem and accepting everything that transpires with love. So what comes first - the chicken or the egg? If teshuva depends on joy and gratitude, and joy and gratitude depend on teshuva – where does one begin?

Even though it's difficult to attain joy without teshuva, we must still begin with happiness. A person must cling to whatever happiness he can grab onto with all his might, as if he's clutching a piece of driftwood in a raging river. He must thank Hashem for all of life's bright spots and rejoice in them. He surely must sing and dance, and thank Hashem for the great privilege of performing any mitzvah. Rebbe Nachman teaches (Likutei Moharan, I:282) that a person taking stock of his own good points will be able to sing praise to Hashem and do true teshuva.

Why So Hard?

Rebbe Nachman also teaches that people often have difficulty confessing their sins (ibid, 178). One person has sins which he has forgotten, another is over-burdened by his sins, and a third person is embarrassed. Therefore, we need something to stimulate our joy to help us do teshuva like we should. But wait – what if there's no stimulus? What if there's no wedding or joyous occasion coming up in the next month or so? What should a person do?

Even without outside stimuli, a person must do what he can to attain the necessary sense of happiness. He should contemplate his positive points and ask Hashem to assist him in attaining emuna and joy. Hashem will undoubtedly help, and soon the person will be able to confess without problems.

Faith is Our Bridge

We must turn to Hashem and ask Him to strengthen our faith that everything is for the best. Emuna is truly above all else, and the bridge upon which we should travel in this earthly life. Even a person who has not yet succeeded in doing complete teshuva will be able to perceive that everything is for the best by connecting with the true tzaddik and trusting in his teachings.

Rebbe Natan explains in **Likutei Halachot**: "If we would all heed the voice of the true tzaddikim, who tell us to believe that everything Hashem does is for our own good, and therefore thank Hashem for all things whether they appear to us good or bad, then all tribulations and exiles would be eradicated entirely and the final redemption would arrive!"

Rebbe Natan does not speak of our own personal efforts or knowledge, but rather teaches that it all depends on our trusting of, and adhering to, the words of the tzaddikim. In other words, he connects the way to true emuna and teshuva to our simple faith – not our knowledge. A person can skip the various intermediate steps and enjoy spiritual illumination through the perfect wisdom of the true tzaddik. In this manner, even the simplest individual on a very low spiritual level can realize that everything is for the best and be inspired to thank and praise Hashem. With his sincere expression of gratitude, the tribulations he suffers will be eradicated and he will be able to return to Hashem speedily, amen.

Chapter Five:
The Little Things Count

Here's an important spiritual rule of thumb to remember: The more a person believes in Divine Providence, the stronger his trust in Hashem. And the more a person trusts in Hashem, the more he will invoke enhanced Divine Providence in his life.

Rebbe Nachman explains (Likutei Moharan, I:76) that when a person looks to Hashem for everything he needs, then in measure-for-measure fashion, Hashem "looks" at that person through enhanced Divine Providence.

Looking and Seeing

The human eye operates like a light beam: The beam exits the eye, "strikes" an object, and bounces back. The result enables a person to see the object.

The beam that emanates from the eye and is directed toward the object is called *direct light*. The beam then comes in contact with the object and bounces back to the eye just as a ball bounced off a wall returns to the person who threw it. This is called *returning light*. Once the returning light reaches the sender's eyeball, the image is instantly processed in the brain, and the person sees. The sight process is so miraculously speedy that it's virtually unnoticed.

This explains why a person doesn't consciously see something that's flashed before his eyes. If the object whizzes by faster than the beam can be transmitted from the eye, which in turns receives the reflected returning beam and processes the image in the brain, then he won't succeed in seeing the object. For the same reason, we can't see past our range of vision, for the outgoing beam will disperse before it even hits the object.

With this principle in mind, arrogant people have difficulty accepting Hashem's influence in their lives. Since arrogant people are spiritually far from Hashem, they can't "see" Hashem. In contrast, the humble person is close to Hashem, easily acknowledging Hashem's influence in his life and seeing His hand in every detail of it.

Look to Hashem

Rebbe Nachman further explains that viewing an object creates a finite image. How? Something unseen has no definition or limits. Say you describe a foreign country to a person who has never been there; his imagination is boundless when he thinks about what it's like and how it looks. Yet, once he sees a photo or – better yet - visits that country and sees it with his own eyes, the image he'll retain will be finite and precisely detailed.

The spiritual eyes of the soul also create finite images in a person's mind. By looking to Hashem for salvation and for all our needs, we create a fixed spiritual image that serves as a worthy vessel to contain the Divine light of abundance. Looking to Hashem, therefore, has the power to bring previously unlimited and infinite Divine abundance from the upper spiritual realm right down to a limited and finite form that a person can use in the material world.

King David mentions this phenomenon (Psalms, 145:15), "The eyes of all look to You with hope, and You give them their food in its proper time." By looking to Hashem, unlimited Divine abundance translates into finite food on our table, the mortgage payment, a cure to a sickness, or anything else we need in life.

Hashem sends Divine abundance down to the material world continuously, but this abundance is not definitive in time or space and, therefore, is not optimal. For example, if someone lives his life without "looking to Hashem" - in other words, without prayer, emuna, and trust – he'll attain his portion of Divine abundance, but not necessarily get what he needs at the opportune time. He may receive money when he doesn't need it, squander it, and subsequently end up helpless when he needs that exact sum. Or he may urgently need a sum of money, but it only reaches him several months later. Meanwhile, he has to resort to financial acrobatics in order to secure the amount he needs. Such is the practical consequence of lacking a suitable spiritual vessel that transforms unlimited Divine abundance into definitive and readily available fulfillment of our needs.

Let's take a closer look at what King David taught us: "The eyes of all look to You with hope, and You give them their food in its proper time." We humans receive what we need and when we need it only when we look to Hashem.

Emuna and *bitachon* (trust) in Hashem are our spiritual vessels for showering Divine abundance on the material world. With emuna and *bitachon*, a person receives what he needs when he needs it, no earlier and no later, in the definitive amount that's beneficial for him.

The principle of the finite image and definitive spiritual vessel also testifies to the advantage of being connected to a true tzaddik and spiritual guide. When a person first comes in contact with spirituality, he might receive Divine light in a measure that's far too great for him to handle. That's why some people do crazy things, develop eccentric habits and opinions, or have violent ups and downs when they are first exposed to Torah. But, when a person receives Divine light under the direction of a tzaddik and spiritual guide, that light is beneficial. Just like an unlimited dose of antibiotics is detrimental to a patient with a bacterial infection, so too one's spiritual health depends on receiving the right "dose" of Divine light as prescribed by the tzaddik and spiritual guide, who in effect is the doctor of the soul.

Thus, the very best way to enhance one's livelihood is to look to Hashem with increased emuna and *bitachon*.

Divine Supervision

Once again, the more a person believes in Divine Providence – knowing that his fate lies solely in Hashem's hands - the stronger his trust in Hashem. The Almighty's Divine Providence is manifest in His minutely detailed Divine Supervision over every creation, from the greatest of galaxies to the tiniest microscopic creatures - with no exception. Hashem decides which stars will explode and which particular grain of pollen will be picked up by a certain bee. In short, "mind-boggling" is an understatement for Hashem's Divine Supervision over every single creation in the world.

Stop and think how no two snowflakes are alike. Ponder the fact that every person has their own unique fingerprints. These are two amazing examples of Hashem's individual and precisely guided supervision.

Awareness of Hashem's Divine Supervision is conducive for emotional health. The more a person has faith and trust in Hashem, the less he'll worry. Such a person doesn't readily succumb to hopelessness, despair, and depression, even under the most difficult circumstances. He turns to Hashem for all his needs and is in constant dialogue with Hashem, not just at prescribed times of prayer.

Torah and Divine Supervision

Rebbe Natan of Breslev teaches (Likutei Halachot, Laws of Negotiations, 4) that belief in Divine Supervision is the foundation of the entire Torah. Divine Supervision is the result of Hashem's ability to see and direct every occurrence in the universe. Without belief in Divine Supervision, a person cannot believe in reward and punishment, since there cannot be a framework of reward and punishment if Hashem doesn't see and know everything.

Some people have a general belief in G-d, but they don't think He is involved in the day-to-day occurrences of our lives. It is difficult for them to fathom that Hashem controls the function of every single cell in our bodies. King David therefore testifies, "Who is like Hashem, our G-d, enthroned on lofty heights? Yet He lowers Himself to see [everything that happens] in the heavens and on earth." (Psalms, 113:5-6)

Rebbe Natan concludes that the slightest doubt in Hashem's precise Divine Supervision constitutes a total denial of Hashem, G-d forbid.

The barometer of true emuna, and particularly emuna in Hashem's Divine Supervision, is an even emotional keel, void of anger and anxiety, leading a person to a worry-free existence. How can this be achieved? Someone who believes in Hashem's Divine Supervision doesn't look for scapegoats when something doesn't go according to his plan or desires. He doesn't persecute himself, nor does he torment his wife or children. He plays no blame games with people. He believes that everything in his life is the product of Hashem's Divine Supervision – and it's all for the very best.

Internalizing the Torah

A person can learn Torah day and night, but he won't internalize his Torah learning without firm belief in Hashem's Divine Providence, His detailed supervision over every creation in the universe. Many people have learned Torah throughout the generations, but the select few who succeeded in internalizing the Torah to the extent that the Torah permeated every fiber of their thoughts, speech, and deeds, were the ones who developed steadfast emuna in Hashem's Divine Providence.

Genuine emuna in Hashem's Divine Providence means that we see Hashem's hand in everything that happens to us and around us, no matter how big or small. For example, if a person has a chronically itchy scalp and he attributes this to anything other than Hashem, he has not yet internalized his Torah learning. Sure, this young man might be one of the brightest students in his Yeshiva, but he doesn't yet live and breathe his Torah.

Divine Direction

People ask: If everything Hashem does is good, then why the punishments? The answer is simple: Hashem, like a loving parent, sometimes reprimands us in order to direct us to our optimal path in life - the path that both leads to our soul correction and enables us to perform our designated individual missions on earth. So, when things don't go our way or we experience difficulties and the like, Hashem is merely stimulating us to assess ourselves. As such, life's tribulations are not punishments, but a mechanism of Divine direction to arouse us from spiritual slumber and lead us on the right path.

We can now understand the seemingly harsh view of Rebbe Natan when he said that the slightest doubt in Hashem's precise Divine Supervision constitutes a total denial of Hashem, G-d forbid. A person who considers tribulations and suffering to be random and illogical is spiritually blind. Like the wicked Esau, he fails to see the Divine wisdom within each occurrence and creation (Likutei Moharan, I:1).

The minutest stimuli in our lives are designed to bring us closer to Hashem. Those who ignore Hashem's messages – the tiny and/or subtle wakeup calls from Above that are designed to bring us closer to Hashem and keep us from straying off the right path – are inviting upon themselves louder and more severe wake-up calls in the form of troubles and tribulations. The Gemara teaches us that when we reach into our pockets to pull out a dime and instead we pull out a penny, forcing us to reach into our pockets a second time to pull out the dime, the experience is a tribulation. When we ask ourselves why Hashem is troubling us by the need to put our hands into our pockets twice for what we could have achieved once, and we assess ourselves and do teshuva accordingly, we save ourselves untold difficulties.

If a person wakes up in the morning when you merely whisper his name, then you don't have to pour a bucket of water on his head to get him out of bed. In identical manner, when we heed Hashem's "whispers" – his subtle wakeup calls – we spare ourselves the louder and more megaphone-type tribulation wakeup calls.

Someone came to me with inexplicable knee pain after having been fully examined by an orthopedic specialist who found nothing wrong. The word for knee in Hebrew is *berech*. I asked the person if he'd been careful with the way he makes his blessings before and after eating. The Hebrew word for blessing is *bracha*, from the same root word as *berech*. This seemed to me to what Hashem was hinting here by way of the knee pain. Sure enough, the young man admitted that he was slipshod in that area. I suggested that he make a concerted effort to make the proper blessings at the right time and with intent. He did and the pain soon left him.

One doesn't have to be a big tzaddik or kabbalist in order to interpret Hashem's subtle messages. The more a person enhances his or her spiritual awareness - emuna in Hashem's total Divine Providence and individual supervision over every single creation in the universe from greatest to tiniest - the more he or she will be sensitive to Hashem's messages. We can all improve our spiritual receptors by strengthening our emuna in Divine Providence.

Each part of our body corresponds to a certain commandment of the Torah. An ailment of the body is likely to be a message that we must rectify a violation of a certain commandment. Anytime a person doesn't feel well, he should put serious effort into personal prayer and self-assessment, asking Hashem to help him understand what he must correct. Asking a tzaddik or a reputable spiritual guide is also beneficial.

Everything that happens to us – both good and seemingly bad, both reward and seemingly punishment – comes from a loving Father in Heaven who wants us to maintain healthy and unblemished souls that are worthy vessels for Divine light. Like fine wine, Divine light would be wasted in a dirty receptacle. A sparkling crystal goblet is worthy of a thirty-year old Bordeaux; a shining and unblemished soul is worthy of Divine light.

Entering the Land of Israel

Our sages teach us that three things don't come easy to a person: Torah, the World to Come, and the Land of Israel. Consequently, in order to obtain one of these wonderful gifts, a person most certainly experiences difficulties; comfort-zone efforts won't get him anywhere. Even if he is pious and free from sin, he won't merit his portion in Torah, the World to Come, or the Land of Israel without paying a spiritual price.

"Wait a second," you may wonder. "If someone lives an upright life and does their very best to walk a straight path, must he still suffer?"

The holy *Sfas Emes* of Gur has an answer. First, he asks this question: Why does the Gemara list the Land of Israel as one of the three things that don't come easy? The Children of Israel made the eleven-day walk from Horev (Mount Sinai) to Kadesh Barnea on the southern border of the Land of Israel in only three days! Hashem wanted to make life easy for the Children of Israel, bringing them quickly to their holy homeland, but because of the sin of the spies, they ended up sojourning for forty years in the desert. So we see that we didn't necessarily have to suffer to obtain the Land of Israel. How is that possible?

The Sfas Emes answers both his own question and our previous question with one amazing explanation: As swiftly as the Children of Israel made the eleven-day journey in three days, they were still on the road and in the desert. They weren't in the comforts of their own home. No travelling with babies and small children is ever easy. Each family certainly had to cope with a long list of minor difficulties and tribulations.

Even today, we know how difficult a three-day road trip can be even in an air-conditioned family vehicle. The baby wails because he can't find his pacifier. The kids fight in the back seat. Mom needs a restroom but the nearest gas station is sixty miles away. These are all genuine – although minor – tribulations.

The Sfas Emes says that had the Children of Israel accepted the minor tribulations with emuna and love, not only would this have atoned for their previous sins – it would have also prepared them to receive the holy Land of Israel. Minor tribulations that are accepted with love spare us from much greater suffering.

The Gerrer Rebbe's eye-opening conclusion is that the minor tribulations we accept with love save us inestimable torment - the type that people battle when they don't accept life's difficulties with emuna and love.

The Children of Israel whined and complained instead of accepting their reality. This transformed a potentially miraculous three-day journey and peacefully swift conquest of the Land of Israel into a forty-year trek in the desert and endless wars that we are still fighting to this very day. Centuries of inquisitions, pogroms, torture, exile, terror, mass murder and suffering can all be traced back to the root cause of not accepting life's minor difficulties with emuna.

Think about it – the difference between accepting one's difficulties in life with emuna and complaining about them is at least the difference between a three-day trip and a forty year journey! Forty years equals 14,600 days (40 multiplied by 365). Forty years is a period 4,866 times longer than 3 days (14,600 divided by 3). The Torah is telling us that if a person doesn't accept his minor difficulties in life with emuna and joy, he'll have to suffer 4,866 times more!

Continuing the holy Gerrer Rebbe's line of thought, we can also conclude that accepting our minor difficulties, tribulations, and suffering in life with emuna and love also qualifies as legitimate hardships that earn us the Torah and the World to Come.

Accepting life's minor hardships with emuna and love cleanses us and atones for our misdeeds. It also prepares us as worthy receptacles for Divine abundance and particularly Torah, the Land of Israel, and the World to Come. Nobody can circumvent life's challenges. But, by accepting them lovingly and with complete emuna in Divine Providence, we sweeten our lives in this world and in the next.

Tiny Tribulations

The Gemara asks what qualifies as tribulations. We previously mentioned the example of reaching into your pocket to pull out a dime, and instead pulling out a penny. Yes, accepting such a minor inconvenience with emuna and love is enough to save a person from many more severe tribulations.

The Gemara gives another example: A person goes to a tailor and orders a suit. The tailor summons him a few days later, saying that the suit is ready. The customer tries the suit on and it doesn't fit well – the jacket is much too narrow.

According to everything we have learned, this is a bona-fide tribulation. If the customer accepts it with emuna and love, it will atone for all his sins and save him from many more severe tribulations in quantity and in quality.

What does a loving and emuna-filled reaction mean in this case? The customer doesn't yell at the tailor; he realizes that his frustration over the ill-fitting suit comes from Hashem. The tailor is only a pawn in Hashem's hands. The customer looks in the mirror and says to the tailor, "You're a great tailor. The suit is wonderful!"

The tailor is not blind. He sees that the jacket is too narrow and the sleeves are too short. He knows that his measurements and his cloth-cutting were not accurate. He stutters, "B-b-but the suit didn't turn out quite right…"

The customer reassures the tailor, "You did your best. But Hashem decided that this was a good way to help me atone for my sins. It's not your fault the suit doesn't fit properly – that's the way Hashem wanted it to be!"

Wait a second, you're probably saying. Isn't the customer lying when he says to the tailor, "The suit is wonderful"? No, it is not a lie. Since the customer has strong emuna, he sees that everything Hashem does as wonderful because he knows that everything is for the best. The customer knows that the ill-fitting suit might have saved him from being in traction for a month after a crippling automobile accident. With that in mind, the suit is surely wonderful!

Now let's look at a different type of customer reaction: "Customer B" believes in G-d in a general way like many others do, but he doesn't believe in Hashem's Divine Providence. Customer B doesn't believe that Hashem had anything to do with the ill-fitting suit. He doesn't accept this situation; much less accept it with love and emuna. He's peeved with the tailor and thinks the tailor is cheating him. He humiliates the tailor, insults him, and threatens him. He wants his down payment back or else. Not only have Customer B's sins gone without atonement, but he's accumulated a whole new stack of spiritual debits for the verbal abuse and the false accusations he hurled at the tailor. What a lost opportunity…

Many of life's minute inconveniences qualify as tiny tribulations which can literally mitigate stiff judgments. And, as we've already learned, tiny tribulations can neutralize, mitigate, and atone for tribulations and stern judgments almost 5,000 times greater in magnitude! Do you realize what that means, dear reader? Accepting a tiny tribulation with emuna and love can save lives!

Let's observe a hypothetical day-to-day situation from two different vantage points, up in Heaven and down on earth:

Hypothetical case study – view from Heaven: Arthur has inadvertently done a misdeed that is punishable by burning. The Heavenly Prosecution demands that he receive third-degree burns; Hashem in His infinite mercy 'grabs' Arnold's file and instead gives him a mild surrogate punishment of a minor inconvenience with something too hot. If Arnold accepts Hashem's tiny tribulation with love, the serious misdeed that accrued the severe burning punishment will be completely mitigated.

Hypothetical case study – view from earth: Arthur's favorite breakfast beverage is English tea with milk. His wife, in the morning rush of trying to prepare breakfast and getting the children off to school, serves Arthur his tea much hotter than he likes it. It doesn't even burn his lips, but it's too hot for him.

Hypothetical scenario #1: Arthur is fortunate; he has read **The Garden of Emuna**, **The Garden of Peace**, and he's now half way through **The Garden of Gratitude**. He smiles to himself. He sees how busy his wife is. He knows that if he waits patiently for another two minutes, the tea will be sufficiently cooled down. He thanks Hashem in his heart for the tiny tribulation, which neither affects neither his health nor his income. Meanwhile, up in Heaven, the case against

Arthur is closed and the Prosecutor's writ of accusation goes into the shredder. Back down on earth, Arthur has a wonderful day.

Hypothetical scenario #2: Arthur blames his wife and yells at her. Not only does he ignore Divine Providence and fail to accept the tiny tribulation with love, but he accumulates a dozen additional serious transgressions in rapid succession. He could have picked himself up, gone to the fridge, and added a little more milk to his tea, but no – in his arrogance, he insults his wife. He loses his temper, which the Gemara compares to idolatry. He uses language that should never be used, especially in front of the children. He wastes the opportunity to atone for a serious misdeed at a below bargain-basement price. In rejecting Hashem's mercy, Arthur's case goes to the Heavenly Court, which now tries him according to the letter of the law. Later in the week, there's an article on Page 2 of the London Times about a fatal car accident in which one of the vehicles burst into a ball of flames...

The above hypothetical case is no joke! The Gemara teaches us that being served a cup of coffee or tea that's a little too hot or too cold than what we like qualifies as a legitimate tribulation. And don't forget - these tiny tribulations, when accepted with emuna and love, can mitigate severe judgments that invoke tribulations and suffering that's 5,000 times greater!

Think about this, cherished reader, the next time something happens in your life that's not exactly convenient or to your liking. It's a gift from Hashem and a product of His mercy! It's a tiny tribulation that's worth its weight in gold and diamonds. Smile and thank Hashem for it; by accepting our tiny tribulations with emuna and love, we spare ourselves much greater anguish in life.

Attention to Small Details

Here's a partial list of common inconveniences that qualify as bona-fide tribulations, even though they seem minor:

- You open a book to the wrong page.

- You can't find your slippers.

- Your spouse has squeezed the toothpaste from the top of the tube and you prefer to squeeze from the bottom of the tube.

- You dial your friend and get a busy signal.

- The soup doesn't have enough salt to your taste.

- Your morning newspaper got wet from the rain on your front doorstep.

A person who lives with emuna, and particularly emuna in Hashem's Divine Providence, sees life's mini-inconveniences as great gifts from Hashem and all for the very best. These tribulations qualify as sufficient difficulties for earning Torah, the Land of Israel, and the World to Come. Such a person won't be required to suffer more serious tribulations according to everything we've learned from the Gemara and from the Sfas Emes, of blessed and saintly memory.

Some people are patient and even-tempered; they don't get angry about life's tiny inconveniences. Even so, if they don't accept them lovingly and with emuna, their patience won't be enough to mitigate harsh decrees and judgments.

Cherished reader, please remember: If you don't accept life's tiny tribulations with love and emuna, you might have to suffer tribulations 5,000 times worse! Learn and review this chapter until it becomes second nature, and your life will become a heaven right here on earth.

Emuna on the Road

During the very same days when I was working on this chapter, I was driving on a four-lane highway at the maximum permissible speed. I was in the right northbound lane, and a taxi was in the process of passing me in the left lane. All of a sudden, a car that was on the shoulder of the road pulled out right in front of me. There was no time to slam on the brakes; if I had dodged the car so carelessly pulling out by swerving into the left lane, I'd have collided with the taxi that was passing me, which was travelling at about 80 mph. Miraculously, the careless car returned to the shoulder in an instant, right before my car would have collided with it, thanks to Hashem!

Suppose that I didn't have in emuna in Divine Providence; how would I have reacted? The careless driver could have killed me! What would I have done, yell at him? Chase him? Hit him? No. Emuna dictates that this is what Hashem wanted. If Hashem wills, even the best driver can make a near-fatal mistake.

Sure, my heart skipped a beat or two. After calming down by reminding myself that this is what Hashem wants and it's all for the best, I thanked Hashem profusely, did some serious self-assessment, and resolved to improve in an area that seemed to need improvement.

A person devoid of emuna can lose his temper and his mind from the anger and frustration of something similar to my near-accident. This is the result of attributing tribulations to anything or anyone other than Hashem. Rebbe Natan teaches that any doubt in Hashem's total Divine Providence is outright denial of G-d altogether.

Happy with Every Detail of his Lot in Life

A person who believes in Hashem's Divine Providence is always happy. As soon as he believes that every detail of his lot in life is the product of Divine Providence, he is happy. He knows that Hashem is doing everything for his ultimate benefit, to facilitate both his mission in life and his soul correction. This saves untold emotional wear and tear and is conducive to clarity of thought and self-composure. In addition, his cognizance that Hashem is directing his life is the best guarantee that he'll pursue his optimal path in life. A person with developed emuna in Hashem's Divine Providence is also proficient in finding the intrinsic Divine wisdom and message in everything that happens to him and in every occurrence around him.

In stark contrast, one who doesn't believe in Divine Providence is never satisfied with his lot in life. Anything unfavorable that happens to him will cause him distress and anguish. He worries about the future and is apprehensive about the economy, the security situation, and a long list of other things. He can't understand how anything – much less everything – is for the best. He sees injustice everywhere and has no idea what Hashem wants from him. Rather than living a life of emuna and spiritual awareness, he's in his own fantasy world.

Here's a concrete example: Michael believes in Hashem's Divine Providence, and has a teenage son who willfully has just shown him blatant disrespect. He neither yells at his son nor reacts in the slightest negative manner. He says to himself, "Hashem has arranged that my son should give me a hard time; if this is what Hashem wants, it's certainly for my benefit." Michael looks for the intrinsic message. He realizes that Hashem runs the world in a measure-for-measure fashion. He assesses himself while assuming that if his son was disrespectful to him, then he must have been disrespectful to Hashem. Michael then recalls that he was chatting in the synagogue on Shabbat during the Torah reading, an act of gross disrespect to G-d. He asks forgiveness and resolves to do better. Soon thereafter, Michael's son asks him for forgiveness.

Were it not for Michael's son being disrespectful to him, he may never have atoned for his disrespect to Hashem. He'd be walking around with a blemish on his soul. Hashem, in His loving mercy, helped His beloved and spiritually-sensitive son Michael rectify a wrongdoing, thus sparing him the potential tribulations that result from an uncorrected misdeed. We see that everything is truly for the best! Michael knows this, and is therefore happy all the time.

Dan lives across the street from Michael and attends the same synagogue. Dan defines himself as "Orthodox" – he observes the Sabbath and eats kosher food. Michael considers himself a strong believer in G-d too, but put to the test, he's still light-years away from believing in Hashem's tailor-made per-individual Divine Providence.

Dan, like Michael, has a teenage son. Before Dan left for work on Friday morning, he asked his son to do a certain chore in preparation for the Sabbath. His son forgot, and he came home from work an hour before the Sabbath, only to find that the chore wasn't done. Without asking for any explanation, Dan flew into a tirade. He called his son irresponsible, disrespectful, and an idiot. The boy was so upset that he locked himself in his room and refused to accompany his father to the synagogue. The tension in the family ruined the festive Friday night meal. Dan's wife tried to come to her son's defense and incurred a double portion of her husband's wrath.

Dan's household became not only a battleground but an emotional burial ground. Why? 16-year old Dan Junior forgot to shine Daddy's shoes before the Sabbath. For this youthful oversight, his father sentenced him to the worst form of degradation and verbal abuse. The father's wrath – tantamount to idolatry – shattered both his marital peace and the sanctity of the Sabbath.

Little does Dan realize that the Heavenly Court will now judge him with the same harshness by which he judged his son. That's scary, since the Heavenly prosecutors have an entire dossier of chores that Dan should be doing for his Father in Heaven...

It's no surprise that Dan is always suffering and complaining. There's no end in sight to his troubles.

From the sidelines, we shake our heads in astonishment. If Dan would only have believed in Divine Providence and realized that everything Hashem does is for the very best and for a purpose, how many headaches he might have spared himself! His son now has severe emotional problems due to his father's repeated abuse. His marriage is on the rocks. He is confused and depressed, since he doesn't understand why he suffers.

Those who aren't happy with every detail of their lot in life are the ones who suffer in this world. Those who ignore and complain about Hashem's subtle wakeup calls end up dealing with screaming siren-level arousals.

A person's entire mission on earth is to learn emuna, and particularly emuna in Hashem's Divine Providence. In addition to this book, we strongly suggest that readers go back and review **The Garden of Emuna** and **The Garden of Peace** (for men only) or **Women's Wisdom** (for women only).

Believing in Divine Providence

Let's examine the ramifications of Rebbe Natan's far-reaching definition of belief in Divine Providence; namely, that disbelief in Divine Providence and Hashem's personal supervision and direction of every phase of our lives constitutes outright heresy.

Imagine an individual who learns Torah all day long. He gets up at midnight to lament the destruction of the Holy Temple and frequents the hallowed gravesites of the great tzaddikim. Add to this your own ideas of a seemingly perfect pious person.

The apparently "perfect tzaddik" comes home at the end of the day, and his 10-year old son is impudent. The apparently "perfect tzaddik" cannot believe that Hashem decreed that the little boy should be insolent and disrespectful toward him. He yells at the child and threatens him with the worst punishments, totally losing his temper.

Huffing and puffing into the kitchen, the apparently "perfect tzaddik" – stomach grumbling - demands dinner. His wife had a hard day; it was her turn to drive carpool and she spent three hours finding a plumber who could fix a cracked pipe that flooded the laundry room. She apologizes to her righteous and scholarly husband that dinner isn't ready, and before she has a chance to explain, he is now chastising her in the worst way.

The apparently "perfect tzaddik" can't believe that Hashem would delay his dinner. He believes that his wife is slovenly and negligent when, in actuality, she is a true woman of valor.

Our apparently "perfect tzaddik" is overcome with anger and frustration – even when he doesn't show it with an outward display of temper – every time that life doesn't go according to his plan. Rebbe Natan would call this individual an outright heretic. The extremely negative reactions of the apparently "perfect tzaddik" only show that he doesn't believe in total Divine Providence.

We now can understand that a true "believer" is not just one who says that he believes. The real believer is one who believes in Divine Providence, and it is this definition that should be engraved on our hearts.

The ultimate purpose of learning Torah and fulfilling its commandments is to enhance our belief in Divine Providence and thereby strengthen our bond with Hashem. If a person doesn't believe that every tiny detail of his own existence and that of the entire universe at large is a product of Divine Providence, then he lacks the very foundation of Torah.

Acknowledgement of, and belief in, Divine Providence is the key to our learning all about gratitude to Hashem. When we regard all of life's periodic aggravations – no matter how big or small – as the products of tailor-made individual Divine Providence which are all for our best, we mitigate all severe judgments.

This is the secret to a pleasant life.

Radical?

Some people think that Rebbe Natan's definition is radical. They think that a heretic is one who denies the existence of G-d, Heaven forbid. On the contrary – acknowledging the existence of G-d, yet believing that any event or occurrence is exclusive of His Divine Providence, constitutes total heresy.

Why?

The slightest denial of Divine Providence means that a person regards certain events as exclusive of Hashem's control. If a person thinks that there is any additional power or powers that govern the universe other than Hashem, then he is a total heretic! Let's remember that the very first tenet of our faith – the first of the Rambam's Thirteen Principles – says: "I believe with complete faith that The Creator blessed be He is Creator and Director of all of creation; He alone did, does, and will do all actions."

The Rambam removes all doubt in the very first principle. Creator means that Hashem creates everything - always did and always will. Director means that He supervises our lives down to the tiniest detail in precise Divine Providence. To qualify as a believer, one must therefore have complete belief in Hashem both as Creator and as Director. Hence, Rebbe Natan's definition is not radical at all, but completely consistent with the Rambam's first principle.

Smile and Leave Purgatory Behind

Belief in Divine Providence is vital for our emotional wellbeing. Imagine that you're driving down the highway and a careless driver passes you dangerously, nearly colliding with you. Without belief in Divine Providence, you'd be angry and upset. You might even roll down the window and let the other driver have a piece of your mind. A person with a shorter temper might even yell unpleasant words. There are plenty of road-rage cases resulting in fights. All these negative reactions result from a lack of belief in Divine Providence.

Now, imagine that a different driver has complete faith in Divine Providence. He's driving to work and he's stuck in a massive traffic jam. He knows that he'll be late to work and he might miss an important meeting. Rather than being frustrated and angry, he thanks Hashem, since he knows that Hashem is doing everything for his benefit. He knows that Hashem caused the traffic jam for an infinite number of good reasons. Such a person goes through life on an even emotional keel, with minimal wear and tear on his heart, nerves, and digestive system.

Let's remember what the holy Sfas Emes of Gur taught us – tiny tribulations save us from major suffering. By accepting the traffic jam and subsequent delay with joy and emuna, a person could be saving himself a much more severe decree, such as a six-week "delay" in a hospital bed. As such, when we remind ourselves that every seemingly uncomfortable, unfavorable, or upsetting situation is a product of Divine Providence, we can profusely thank Hashem. Life's thorns are really from Hashem that atone for our sins and cleanse our souls.

Jewish law (Code of Jewish Law, Orach Chaim, 230) requires that we always say, "Whatever Hashem does is for the very best!"

Caution – Breakdown!

Another phenomenon that we unfortunately see ever too often is a total breakdown of faith when a person without strong faith in Divine Providence is faced with a challenge. Let's look at a few examples:

Income: Probably the most common occurrence of faith breakdown results from financial difficulties that a person doesn't accept with love. People with weak faith in Divine Providence lose their will to pray and learn Torah altogether. Just as Rebbe Natan warned, the slightest doubt in Divine Providence is liable to develop into total heresy. A person who forgets that his current predicament is exactly the way Hashem wants it to be, for his ultimate good and to facilitate his soul correction, will not only miss an opportunity for personal and spiritual growth, but is liable to fall into despair, chronic worry, and depression. Such a person will experience a dangerous spiritual slide, if not a total breakdown in faith altogether.

Marital Peace: A couple with temporary marital difficulties will be able to get back on the track of peace in the home when they live with emuna, particularly emuna in Divine Providence. They emerge stronger from their difficulties, since they see them as messages from Hashem that certain aspects in their character in general and in their marriage in particular need reinforcement. Having weathered a difficulty with emuna, a couple emerges with a solid bond and a more loving relationship.

Those unfortunate individuals who lack faith in Divine Providence will retaliate bitterly against their partner when they perceive their partner has mistreated them in the slightest. In denying that their marital difficulties are from Hashem, they fall into a downward spiral of anger, fighting and negative emotions. Ultimately, many end up both in divorce court and in total spiritual breakdown.

Build or destroy? The rule of thumb we learn here is that life's difficulties and challenges build those with strong emuna but destroy those with weak emuna. By strengthening our emuna, we better our lives in every single aspect.

Emuna and Patience

Let's ponder the above rule further. When we look at life's trivial tribulations with emuna, it doesn't seem proper to call them tribulations anymore. On the contrary, a person's lack of emuna leads to the type of frustration and impatience that turns miniscule inconveniences into major crises. An inability to accept the small things in life that aren't to his liking or exactly according to plan is an expression of weak or no belief in Hashem's individual Divine Providence. As we learned earlier, by not accepting these tiny tribulations with emuna and with love, a person invokes upon himself much more difficult tribulations.

For example, if a person lacks patience with his children and is unwilling to live happily with such tiny inconveniences as their periodic pillow fights, a glass of spilled milk, or cookie crumbs on the carpet, he may have to suffer many more severe tribulations, such as their going off the right path altogether.

So many people cry out when their children go astray, "What did I do to deserve this?" or "How could this happen to my child?" Maybe those parents didn't have the emuna that enabled them to raise their children with patience. A parent needs strong emuna – particularly emuna in Divine Providence – to be able to accept even small tribulations with patience. A parent who lacks patience reacts with yelling, screaming, verbal abuse, and even physical abuse. If a child gets scolded and/or slapped all the time, he'll soon be looking for the love he needs in the wrong places. Once again, the parent's inability to lovingly accept the small tribulations of child-rearing will be faced with the heartbreak of much more difficult problems.

The same applies to marriage. With emuna in Divine Providence, a person who suffers any slight grief from his or her partner turns to Hashem and asks, "Hashem, what's the message that You're conveying to me?" Without emuna, friction, tension and outright confrontations develop that ever too frequently lead to separation and divorce, Heaven forbid.

The Gate to Heaven…or Purgatory

This principle of accepting tiny tribulations with emuna and love applies to virtually every situation in life. With emuna, we're calm, collected and always smiling. Without emuna, we're a bag of frayed nerves.

Imagine that a person without emuna is going through airport security. He forgets to remove all the contents of his pockets and walks through the metal detector. The buzzer sounds off. The security guard says politely but firmly, "Sir, go back through, check your pockets, and enter again." The person finds a key in his pocket, puts it on the conveyer tray, and tries walking through the metal detector again. Once more, the buzzer goes off. The guard sends him back, and this time he discovers something else that he left in his pocket. He walks through a third time, and again the buzzers buzz.

Another security officer arrives, and begins to do a body-check on the passenger. The passenger – failing to see Hashem's involvement in everything that's happening to him – is becoming angrier and more frustrated by the minute. He yells at the two security guards, "Do I look like a terrorist? When the real terrorists come along, you flunkies don't catch them because you're busy tormenting innocent passengers like me!"

Soon, the supervisor arrives on the scene and the bellicose, emuna-lacking passenger is detained for obstructing a security officer in the line of duty. He even misses his plane.

A person with emuna doesn't blame the keys in his pocket, the buzzer, or the security personnel for his problems. He knows that it's all from Hashem, so he accepts whatever transpires with emuna and love. He suffers fewer headaches and digestive disorders. Whereas the other passenger's life is a purgatory on earth, his is a most pleasant Heaven on earth.

Don't think that the ability to accept life's difficulties with love is limited to the select few. This is actually a requirement in Jewish law. The Code of Jewish Law states (Shulchan Aruch, Orach Chaim, 222), "the [seemingly] bad for servants of G-d are their happiness and their credit; since they accept with love everything that Hashem decrees, they are thereby using these difficulties to serve Hashem with joy."

Stop and think of all the other daily aggravations that upset us. The teller at the bank refuses to cash a check. Someone is sitting in your synagogue seat. Your brand new washing machine is not functioning properly.

The choice is ours – emuna or no emuna, Heaven or purgatory. By accepting life's tiny tribulations with love, we're doing ourselves the greatest favor in the world.

Don't Cry over Spilled Milk

Rabbi Yisrael Salanter of saintly and blessed memory was an immensely pious man, but a he lived a life of poverty. His wife once heated up some milk that they could barely afford; the milk came to a vigorous boil, overflowed, and spilled onto the floor. A person with no emuna would have likely yelled at his wife, "Idiot! Why are you so careless?" One can imagine how a bit of spilled milk could trigger a domestic war...

No, there was no war in the Salanter home. Rabbi Yisrael asked his wife, "Sweetheart, what do you think we did wrong to deserve the milk being spilled?" His wife pondered for a moment and remembered that she forgot to leave the payment for the milk in the prearranged hiding place for the milkman. If the milk hadn't spilled, she would have forgotten to pay him entirely. Negligence in paying a debt is a serious violation of Torah. What's more, the milkman – out of respect to Rabbi Yisrael – might have been embarrassed to claim what's due. Then, the Salanters would have been guilty of swindling the milkman, G-d forbid. As such, they were happy that the milk spilled because it saved them from serious transgressions.

The Salanters' story has a happy ending because of emuna. Without emuna, little stories with happy endings become major dramas with tragic outcomes. Walking the path of emuna is like walking in a flowering botanical garden where one flower is prettier that the next. The path without emuna is a perilous jungle of negative emotions - snake-pits of anger, quick sands of depression, poison spiders of anxiety, and torturous nightmares.

We frequently perpetuate our own suffering. Rather than accepting tiny tribulations with emuna and love, we fight them, get upset about them, and blow them up to such inflated proportions that we suffer from them for forty years rather than for three days.

Remember that three days atones for forty years, and that tiny tribulations atone for things 5,000 times worse. Do you know what that means? If a person accepts losing a twenty dollar bill with emuna and love, he won't have to lose a sum 5,000 times greater! A twenty-dollar loss is sufficient to atone and much easier to swallow than a $100,000 loss!

Dear reader, from now on, be happy about the burnt toast or the flat tire. Imagine that the burnt toast is in lieu of a fire in the house or that the flat tire is Hashem's loving substitute for a car accident. From now on, let's not only stop our complaining about life's minor tribulations - let's thank Hashem for them.

A Turn for a Turn

Accepting tiny tribulations with love and emuna is not only laudable, but it's highly beneficial as we've learned. However, it's not enough; we have to remember that every minor detail is Hashem's will. Things happen because that's the way Hashem wants it to be. And since we know that Hashem does everything for the best, we should thank Him for everything, even when it's not exactly what we want. If accepting a given situation of suffering or tribulation with love and emuna has a 5,000-times power of atonement, then thanking Hashem for that same situation has an unlimited power of atonement.

Hashem runs the world in "ATFAT" fashion (a turn for a turn). Since it's unnatural to thank Hashem for our difficulties in life, once we thank Him, Hashem also responds in an "unnatural" fashion, doing favors for us that transcend the limits of nature.

There's No Mistake

The Gemara in Tractate Bava Batra explains that when Job's tribulations worsened, Job lost faith, especially in Divine Providence. He thought that perhaps Hashem sent the tribulations to the wrong address or to the wrong Job.

Hashem had many answers for Job. There are many pores in the human body, and each has its own source of nutrition. Hashem said, "If I can differentiate between two tiny pores in a person's body, giving each its own nutrients, then I can surely differentiate between two Jobs." Hashem went on to tell Job how every raindrop is unique.

Hashem's amazing Divine Supervision is not only over every human, but over every mosquito. Let's go further – Hashem decides what every one-celled ameba will have for dinner tonight. There is no mistake in Hashem's Divine Providence. The fact that every single snowflake has its own unique, exquisite design is no quirk of nature but precise, mind-boggling Divine Providence.

Forty Quiet Days

The same Gemara (Tractate Arachin) that taught us earlier about "tiny tribulations" also teaches us that if a person has "forty quiet days" free of tribulations, then it's a sign that he's receiving his portion in the world-to-come in this world. That's not very good news, to say the least.

Our sages go a step further: They explain that if a person has forty tribulation-free days, then he's liable to be hit with a massive tribulation all at once.

We can now fully realize the value of tiny tribulations, even if we haven't until now. They are a wonderful favor from Hashem to keep our spiritual slates clean.

The Gemara in Tractate Avoda Zara makes an interesting observation: If someone whom you love owes you money, you'll accept payback little by little over a period of time. But, if someone you can't stand owes you money, you demand payback immediately, in one lump sum.

People often point out the cruel and wicked tyrants who seem to be getting whatever they want in this world, while the gentle, kind, and upright seem to live lives of suffering. With the above principles in mind, such a phenomenon is crystal clear: The kind and the upright suffer from periodic tribulations, since Hashem guards them from accumulating spiritual debts. These are the beloved who pay their debts little by little. The cruel and wicked aren't given the gift of atonement at bargain-basement prices by way of small and periodic tribulations; they end up paying their debts in one tragic fell swoop.

Thanks for the Little Details

The Gemara teaches that if we encounter tribulations, then we should right away begin a process of self-assessment. The Gemara adds that if, after self-assessment, a person still can't put his finger on what he did wrong, he should attribute the tribulations to *bitul Torah*, or neglecting to study Torah in his free time.

If a person knows that he hasn't done anything wrong, nor has he wasted Torah study time, then he should attribute his tribulations to Hashem's love. King Solomon says in Proverbs, Chapter 3, "Hashem chastises those who He loves."

The Meiri, one of the great medieval Talmud commentators, reminds us that suffering and tribulations are all part of Hashem's Divine Providence. Since tribulations come from Hashem, a person is best advised to perform comprehensive self-assessment and teshuva. Once a person corrects what needs to be corrected, the tribulations are rendered superfluous.

Since each little detail of discomfort in life is a wakeup call intended to initiate self-assessment and the subsequent teshuva process, then it's certainly a gift from Heaven that we should thank Hashem for!

Like a Garden of Eden

Maybe you're saying to yourself right now, "Fine and dandy – we've learned all about tribulations in this book; but why in the world did Hashem create a universe that needs tribulations?"

The answer is amazingly simple: Hashem created the universe with no need for tribulations. Man brought upon himself the need for tribulations when he first sinned by eating from the tree of knowledge.

When Hashem first created Adam, the latter lived a tribulation-free existence in the Garden of Eden. Indeed, he was pampered in the most lavish ways that defy description. Yet, when he sinned, he was exiled from the Garden of Eden immediately. Why such seemingly excessive punishment, and for a first offense at that?

Hashem knew that Adam could neither fulfill his personal potential nor attain his soul correction if he had remained in the Garden of Eden. Adam's exile and subsequent hardships would force him to yearn for Hashem and pray for His guidance and assistance; this kept Adam from sinking into a material-oriented existence and a deep spiritual slumber.

Hashem knows that with a life of pampered pleasures, a person won't make any character improvements, won't fulfill even a small portion of his personal potential, and certainly won't seek Hashem. He'll be light years away from teshuva and spiritual awareness. Such a person will be spoiled and weak; he'll probably develop an over-inflated sense of entitlement and an intolerable personality. Therefore, a life of constant pleasures is certainly not in a person's ultimate best interest.

On the other hand, life's difficulties not only strengthen a person but stimulate his search for meaning and spiritual growth. Once a person grows sufficiently in spirit to realize that everything in his life is under Hashem's direction of Divine Providence, he can accept his tribulations with love and even thank Hashem for them. In that respect, tribulations are no longer tribulations!

Also, as soon as a person seeks Hashem and does teshuva on his own accord, Hashem doesn't need to implement the harsh wakeup calls of tribulations to bring that self-starting individual close to Him. So, with emuna in Divine Providence, there are no tribulations! Rebbe Nachman says explicitly (Likutei Moharan, I:4), "When a person knows that every occurrence in life is for his ultimate benefit, then this world becomes tantamount to a Garden of Eden."

A Little is Sufficient

Some people become confused at this point; they ask: "We've already learned that Hashem runs the world according to the ATFAT principle, a turn for a turn. If that's the case, shouldn't we expect serious tribulations for serious transgressions?"

Fortunately, Hashem is a loving Father who avoids using harsh measures whenever He can. The beauty of emuna in Divine Providence is that we begin to see with our own eyes how Hashem uses the tiny tribulations to stimulate us. Although each of us are on different levels of spiritual awareness, Hashem "speaks" to us in such a way that we can understand what we need to correct. Here's an example:

A person has an inexplicable recurring headache. Medically, nothing seems to be wrong. He turns to Hashem, begging for help. All of a sudden, he gets the idea to have his tefillin checked. Sure enough, the *shel rosh* – the tefillin that are worn on the head – has a mistake on one of the parchments and must be replaced. The person has his tefillin fixed, and the headaches go away completely...

Were it not for the headaches, the person in the example above may never have fathomed that anything was wrong with his tefillin. He might have continued to wear the unkosher tefillin for another forty years. But, by virtue of his emuna in Divine Providence, he realized that his tribulations came from Hashem and for a good reason. The headaches were a catalyst for needed soul-searching and subsequent rectification. Without them, the person might have gone for decades without fulfilling the important mitzvah of tefillin.

As soon as we recognize that everything in our lives is the product of exact, individually-tailored Divine direction and Providence, we use our daily difficulties as tools for introspection, implementation, and subsequent personal and spiritual growth; each person in accordance with his current spiritual level.

Mitigation of all Stern Judgments

Some two hundred twenty years ago, there was a five-year drought in Yemen. Rabbi Yechia Tzalach of saintly and blessed memory, the righteous local rabbi and spiritual leader, told the community that the harsh decree was originally intended to be much shorter. But, since the community cried and complained about the drought, it was prolonged. "As long as the entire community refuses to accept the decree with love and faith, it will be impossible to mitigate it," declared the Rabbi.

The community agreed not only to accept the decree with love and faith, but to thank Hashem for his justice and loving-kindness, acknowledging that the drought was beneficial in stimulating everyone to do teshuva. In unison, they began to praise Hashem's Name and thank Him. Heavy clouds gathered and within minutes, the rain poured forth.

Mazal Tov!

Rebbe Baruch of Medziboz of saintly and blessed memory once sat around the table with his disciples. Suddenly, his glass fell off the table and shattered on the floor. Rebbe Baruch immediately gave thanks to Hashem and began a process of self-evaluation in search of a misdeed that he might have done.

His disciples were stunned. "Rebbe," they said, "usually when a glass breaks, we all yell out 'mazal tov' and that's it. Why is the Rebbe looking so serious, as if it were Yom Kippur right now?"

Rebbe Baruch answered, "Do you know why we say 'mazal tov'? Who knows what should have been broken as a result of some harsh decree against me? But, Hashem in His infinite mercy, decided to break a glass instead of breaking something on my body. That's why we say mazal tov. I still have to do teshuva for whatever led to the stiff judgment in the first place."

Remember this rule: Whenever things don't go the way you want them to, look at Hashem! Don't play the blame game and don't look at anyone else. A broken glass or a cup of spilled milk is the type of minor tribulation that people fail to accept with love and emuna. Stop and think - granted, your brand new carpet is blemished because little six-year old Aaron, your own beloved little boy, was careless and spilled a glass of chocolate milk. But does he deserve to be abused for that, verbally and physically? Does he deserve to have his tender little soul virtually slaughtered by an irate mother or father who doesn't believe in Divine Providence? Sure, we can educate little Aaron to be more careful, but education has to be with love, not with anger. Rather than calling Aaron "stupid" or "klutzy," the parent should thank Hashem for the minor tribulation. The shining personal example of a parent with emuna who thanks Hashem for the good and for the seemingly bad is the very best way in the world to educate a child.

When life's tiny tribulations are sufficient to spiritually arouse us, Hashem has no need to stimulate us with greater and more difficult tribulations.

Wake Up

As opposed to the spiritually aware who use every tiny tribulation as a growth opportunity and as a window for self-assessment and subsequent teshuva, the rest of the world is in deep spiritual slumber. People are still light years away from emuna and particularly emuna in Divine Providence. They go through life like the proverbial little metal ball that gets kicked around from side to side in a pinball machine. They have no direction and certainly no understanding of why they suffer all the time. Sadly, such people are at the mercy of natural forces, beyond which they simply don't see Hashem.

Teaching Everyone to Say Thank You

A woman came to me complaining that she had moved ten times in ten years. I told her that in the World to Come, everyone will be jealous of her, because each move was an absolution of her sins. Hashem was helping her maintain a completely unblemished soul.

Remember, if you accept the minor aggravations in life with love and with emuna, you're saving yourself much greater suffering. If the woman in the above example would have accepted moving from place to place with love the first time she had to move, she might have saved herself from moving the other nine times.

A devastated young lady came to speak to me after her second engagement was broken off. She cried bitterly. I told her how lucky she was for all kinds of reasons: Spiritually, her suffering atones for her sins in this world at a bargain-basement price. I asked her how she'd feel if right after the wedding, she discovered that her husband was abusive or dishonest or maybe something much worse. "You should be singing and dancing," I told her. "Thank Hashem."

As in our previous example of the lady that moved ten times, if this young woman would have thanked Hashem after her first engagement was broken off, then she might have spared herself from a second broken engagement.

Let's never forget the lesson of the Children of Israel in the desert: If we don't accept three days of tiny tribulations with love and with emuna, we could end up suffering for forty years! Do you know what that means?

You missed the chance to make a tremendous deal. You had a broken engagement. You failed your driving test. G-d forbid, you had a miscarriage. Stop tormenting yourself! Stop looking for someone to blame! This is Hashem's will and for your absolute benefit. Accept this tribulation with emuna and joy in your heart, for Hashem is doing the very best. Wait and see how soon you'll be blessed with whatever you need when you thank Hashem for the seemingly bad as well as for the good.

The entire purpose of this book is to help you - the reader - accept everything with a smile and with emuna, thanking Hashem for everything. With such a mindset, you'll see phenomenal miracles and salvation from the most difficult of problems in your life. When we thank Hashem for everything, Hashem gives us many more wonderful reasons to thank Him.

Chapter Six:
Rectifying our Lives

In the future, our Sages say, all the sacrifices will be nullified – except for the thanksgiving offering. In other words, when our righteous Moshiach will come, in the very near future, and the holy Temple will be built in Jerusalem, no other sacrifices will be offered there – not sin offerings and not guilt offerings. The only sacrifices will be thanksgiving offerings. Rabbi Yosef Chaim of Baghdad, better known as "The Ben Ish Chai," writes that all the Psalms will also be nullified except for the hymn of thanksgiving. In other words, anyone who wants to say Psalms to G-d will have nothing to say but the hymn of thanksgiving.

What will we have that will necessitate so much thanks to G-d? Why will we be saying thank you exclusively?

If we would really see the truth, we would be thanking G-d endlessly right now, even before Moshiach comes. We should be thanking G-d for everything – including His smallest gifts – whether spiritual or material. We should take nothing for granted, even the most mundane details of life. A person must believe and know that G-d is watching over him and has given him all the necessities in life for use right now.

For this reason we must thank G-d every time that we enjoy the use of an item. For example, every time we sit on a chair, we should thank G-d for the chair. And every time we use a certain tool, we should thank G-d for the tool. And so on and so forth: "Thank You, G-d, for the shoes. Thank You G-d, for the coat. Thank You G-d, for the car." Sound exaggerated? This helps us appreciate everything we have while taking nothing for granted.

When we enjoy the use of something, we must believe that it is G-d's Divine Providence that gave us, specifically, the article for our utilization and benefit. We must thank G-d in detail for His personal guidance. Just as the Creator's guidance includes the smallest details, so must our thanks to Him be for the smallest details, each and every time we enjoy the use of something.

Even now, we must thank G-d for everything. There is a difference, though, between now and the future. Now, the service of G-d with faith and thanks is more or less concealed; not many people live the truth of giving thanks to G-d for every detail. But in the future, spiritual awareness will greatly expand and we will see that we must thank G-d all the time. We will say hymns of thanksgiving repeatedly – each time with a new awakening of the soul.

The Good Who Does Good

In the future, we will understand how little we praised the Creator for His revealed kindness. But we will also realize how all the seemingly bad things were actually acts of profound loving-kindness. When Moshiach comes, he will show every person how everything was all for the best. At that point, everyone will give thanks for all the things for which they hadn't thanked G-d and for the things about which they had been unhappy.

We'll then come to remarkable realizations: Remember that time when I was so upset? I see that it was all for the very best and that I should have thanked G-d. Now I will bring a thanksgiving offering to make up for what I missed. And remember the other time, when I cried over what had happened? Actually, it was a wondrously good turn of events. It's just that I was clueless and didn't thank G-d. Now I will bring a thanksgiving offering.

Each time that a person will bring a thanksgiving offering, he will become aware of new instances for which he should have been thankful, but was not. And for every new instance, he will bring another thanksgiving offering. And for every thanksgiving offering that he will bring, he will understand how even more seemingly negative experiences worked out for the best. He will see how G-d did him a huge favor here, and how He had mercy on him there. In this way, everybody will be bringing thanksgiving offerings to the Temple day and night. They will thank G-d time and again for all events throughout their lives and for all the times they did not understand, did not thank G-d, and even cried and felt sorrow. They will thank G-d for every breath they take.

Don't wait for the Moshiach to come to thank Hashem. Instead, reflect on your life today and thank Him for every last detail: For the fact that you were born on a certain day, thank You! For your particular parents, thank You! For being raised in a particular manner, thank You! Thank G-d for every stage of your life and for every day, and every detail of every day. In particular, thank G-d for all the hardship that you have endured, for all the things that brought you sorrow or confusion, for all the things that you did not believe were for the best. Now review it all in your mind and thank G-d for everything. In this way, you will rectify your entire life!

Thanking and Rectifying

When a person reviews his life and thanks G-d for things he had not been previously grateful for, he rectifies his entire life. He performs a remarkable spiritual correction of the stages in his life he had not lived with faith in G-d.

When we review our lives in detail and give thanks for the past, we rectify all of those details for which we had not thanked G-d when they actually occurred. By not thanking G-d, we were actually living a life devoid of emuna: We didn't believe that the positive circumstances were the result of Divine Providence; rather, they were just natural or the result of our own efforts. Or we simply didn't relate to them and took them for granted. We also did not believe that the negative circumstances of our lives were the will of G-d and for our ultimate good; we only cried and complained. Thanking Hashem is the best remedy to retroactively repair our past.

Channels of Abundance

Giving thanks opens all the channels of spiritual and physical abundance that had been closed off to each of us. When these channels are clogged, the abundance that the person needs for his vitality – both spiritually and physically – do not reach him. This deficiency results in all sorts of troubles. As such, the underlying reason for most of the suffering in the world - illnesses, G-d forbid, serious financial difficulties and other acute problems – are congested and closed channels of abundance.

Honoring Parents

The first channel through which a person receives his abundance is his father and mother. When a person merits continuous blessings from his parents, he succeeds above and beyond his normal capabilities. Blessings accompany him on all sides and everything is open before him. For this reason, a person should do everything in his power to merit the blessings of his parents. Even the evil Esau knew this and was aware of the importance of his father's blessing. That is why, when he did not receive Isaac's blessing, he cried "a very great and bitter cry" - the most intense form of wailing defined in the Torah.

Many people who suffer are disconnected in some way from their parents. They may feel resentment or anger toward their parents, or vehemently disagree with their parents' behavior or opinions. This causes the major parental artery of abundance to be closed.

This is not an assumption, but tried and true knowledge. Lack of peace with parents destroys people's lives! Even if the Torah had not commanded us to honor our parents, common sense would dictate that a person must be perpetually indebted to his parents, who brought him into this world, and raised and supported him. Surely the fact that this directive is written in the Ten Commandments reinforces the certainty that we must thank our parents wholeheartedly daily: Thank you, dear father! Thank you, dear mother!

A foundation of emuna and simple ethics requires that when a person has done tremendous favors for us, even if he causes us pain, we must remember the kindness that he did for us and tolerate the pain that he causes. A person should not feel resentful toward his parents – not even a bit – even if he believes he is right. If he is not right, it is certainly a terrible fault to resent his parents. Even if his parents caused him pain, abused him, and did not give him enough love – although this certainly hurt him - it is forbidden to resent his parents because of it. A person can be completely justified. But as long as he nurtures his resentment, his channel of abundance will be closed. In fact, we should never resent someone who causes us pain, because he is no more than G-d's messenger to cause us pain, as explained below and in **The Garden of Emuna** in detail.

The Rectification of Thanks

The only way to rectify all this and to open our channels of abundance is to start to do some serious thanking. In this way, we repent for our lack of faith. Giving thanks also teaches us to be better, more gracious people.

Even the worst parent deserves wholehearted thanks daily. The accounting of good that a person does must be kept separate from the accounting of the bad. The bad actually comes from G-d as a correction and purification of one's soul. The person who was the conveyer of the bad was simply chosen to act as a rod of reproof in G-d's hands. If not grief from this "rod," one would have had grief from another "rod," so why be angry at the rod? And even if we cannot accept the seemingly bad with complete faith, we are still obligated to show appreciation for the good.

Hashem doesn't make mistakes. Abusive parents are sticks in His hands. The victim of the abuse was judged in the most exacting way in the Heavenly court. On the other hand, the parents who sinned – if they do not repent - will certainly be severely punished for causing their child pain instead of giving him warmth and love.

This is one of the reasons that severe punishments – such as imprisonment - are meted out to many people who are parents. Heavenly mercy is removed from them and all the gates are closed before them. There is a rule: He who has mercy on G-d's creations will be the recipient of Heavenly mercy. When a person is cruel to G-d's creations,

G-d's mercy is closed to him. This is truer of a parent who should naturally have mercy on his children. Even wild animals have mercy on their offspring. Heavenly mercy is completely closed before parents who do not have mercy on their children. They are punished in this world for harming their children and have purgatory to look forward to after their deaths, if they do not do teshuva.

This is G-d's accounting with the parents. But the victimized child must know that his parents are G-d's rods of reproof and should not resent them. Victims of child abuse carry indescribable pain in their hearts. This pain distorts their lives and is often the prism through which they see reality. Despite the pain, it is G-d's Divine Providence that determined that the victim would be born to those parents who abused him or caused him pain. This is his soul correction according to his past incarnations. He must make a concentrated effort to overcome all the bad that they did to him, remember only the good and be eternally grateful for it. If one manages to do so, it will help heal his soul and creates a cosmic rectification.

Thanksgiving

We must believe that all our suffering is for the best and thank G-d for it. This mitigates the suffering. When we accept everything – even excruciating situations like parental abuse - with emuna and love, and thank G-d for all suffering, we sweeten the entire situation and do not suffer. Thus, the main reason for our suffering is lack of emuna.

It is highly likely that a victim of child abuse was still small when he suffered the abuse. At that point, he did not have the intellectual capacity to understand that everything is from G-d. The problem is that he perpetuated his anger and resentment for all the years he was abused. Every time those memories of abuse enter his mind, he feels pain and anger once again. Why? Because he still has not acquired the belief that there is nothing but G-d, and that this is what G-d wanted. Even more, that everything is for the best and that we must thank Him for everything. He must believe that G-d willed him to grow up in this abusive situation for his eternal good.

Now that the adult victim of child abuse has the opportunity to learn this book – and he already knows that everything is for the best - he can finally do teshuva for his past and say the following to G-d:

"Master of the Universe, pardon me, forgive me for the past. For I did not know then, when I was suffering, that everything is from You and that everything was for my own good – and I did not thank You for the suffering. I should have said to You 'thank You very much' for my suffering at the hands of my father, and 'thank You very much' for my suffering at the hands of my mother. But in my sins, not only did I not thank You, but I was even angry and carried years of anger and resentment with me. But now that I have emuna, I am returning to You. And I thank You for all the suffering that I have experienced from then until today. Because everything is exact and for my eternal good."

When the victim will do deep, serious thanksgiving for everything that has transpired; for every bit of sorrow, for every lack that he experienced – until the impression that life was bad is erased – he will have rectified his past. Now he will begin a completely new life. The channels of abundance will open for him and will shower him with plenty until his "cup runneth over."

Tzaddikim

The important next channel of abundance for every person is his rabbi and spiritual guide, as well as all the rabbis and tzaddikim of this generation and all previous generations. If a person is disconnected from them, all the channels of abundance are tightly closed.

One must never disassociate himself from his main rabbi. The Mishnah tells us that a person's rabbi brings him to the World to Come. Our Sages relate that every student is sustained in the merit of his rabbi. The rabbi's guidance protects him from the pitfalls of this world. As long as the Heavenly Court sees that the student has a rabbi who leads and guides him, it does not judge him. Instead, it leaves it up to the rabbi to correct his student's soul. The rabbi prays for his students continuously, focuses on how to better their situations, and more. How can a person separate himself from his rabbi, from whom he receives his vitality?

The Evil Inclination works extra hard to distance a person from his rabbi. It knows that the person's entire soul correction depends on this connection. Therefore, it plants dissension in the heart of the student, distorts his vision of his rabbi and incites him to turn his back on all the good that his rabbi has done for him. A person whose life is dear to him must thank G-d daily from the bottom of his heart for his rabbi and constantly remind himself from where his rabbi extricated him – from what depths of depravity – and how much he helped him, brought him close to him, counseled him in his relationships and more. He must thank G-d for all of this with all his heart and pray that his source of vitality is never shut off.

The same is true of every tzaddik or Torah scholar that ever lived or is still alive. One should never engage in dispute with them or discuss them in a negative light. Every tzaddik draws spiritual and physical abundance down to the world. If a person creates a dispute concerning a tzaddik – or even worse, if he hates or speaks negatively of him - he closes his channels of abundance from that tzaddik. Is it any wonder that afterwards he becomes ill or sinks into debt?

The general rule is that a person should be connected to all the tzaddikim. Nonetheless, it is good and worthy for a person to have one main rabbi from whom he receives guidance in life and in his service of G-d, as our Sages say: "Make a rabbi for yourself and be absolved of doubt." If a person asks the opinions of many rabbis all at once, he can create confusion. Rebbe Nachman writes in **Sefer Hamiddot** that if a person learns from many rabbis, it negatively affects his faith in G-d's oneness. In general, though, every person must be connected with bonds of love to all the sages of Israel, with no exception. Certainly, he should not engage in dispute with any of them, G-d forbid.

The fact that a person is connected to a certain rabbi does not mean that it is permissible for him to think or speak derisively of other rabbis, G-d forbid. A person becomes close to a particular rabbi because G-d guided him so. This is his path to achieving closeness with G-d. But he must love all the other rabbis, including those to whom he does not feel close. In addition, he must love all the holy books that were written by the rabbis and not denigrate them, G-d forbid.

A person should not close off the channels of abundance of the Nation of Israel's tzaddikim, rabbis and Torah scholars. Instead, he should accustom himself to thank G-d daily for the tzaddikim and sages. In this way, he will surely not engage in dispute with any tzaddik. We must thank G-d profusely for the tzaddikim in our own generation and pray that G-d will give them strength, health, wisdom, and understanding so that they may bring Jews close to Him and infuse the Nation of Israel with emuna.

One should also thank G-d for every tzaddik who ever lived. He should thank G-d for bringing tzaddikim to the world so they could become conduits for wonderful things for the world. This reminds us once again of the story of the Seer of Lublin who, for fifteen years daily, thanked G-d for bringing the soul of Rebbe Elimelech of Liszansk to the world. Every person must thank G-d daily for the tzaddikim who brought him close to Hashem. How much we must thank G-d for the tzaddikim who bring us to the truth and enlighten our eyes!

Spouses

The next channel of abundance closest to a person is his or her spouse. A person who closes this channel with anger, criticism, and insults not only siphons off all the physical and spiritual abundance that should have been flowing through this channel - he also brings pain and suffering upon himself.

A couple once came to me with marital problems. I sat and listened to them. The husband accused his wife of all sorts of wrongdoings, definitively proving that their marital difficulties and problems with their children were all her fault. In truth, he was most convincing…

Then it was the wife's turn and she had plenty to say. She clearly explained why all their problems were her husband's fault. She was also very convincing…

I couldn't help them; all I could do was listen. I was very saddened by their home, in which everyone – husband, wife and children – were all suffering. In my personal prayers to G-d that day, I begged Him to show me what this couple was missing. Why didn't they merit marital peace? Why was everything closed before them? They were making huge amounts of money, but they had nothing and were still living in a rented home. There was no blessing in their lives – just mutual accusation and pain. Ironically, they could have lived royally. What was the problem?

Then G-d opened my eyes and I understood that what they were missing was our series of CDs on thanksgiving: **It's Good to Thank Hashem**, **We Thank You**, **Stop Crying** and **Learn to Say Thank You**. Whoever listens to these CDs should really listen to them all – not just one or parts of one. Each illuminates a different, crucial point. Of course, now that this book has been published, I'll add that it's vital to study it well, review it and pray to fulfill everything that is written here.

Getting back to our couple, I understood that what they were missing was guidance on thanksgiving. Why? Being happy with everything means being happy with our lot. Clearly, if the husband would be happy with his lot, which, in this case, was his wife – and all her shortcomings in his opinion - he would no longer experience pain and grief.

Had he adopted the emuna approach to his marriage, he would have decided: This is my wife. She has shortcomings x and y. But she is my wife, which means that she is my lot in life…and I must be happy with my lot in life.

At that point, he would have accepted her shortcomings with love, as everything about her is for his good. G-d knows that only with this woman will he make his soul correction and fulfill the purpose for which his soul came down to earth.

Emuna is the belief that there is nothing else but G-d. Emuna means that all is for the best. Being that there is nothing else but G-d, then his wife is also part of G-d's plan for him.

If the husband would believe this, he would see all the good in his wife and all the good the she does for him. Not only would he replace his complaints with thanksgiving, but he would do teshuva for all the shortcomings that he saw in her, since a wife is a mirror image of her husband. Every shortcoming in her points the husband to his own shortcoming. Every bit of pain that he has from her points to his own sins, as is explained in the book **The Garden of Peace** (and for her, **Women's Wisdom**).

Complaints Transformed to Thanksgiving

The wife must also have emuna and be happy that the Creator of the world designed her husband especially for her soul correction. She must also thank G-d.

Periodically, I lectured in a town in Israel's south. Every time that I would go to this town, a particular woman would approach me after the lecture and tell me how her husband humiliates her, causes her pain, degrades her, and generally makes her life miserable.

This time, she approached me and was all smiles. She told me that for years she had heard my Torah lessons but had not really listened to their message. She was always engrossed in her pain and would just wait for the opportunity to pour her heart out following the lesson. But recently, she decided to truly study **The Garden of Emuna**. Upon learning the book, she began to understand what she had heard so many times - that everything is from G-d, and that it is not her husband who is humiliating her, but rather her suffering is a message from G-d and all for her own good. She integrated these ideas and began to spend time in personal prayer to G-d, thanking Him for half an hour daily for this particular husband - for all the humiliation, degradation and curses, for all the pain that she had suffered at the hands of the rod of reproof that was called 'husband.'

The woman reported that in every session of personal prayer, after she thanked Hashem for one half hour from the bottom of her heart, she asked His forgiveness for all the years she didn't believe that everything is from Him and all for the very best. She did teshuva for all her needless crying and complaints, and the fact that she lacked true appreciation for her husband, children and home. After all, she knew she had the suffering coming to her, for she had sinned a lot in her youth. Once she started giving thanks, she became happier than she had ever been in her life.

She also told me that her husband noticed the change in her and asked her, "What happened? Something changed in you. You don't complain, you don't protest, you don't cry…"

She answered, "I'm now happy. I'm glad that I don't have marital peace."

"What?" her husband asked in surprise. "You're happy that you don't have marital peace?"

"Yes," she answered. "It brings me closer to G-d. I thank G-d for all the humiliation and sorrow that you cause me. I am glad that you degrade me, because all you are is a rod of reproof in G-d's hands. I deserve all of your insults. If you wouldn't do this, then G-d would have someone else do it. This way, I repent every day and get closer to G-d. Every day, G-d opens new gates for me, and I happily do teshuva. I don't care that I do not have marital peace because I am getting closer to G-d. I am fulfilling my ultimate purpose; what do I care about the rest?"

Afraid of Marital Peace

This case is similar to what I experienced myself, when I had a large debt on my shoulders. I would dance with joy all the time because I saw with my very own eyes how the debt was bringing me closer to Hashem. I would do teshuva every day. Daily, new opportunities would open up for me, both materially and spiritually. Every day G-d would guide me to do teshuva again and again. When I would see this, I would say, "How wonderful it is to be in debt! How wonderful it is to be in a constant state of teshuva!"

This woman also told me that as a result of the fact that she stopped viewing her husband as the source of her suffering and began to view him as G-d's rod of reproof, her husband also woke up and did teshuva. He made a simple calculation: "What? I am G-d's rod? I prefer to be G-d's messenger of good and not his punishment rod." This woman became worried - now that her marriage was improving, how was she going to continue to get closer to Hashem every day with the same strong feeling?

I told her that she should not worry. If she'd make a personal accounting of her deeds every day and fix what needs to be corrected and progress in spiritual matters, she won't need suffering to motivate her to come closer to G-d, as is explained in the book **In Forest Fields**.

A couple who lives with emuna and is sure that everything is for the best will be blessed with marital peace.

Hashem's Blessing

The source of a couple's abundance is the broad feeling of joy that the wife feels from the illumination of her soul, as Rebbe Nachman explains in Likutei Moharan I:69. The Talmud teaches that the blessing in a man's house exists as a result of the honor that he gives to his wife.

Abundance is Spiritual

Back to our original couple: They had a hefty income but couldn't afford to own their own home. They hardly had food to put on the table. How could that be? What happened to their wealth?

A person's abundance is not material. It is spiritual and depends on Divine input, as King Solomon says in the Book of Proverbs, "Hashem's blessing brings wealth." I have seen people who have a small amount of money, but never go into debt and lack nothing. They have Hashem's blessing. How do they manage? No one knows. The plain facts are that they have very little money but have it all. That is the reality and we cannot argue with it. On the other hand, there are people who earn huge amounts of money but have nothing – they have to borrow money to buy food!

From an emuna perspective, this phenomenon is simple to understand. The world operates according to Hashem's laws as elaborated in the Talmud, which says that blessing resides in a person's house in the merit of the honor that a husband gives his wife.

In the Mishnah, Rabbi Shimon ben Halafta gives us another important tip for life: "The Holy One, Blessed Be He did not find a vessel to sustain blessing other than peace." When a person closes his channels of blessing by not honoring his wife sufficiently and damages the vessel of peace –

even if he is one hundred per cent justified – they remain hermetically sealed. The fact that he is justified does not help him.

If the husband would see G-d and not the "rod of reproof" - the role that his wife is currently fulfilling - he would know that he is the one who is at fault. He would not be angry with the rod at all and would not be upset in the slightest with his wife. Certainly, he would not be angry with G-d, Who wielded the rod. Rather, he would submissively take an accounting of his actions and attempt to rectify them.

Love of Israel

These are all important channels of abundance for every person. If someone feels any type of resentment against these channels, abundance ceases its flow. A person's lack of joy, or feeling that he has nothing to live for, is a sign of clogged channels of abundance.

There is another, more general channel of abundance: The Nation of Israel. Every Jew is a channel through which abundance flows to the world. The Nation of Israel is one nation, one soul and one body. Thus, when a person resents a Jew anywhere in the world, he closes the flow of abundance that he received from that Jew's channel.

Rebbe Nachman explains this as follows (Sichot Haran, Discourse 91):

"A propitious action to encourage diligence, so that a person will be diligent in his [Torah] study, is to be careful not to speak[ill] of any Jew. Just as when the bride is beautiful, then the love is perfect. But when the bride has a flaw or blemish, then certainly the love is not perfect. Thus it is with the Torah, which is called a bride, as is written (Deuteronomy, 33:4): 'Moses commanded the Torah to us, an inheritance of the Congregation of Jacob.' And our Sages of blessed memory expounded (Brachot, 57:A; Pesachim, 49:B) 'Do not read it as 'inheritance' but rather as 'betrothed.' Every Jew has a letter of the Torah, for the Torah has six hundred thousand letters, parallel to the six hundred thousand soul roots of Israel. When there is a shortcoming in one Jew, it would mean that there is a shortcoming in the Torah, where the soul roots of Israel are. Certainly, it is impossible to love the Torah perfectly. But one should be careful not to speak [ill] of any Jew and not to find any shortcoming in any Jew. This will lead him to realize that there is no shortcoming or blemish and then he will love the Torah very much. And then he will study the Torah diligently, out of his great love, as above.

This is the meaning of 'The Torah of G-d is perfect' (Psalms, 19:8). In other words, the Torah of G-d is perfect with no shortcoming or blemish. When a person is careful not to find fault with any Jew, who is a letter of the Torah, then the Torah is perfect, with no shortcoming or blemish. The Torah then restores the soul, because then, specifically, we merit to love the Torah and feel the sweet taste of Torah that restores the soul – because it has no shortcoming, as above. And then we merit diligence, as above."

This is written about the spiritual abundance of the Torah, which is certainly closed if a person enters into a dispute with any Jew in the world. Material abundance is drawn down by spiritual abundance. When the channel of spiritual abundance is closed, material abundance immediately dries up. Thus, a person should thank G-d daily for all Jews and love all Jews, without exception.

If a person feels anger or resentment, she must work on her emuna and teshuva, as discussed. She must thank G-d for the suffering that she has (or had) from the Jew and believe that the suffering is from G-d and for her very best. She must remember that the person who caused her the pain is there for her to do teshuva and obliterate any anger or resentment that she harbors toward anyone in the world – until her heart is clean and pure, filled with love of Israel.

A Clean Past

To erase all the resentment, residual anger and sorrow of one's past, one must thank G-d for everything and continue to do so until nowhere in his heart does he feel that something is not good, and harbors no negative memories. When he believes that everything that happened to him and all the suffering that he endured until this point was for his eternal good - and when he thanks G-d for everything in his past, he will erase that which he sees as negative.

A person needs to work hard to acquire a clean heart. He must believe that there is nothing but G-d and that it is not a particular person who does him wrong; not his father, mother or wife. He must work on believing that all is G-d and that all the different types of suffering that he endures from various people is G-d's will and for his ultimate good!

G-d didn't will this pointlessly. He willed it for your good. Thank Him, clean your heart so that you will have no bad memories from the past, and you will be pure and all the channels of abundance will open for you!

Thanksgiving Heals the Soul

When a person works at thanksgiving, he heals his soul. By giving thanks, a person is completely healed from all sorts of mental illnesses that lurk within. This is because thanksgiving completely rectifies emuna. Through perfect emuna, we heal from all mental illness, because emuna and the soul are one and the same.

Rebbe Nachman explains this in Likutei Moharan 173:

"Through a person's writing, the true tzaddik can discern his soul and inner dimensions of his soul, his emuna and the root of his emuna. Because there is an aspect called 'the root of emuna,' because emuna itself has vitality and a root. In other words, there is a world of emuna from where emuna is taken. The world of emuna also has emuna in G-d. This is the aspect of emuna that is the inner dimension of emuna. It is the aspect of the inner dimension of the soul, because the soul and emuna are the same aspect."

In this paragraph, Rebbe Nachman reveals to us that G-d created an entity called emuna. It is a world in and of itself. From this world, our emuna is drawn down. The world of emuna gets its emuna from the root of emuna, called the inner dimension of emuna, which is also the inner dimension of the soul. Rebbe Nachman has revealed something wonderful: The soul and emuna are one and the same.

Now we can understand that any acquired mental illness, deficiency in the soul or problem in the soul all come from some blemish in emuna. Since emuna and the soul are one and the same, we can now understand that if there is any type of deficiency in one of them, it can easily be detected in the other. Any lack of emuna is also a deficiency in the soul and any deficiency in the soul is a lack of emuna. When we rectify and perfect our emuna, we rectify and cure our emotional problems – big or small.

The Superiority and Inferiority Complexes

Anyone who lacks perfect emuna suffers from these complexes to some degree. Actually, the Superiority

Complex is the flip side of the Inferiority Complex. Someone with a Superiority Complex swings back and forth between feelings of superiority and feelings of inferiority.

A person seeks superiority because he is dissatisfied with his lot in life. The person feels inferior and that he lacks something. This character trait actually stems from a lack of emuna. A person with emuna believes that the Almighty created him, watches over him, and is happy with him just the way he is – even if he is the smallest and lowliest person in the world. This person is happy with his lot.

Being happy with your lot in life means believing, with perfect faith, that G-d watches over you. When you clearly internalize that knowledge – that all your shortcomings, difficulties and problems are from G-d, tailor-made to facilitate your ultimate soul correction - you will be happy with everything that happens to you, and at peace with your shortcomings and difficulties. This is the true character trait of 'happy with one's lot.'

Someone who lives with the awareness that everything in his life is precise Divine Providence, designed for his ultimate good, does not have to think that he is better than anyone else in order to feel happiness. He is glad to live his life within the framework of the circumstances that Hashem has prepared for him. He knows full well that he is riddled with shortcomings, but that's Hashem's will, so he is nonetheless happy.

A person with emuna is satisfied with his lot in life, and not swept up by visions of grandeur irrelevant to his mission on earth and soul correction. He therefore is not influenced by other peoples' circumstances, is never jealous and is always happy. He doesn't have to think that he is better than anyone else to be happy. He doesn't have to brag to be happy, nor does he need praise, recognition or any external input to be happy. Even when humiliated, he remains happy, because he is happy with his lot in life.

By strengthening our emuna and accepting ourselves with joy just as we are, we overcome the Superiority/Inferiority Complex.

Let's take a look at some common mental illnesses. With G-d's help, we will explain how emuna cures these ills.

Paranoia

Almost everyone suffers from some degree of paranoia. Some are unfortunately so ill with this disease that they lose their emotional balance. The only cure for this serious affliction, as in the case of the Superiority/Inferiority Complex, is to thank G-d for it and strengthen emuna.

The root of paranoia is dissatisfaction with oneself. A person thinks, "I am worthless; I am a failure." This internal self-persecution manifests into external paranoia - when a person thinks that others pursue him, hate him, plot against him, and so forth. Someone who persecutes himself is certainly broken inside. When somebody does not smile at him, he immediately thinks: "He didn't even smile at me! I disgust him. He hates me..." And then when somebody looks at him he thinks: "Why is he looking at me? He must hate me..." This can progress to dimensions of insanity, in which the afflicted person imagines in detail how the entire world is plotting against him, may Hashem have mercy on such a person.

Paranoia is also the result of pride, in which a person thinks that others must surely be jealous of him and want to kill or harm him, and the like. If he was not prideful, he would know that other people are too preoccupied with their own lives to pay much attention to his own. They certainly have no intention to plot against him.

The best medicine for paranoia is thanksgiving, acquired by strengthening emuna in G-d. Hashem leads every person in the very best way. So, when a person persecutes himself and is dissatisfied, he lacks the emuna that Hashem does everything for the best. If a person had simple emuna that the Creator is watching over him, he would accept everything and not persecute himself at all. Even if he would stumble or fall, he would be happy with his lot and thank Hashem for all his shortcomings. He would come close to Hashem under any circumstance, even from the lowest of places. As such, paranoia – where one thinks that everyone is plotting against him - is a total lack of emuna. There is nothing but Hashem in this world and everything that He does is for the very best, so what is there to fear? Who is there to fear? Is there anything that can harm us?

He who fears One fears no one. For example, the Talmud (Tractate Sanhedrin, 67) tells the story of Rebbe Chaninah and the witch who tried to surreptitiously collect dust from under his feet so that she could put a spell on him. Rebbe Chaninah noticed her and said, "What do you want? Dust? Come and take some. I am not afraid of your witchcraft, because the Torah says, 'There is nothing but Him...'"

Rebbe Chaninah showed the witch that she was powerless and that her witchcraft was powerless against Hashem's will. If G-d willed it, it would not help Rebbe Chaninah to fight with her or try to get away from her. Only teshuva would help him.

This is the rule: Emuna means there is nothing but G-d. Emuna means everything is for the best. If there is nothing but G-d, who can chase or harm you? If everything is for the best and G-d loves you, then whatever happens to you is good.

All sorts of fears and anxieties that people harbor are also subclasses of paranoia. Some people are afraid of illness, others of their financial future, some of wars, others of murderers or thieves. All these fears are rooted in a total lack of emuna. A person with emuna has only G-d in his world. He knows that everything is for the best and he has no bad in his life, as we sing: "It was the very best in the past, it is the very best now and it will be the very best in the future..."

G-d is only good. All we can do is thank Him for whatever the future holds. If G-d wants it to be that way, then it is very good. When a person believes that whatever will happen will be for the very best, he fears nothing.

If a person begins to fear or worry about the future, he should thank Hashem and say: "Master of the World! Thank You for these thoughts of fear and worry. These thoughts cause me suffering and they came from Your will for my good..." In this manner, he should thank G-d again and again for the suffering that his bad thoughts, fears and worries cause him. After that, he should thank G-d for the future and say: "If it is Your will that such and such will happen to me in the future, I already thank You. For certainly all that will happen to me is only good. So please accept my thanks ahead of time..."

If a person thanks G-d and merits to believe that G-d's Divine Providence guides over him in every single detail of his life and that everything is for the best, he will be completely free of any paranoia complex. He will no longer suffer in any way.

Schizophrenia

Schizophrenia is an illness of split personality. The afflicted person is confused and does not understand who she is. She has a number of "I"s. Every normal person is born with an ego – a product of her imagination - that she must work on throughout her life to nullify, so she can get close to Hashem and attain her soul correction. Not only has the schizophrenic person not nullified her regular ego, but she has a few more egos that are distorting reality.

The only way for a person to be cured of schizophrenia is to strengthen gratitude to Hashem and develop emuna. She must nullify her ego and attain clear emuna that there is nothing in the world but Hashem. The more that she strengthens her emuna, the more she will heal her soul from its state of confusion.

Every time that a thought of "I" enters her mind, enabling her to think that she is personality X or personality Y, she should say out loud: "There is nothing but Him" (In Hebrew, *Ein od Milvado*). Then she should thank G-d for her confusion and say: "Master of the Universe, thank You very much for this suffering, for my multitude of thoughts that "I" am X and "I" am Y and that "I" am such and such. Thank You that it is not clear to me who I am. Actually, what is clear to me is that there is no "me," because there is nothing but You, Hashem. Thank You very much. Surely this suffering is atoning for my sins, particularly for pride."

Neutralizing Post-Traumatic Stress Disorder

Some people live with post-traumatic stress disorder (PTSD) – a deep emotional scar from a traumatic experience in the past. By giving thanks to G-d, a person can heal and neutralize trauma. Intrinsically, "trauma" means that when a person went through a difficult experience, he did not accept it with emuna. Emotionally, he feels that he underwent a "bad" experience. The concept "bad," as we previously learned, stems from complete concealment of emuna. Clearly, if he had accepted what happened to him with complete emuna – no matter what the experience was – he would not suffer any trauma.

Someone once told me that a number of years ago, he almost lost his life, but instead he experienced miracles and G-d saved him. Nevertheless, every time that he thought about the person who threatened him, he experienced anxiety.

I told him that any sorrow that he felt from the past is because he didn't believe that there is nothing but Hashem, and that the perpetrator was nothing more than G-d's rod of reproof. Even now, I continued, every time that he recalls the incident and is fearful or anxiety-ridden, it is because he still doesn't believe that everything comes from Hashem and is all for the best. I told him to strengthen emuna and do teshuva for all the years that he suffered from these thoughts.

People suffer from any type of difficulty because they lack emuna. As Rebbe Nachman of Breslev said: "A person who does not have emuna – his life is not a life." All pain or hardship that a person has comes from a lack of emuna. If he had emuna, he would have no sorrow, because everything that Hashem does is for the very best, in order to facilitate a person's ultimate soul correction.

I told this man that if he wants to erase the trauma and eradicate pain and anxiety from his past, he must spend half of his daily one-hour session of personal prayer thanking Hashem for what had happened. His teshuva should be twofold: For the sin for which Hashem caused him the pain of having his life threatened in the first place, and for not taking it as wake-up call upon which to do teshuva. When the event took place, he should have thanked G-d, analyzed the situation to discover what he had done to cause such pain, and repented. As he did not do so then, he should do it now and say the following:

"Master of the Universe, thank You for all this pain that actually comes from not having believed in You then. For if I had believed in You then, I would have believed that you sent him for my own good. If I had looked for the silver lining in this trial, and if I had looked for what I needed to repent for, I would have been totally saved then – from the threat to my life, from the fear, and from the subsequent anxiety.

But to my sorrow, I did not believe in You. And today, still, I lack emuna and thus I still have fear. First of all, I thank You, Hashem, for giving me emuna to thank You now for what happened in the past. I ask You to strengthen my emuna so that I will believe with perfect faith that erverything was for my ultimate good and I will thank You for the pain and suffering that I endured. Grant me the merit to completely repent for the sin for which You sent me this suffering."

Victims of Abuse

Another person told me that when he was still far from observant Judaism, he had a serious problem and went to see a psychologist. This psychologist was a wicked person. He hypnotized him and while he was under the influence of the hypnosis, abused him. At a certain point, the man sensed that something was wrong. Thanks be to G-d, Who saved him and granted him the merit to return to Him. But he suffered anxiety from the abuse that he endured. I said to him: "You have done teshuva in the merit of the pain that you suffered, so now thank G-d for all of your suffering. Do not focus on the psychologist – focus on G-d, Who knew that you had to endure this exact measure of suffering so that you would have the merit to return to Him."

When we learn about abuse, we wonder: Why does a person have to suffer abuse, G-d forbid? We do not always understand, but we believe that everything is for the best. In the case above, it is quite clear that without this person's suffering at the hands of the evil psychologist, he would not have had the merit to return to G-d.

This is a lesson to be learned by any person who is still plagued with fear and anxiety from the past. One person experiences flashbacks from a serious accident, another of a horrific scene that he witnessed, and the like. All these fears from the past that flood a person are rooted in the fact that when the frightening or painful event occurred, the person did not believe that there is nothing but Hashem and that everything is for the best.

The rectification of this problem is to uncompromisingly believe in Hashem and thank Him for everything, including the traumatic experience: "Master of the Universe! Thank You for all the suffering that I endured all those years. I thank You for sending me this person to scare me. I thank You, Creator of the world, that you made me have this accident, that you showed me this horrifying scene, etc.

I also thank You for the fact that I lacked the spiritual awareness that everything is for the best, since you wanted me to endure suffering. I thank You for all the pain that I suffered throughout the years, because this was also for the best. And now, You have had mercy on me and granted me the merit to believe that everything is for the best. Thank You very much for that!"

If a person will do teshuva in this way and pray for emuna, he will erase all negativity from his past.

World Wide Insanity

Beside the mental illnesses that are scientifically defined, there are many other serious emotional illnesses that lurk within many people. One such illness is jealousy, which causes terrible emotional suffering, Heaven forbid. But a person who believes that everything is for the best is happy with his lot and completely free of this malady.

Another disease is called hatred. But a person who lives with the emuna that there is nothing but Him and that everything is for the best hates no one, not even those people who have been sent by Hashem to cause him pain.

Anger and sadness are additional emotional difficulties that cease to exist once a person strengthens their emuna.

And there is a special mental illness we'll call "crazy righteousness." People afflicted with this disease blame others for their sins. They are always full of complaints against the whole world and grumble that all sorts of people prevent them from being tzaddikim.

It's the wife's fault, for example, for making it difficult to learn Torah, and it is someone else's fault for the sin that he committed.

Once, Rebbe Natan of Breslev was giving a Torah class. In the middle of the class, a mentally ill person entered and disturbed them a bit, as mentally ill people sometimes do. After he left, Rebbe Natan said to his students, "He is not the only mentally ill person - we are all crazy. I knew only one normal human and that was our holy rabbi, Rebbe Nachman of Breslev. If we learn his opinions well, as well as the opinions of all the tzaddikim and genuine Torah scholars who guide us on the path of Torah, we have a chance to live a life of truth and emuna with sanity…"

Whoever lacks emuna espouses some form of insanity. Worries, depression or fears – all are mental illnesses. When a person with emuna lives the reality of the Creator, he is completely filled with happiness and joy. A person who talks about and studies emuna heals his soul.

Thanks in Advance

As previously discussed, many people worry about the future: What will be? Maybe something terrible will happen? In short, they see a dark future ahead, replete with misery. Can you guess at this point what the advice to remedy this is? To thank G-d. If a person has a thought of impending doom, he should say "Thank You, Hashem!" Ultimately, he will live a life of serenity.

Another suggestion for those suffering a sense of foreboding is to thank Hashem ahead of time, with emuna and confidence in Him - for all the salvations that he needs. Then the Creator will afford him those salvations in accordance with his emuna. In other words, a person who anticipates that he'll be in need of a particular salvation in the future should thank G-d for it in advance: "Creator of the world! Thank You for the salvation that you will give me or for providing me with what I will be lacking." He should continue with gratitude until he activates his request.

There are two ways that a person can fulfill his needs: One is by requesting what he needs from G-d. The other is to thank Him in advance. The second method works better and works always. When a person thanks G-d, no prosecuting angels interfere with his words. When a person makes a request from G-d, however, prosecuting angels could very well interfere with his request. The thanks must be heartfelt and uttered with emuna. If a person uses the thanking method as a ploy, without truly believing that everything is for the best, it will not "work." This is what the Sages refer to in the verse in Job, 41: "Who has preceded Me that I should repay, Whatever is under the entire heavens is Mine."

Our Sages explain that "Who has preceded me that I should repay," means: Who can say to the Holy One, Blessed Be He, "I preceded You, I gave You something before You gave me…" Who can say that? Our Sages cite the commandment of mezuzah: Would anybody boast and say to G-d: "Behold I have affixed mezuzot in Your honor. Now pay me my reward!" If so, G-d would say to him: "And who gave you your house so that you could affix mezuzot on it? Was it not I?" G-d always precedes us and gives us what is His. It is only after G-d's initial gift that a person can give back to G-d what He has already given him.

When it comes to thanking Hashem, it is possible to "precede" Him, because we can always say thank You in advance. And then Hashem is obligated, so to say, to pay us back. For G-d says: "Who has preceded Me that I should repay?," Thus, if we thank G-d in advance for what He will do in the future, G-d will have to fulfill his commitment, as it were, and to pay.

In this way, a person can thank G-d in advance for everything that he is lacking. If he doesn't have children, he should thank G-d: "Thank You very much for the children that You will grant me in the future…" He should continue with his thanks for one or two hours or more. G-d will see that he has thanked Him so much for the children that He has not yet given him, and He will ultimately give him children. This is because G-d said, "Who has preceded me that I should repay," and this person has indeed preceded Him. If so, G-d will pay...

Thanks in Installments

A person can also promise G-d that if He will fill his request, he will give thanks for a certain amount of time. For example: A yeshiva student had a constant urge to sleep. It was such a strong urge that he didn't see how he could possibly overcome it. Then he heard a Torah lesson on the power of thanksgiving and he decided to change his approach. In his personal prayer to G-d, he promised that if He would wake him at midnight, he would thank Him for one half hour. Wonder of wonders! That night he got up literally at midnight, with no problem.

Of course, he kept his promise to G-d and thanked Him for half an hour. And then he thought: Maybe this is just a coincidence? So he promised G-d again that if He would wake him up again at midnight the following night, he would thank Him for it for half an hour. Once again, he woke up with no trouble at midnight! And once again he kept his promise and thanked G-d for waking him up for a full half hour.

The next night came, and the student was already tired. After all, he had missed out on sleep the two previous nights and he was used to sleeping a lot. But once again, he promised G-d to thank Him for half an hour and - behold - G-d woke him up exactly at midnight, even though this was against the student's nature.

Since then, he gets up every night at midnight. This is a boy who was hardly able to drag himself out of bed by midday. Every night that he gets up, and thanks G-d for half an hour for waking him.

The book **Siach Sarfei Kodesh** tells the story of Rebbe Yitzchak, the son of Rebbe Natan of Breslev, who was once seriously ill. In his prayers for healing he said to G-d: "Master of the universe, what can I promise You? Can I promise You that if You heal me I will be perfect in my observance? I cannot promise that. But I can promise You that if You heal me, I will never forget it and I will always thank You for Your loving-kindness and goodness." Sure enough, he recovered.

Thanking G-d is the ultimate purpose of creation. G-d created everything - an infinite number of worlds, one above the next. In our world alone, (called the World of Action, *Asiyah*) we have only discovered an infinitesimal fraction of the heavens and heavenly bodies that G-d has created. And all of this was created for one, unique purpose: So that man would know his Creator and thank Him, as explained in the Ramban's elaboration of the Torah portion Bo: "Therefore a person who thanks G-d fulfills his purpose and the purpose of the entire creation. He is worthy of miracles and wonders, and he will merit great salvations."

Someone who trusts in G-d and expects G-d to perform a miracle and grant the needed salvation, is actually saying thank You before she receives the salvation. She already says thank You for the miracles that she will be experiencing. "Thank You very much, Hashem, for the specific miracle that I expect You will do for me!"

In Summary

A person can rectify his entire life. He can eradicate, correct and elevate all his previous heresy by giving thanks to G-d. He can cleanse his entire past – by giving thanks to G-d! He can cleanse himself of all his resentments and anger and of all his interpersonal problems, and thus open all the channels of abundance – by giving thanks to G-d! He can cleanse himself of all his discomfort, depravity and emotional problems – by giving thanks to G-d! He can also cleanse himself of all his fears and emotional scars – by giving thanks to G-d!

We must remember well that we also need to ask G-d to give us the faith that everything is for the best. If a person sees that he does not believe that all is for the best, he should not blame himself. Instead, he should ask G-d for help: "Master of the universe! Give me emuna! Grant me the merit to live the truth – that everything is for the best."

Clearly, if a person adopts this mode of thinking, he will be living in the Garden of Eden in this world.

Chapter Seven:
Miracle Stories

Rebbe Nachman of Breslev teaches (Likutei Moharan, I:91) that although emuna is in the heart, one's emuna should be so strong that it spreads to all the body's extremities.

Rebbe Nachman emphasizes that a person with emuna so strong that it spreads to all the organs of his body will grasp concepts that he initially only believed but did not understand. We can deduce from Rebbe Nachman's teaching that a person must believe in an intangible concept before he understands it. Once he internalizes the concept by way of constantly reinforced emuna, he succeeds in understanding the concept with his intellect. This process continuously repeats itself, going from emuna to intellect and back again, in a wonderful upward spiral of attaining progressively higher spiritual levels. The stronger a person's emuna, the more he will widen his horizons of intellect.

Lights on the Eve of the Passover Seder

The emuna-intelligence connection is vital for thanking Hashem in all circumstances, even when things seem bad. At the time of a challenge or a test of faith, a person cannot comprehend the benefit of such a difficult situation. Thus, it is hard for him to thank Hashem, because on a cognizant level, he perceives the situation as bad. We are used to saying thank-you for something good. During times of trial, there is no logic to attest to the goodness of the situation. But if a person maintains strong emuna, he will eventually understand – on a deeper level - why the difficult situation is intrinsically good.

A man once told me two stories that exemplify this thought: The first took place while he was beginning to strengthen his emuna and Torah observance.

This man's life was very complicated; he had many troubles, debts, a disjointed marriage, and a court order that ejected him from his home. He was on a dangerous downward spiral. Hashem had mercy on him - while he was driving, his car broke down and came to a complete stop right in front of the holy gravesite of Dan, the son of Jacob. Dan ben Jacob's gravesite is also home to a branch of our yeshiva.

The man had no choice but to enter our yeshiva. The young men from the yeshiva befriended him and gave him the book **The Garden of Peace**. He began to read it and in short time made up with his wife, putting his marriage on positive footing. Now he is a happy man, takes an hour daily for personal prayer, and more. His entire life was transformed dramatically for the very best.

This man's second story: His father was supposed to join him for the Passover Seder. The day before the Seder, his father had a stroke and was taken to the hospital. The family was confused and didn't know what to do about the Seder. Who would lead the Seder for their children if they opted to spend the night with their father in the hospital? They finally decided that the entire family would gather together for the Seder near the grandfather in the hospital and somehow they would manage.

They heard that a charitable organization in the hospital was preparing a Seder for patients' families. This calmed them. They relied on the hospital Seder and made no preparations of their own. But at the dining hall, they had a rude awakening. The hall was packed and they couldn't find any place to sit down.

Naturally, these circumstances created a great opportunity for the Evil Inclination, which bombarded our protagonist with negative thoughts: Look at you, on the night of the Seder – the most important night of the year! Look at how sad your children are, how tense your wife is… But this man had heard our CD lesson **Stop Crying** and decided to put what he had learned into practice. Instead of falling into negativity, he started to give thanks. "Thank You, Hashem that we have nowhere to sit at the Seder. Thank You. You know what You are doing, Hashem. Surely all is for the best."

Suddenly, a thought entered his mind. He said to his wife and children, "What is happening here? Hashem sent us here so that we could help the sick people! Forget about our Seder. Let's help serve and make the patients happy. That will be our Seder – helping the patients!"

His feelings and personal prayers of thanksgiving certainly mitigated the severe judgments, and his wife and children were happy to comply. They began serving and forgot about their "troubles." They focused on kindness and giving. After a short while, some seats opened up for them and they held their own Seder with great joy.

The man told me that the illumination and delight he, his wife and children felt are impossible to describe. The entire family agreed that this was the greatest Passover Seder they had ever had. I told him that he will never have another Seder like that, because such a Seder is the result of successfully withstanding a test of emuna, which gives it a completely different flavor.

Later, he understood why his father had to be hospitalized. He had asked his father a number of times to read **The Garden of Peace**. But his father was busy writing a book and didn't have time. In the hospital, though, he found the time to study the book.

After reading the book, the father changed; his wife said, "Something strange happened here. Either they switched him for someone else, or I don't really know him…"

After a few days the father inexplicably regained his health. He said that he understood that the only reason for his hospitalization was so that he had time for **The Garden of Peace**.

Don't be Right – Be a Believer

In the aforementioned story, we tangibly see the power of thanksgiving and believing that everything is for the best. Let's use it to learn more lessons on thanksgiving: Not having a place to sit down for the Seder is a difficult trial. Seeing one's wife and children standing there, embarrassed and confused, is very unpleasant. After all, this was not just a regular night that if worse came to worse, the family could grab a piece of bread or some cake. It was the Seder night – the night that is the archetype for the year - however the Seder goes, so the entire year goes.

On the surface, our protagonist should have felt sad and angry when he discovered that his family had nowhere to sit. However, this is where the power of emuna kicks in. It has no rules, no right and no wrong! Instead, a person has to relinquish his logic, because during a test of emuna, there is no way that the person can understand the logic behind it. All he can do is rely on emuna and believe that all is for the best - without understanding why and for what reason. He should thank Hashem for organizing a different Seder than the one expected, rejoice in the new Seder and believe that this is the Seder that will invoke a blessing for the entire coming year. Incidentally, that's exactly what happened. On this important night, they helped everyone and gladdened the hearts of the patients who were there without their families. These great merits will accompany this family not only for the year but throughout their lives.

This is a story reminiscent of the one we've often shared about Rebbe Akiva, who was traveling and couldn't find an inn in which to sleep. He eventually went to sleep in the field. A lion came and ate his donkey and, one by one, other calamities befell him until he was left in the field with nothing. With every calamity, Rebbe Akiva said: "Everything that Hashem does, He does for the very best," despite the fact that there was no logical reason to say that these occurrences were for the good. In the morning, enemies came and took all the residents of the city into captivity. Rebbe Akiva was saved specifically through the calamities that had befallen him the previous night. Then it was completely understandable how everything was for the very best. Rebbe Akiva believed without understanding. Because he was strong in his emuna, he merited to understand as well.

Be Decisive

Every person who defines himself as a believer must decide that he will no longer contradict himself. Emuna dictates that everything that happens is from G-d. If a person believes otherwise, that Heaven forbid there are things that Hashem does not bring about, he is a first-class heretic. He certainly cannot call himself a believer.

Emuna is not Wall Street or the futures market – you can't hedge it. A true believer accepts that everything is certainly from G-d, and then certainly everything is for the very best!

Everything – not almost everything. As such, we have to thank Him for everything.

There is no bad in the world! If a person says that something is bad, this is heresy. Either he is implying that it is not from G-d, or he is implying that it is from G-d, but that it's bad anyway. In either case, it is heresy.

It's up to every individual to decide: If he believes in Hashem, then he must thank Him. If he doesn't thank Him, then he is weak in his emuna.

Credit Given in Absentia

If a person believes that things are amiss, it is because he lacks emuna. We feel very sorry for people who are suffering, but their suffering is due to not having emuna. All the people who have troubles and great tribulations suffer only because of a lack of emuna. If they would have emuna, their lives would be good.

A woman once asked me, "Why didn't the Creator ask me if I wanted to come to this world?" Of course, I understood from her question that she was miserable and oblivious to the beauty of the world. My heart ached for her and I answered her as follows:

"For a person who lacks emuna, this world is indeed a source of suffering and hardship. Without emuna, a person stands no chance of attaining happiness or inner peace. Yet with emuna, even the seemingly most difficult life becomes a life of meaning and deep satisfaction. Emuna cannot be learned in the upper worlds – for there, the truth is apparent. A person must come to this lowly material world and withstand a series of trials and tribulations that are designed both to perfect the soul and teach and fortify emuna."

It's unfortunate that so many people have not found joy. This simply highlights why everyone must learn emuna and how to express profuse gratitude to Hashem on a daily basis."

The Shadow at Your Right Hand

When a person articulates thanks to Hashem for something that seems bad, he fortifies his belief that everything is from Hashem and everything is for the best. It's very empowering.

In addition, we know that Hashem guides every person according to his own perspective. This is the meaning of the phrase in Psalms 121, "Hashem is your shadow at your right hand." Hashem is like a shadow - wherever a person turns, his shadow turns with him. So the Creator, in His humility, walks with a person as the person, himself, decides. If the person believes in Hashem rather than in natural forces, Hashem corresponds by performing miracles and defying natural forces for that person, according to his level of emuna. If a person believes that Hashem is good, then Hashem shows him that He is good. He merits seeing Hashem's mercy. When a person believes that everything is good, then Hashem's mercy encompasses his life. He experiences Hashem's goodness and salvations at every turn. Every situation turns out for the best. But if a person says that his circumstances are bad, Heaven forbid, Hashem correspondingly shapes this person's circumstances according to his (false) perceptions.

Generally, when a person says that something is bad, it is under one of the following three circumstances: He blames himself, he blames others, or he blames nature. Everyone must be careful not to fall into this heretical mindset. Instead, remember that everything is from Hashem and everything is for the best.

A person suffers because he denies that everything is for his own good. If a person believes this is so, he will see how it is really all for the best. If a person does not believe in G-d, Hashem does not show him how this particular matter is for the best. The result is that the person who does not believe in Hashem remains trapped in his heresy, because Hashem guides him according to his level of emuna (or lack of it), and does not allow him to see that what has happened is actually good.

A person must constantly remind himself of what Rebbe Natan writes in **Likutei Halachot**: "If everyone would believe in this path of thanksgiving, all troubles would be nullified…" If all of us would internalize this principle, life would surely become more pleasurable.

Thanksgiving Pays

Rabbi Chaim Kanievsky, Shlit"a, tells the following story: Two Jews who were destined to die were walking on the road. The Angel of Death had already been dispatched from Heaven to take them both. But then, an old man crossed their path, and one of them gave him some coins. The Angel of Death immediately appeared. He told the person who gave charity that his act of kindness had saved his life. He told the second person that he had come to take his soul. The second man begged the Angel of Death to wait just a moment while he would also give the old man some coins. The Angel of Death told him that it was too late, since he had already missed the opportunity. The Jew said: "If so, then just give me two minutes to thank G-d, because I am accustomed to thanking Hashem daily."

The Angel of Death stepped aside and the Jew said as follows: "Thank You, Master of the Universe, for the life that You have given me. Thank You for everything that You have done for me in this life. Thank You for wanting to take my soul, so that now I will be close to You." He thanked Hashem in this manner for two minutes. The Angel of Death came to him and said, "Not only can I not take your soul now, but you have been given extra years over and above the years of life originally allotted you."

This is a beautiful story that shows how thanksgiving is even greater than charity. Thanksgiving saved the Jew from death even after he "missed the boat" with charity, and also added extra years to his life.

The Light of the Menorah

Our Sages direct us to recite Psalm 67 frequently in our prayers: In the morning before *Baruch She'amar*, in the afternoon after *Kadish Titkabal*, in the Midnight Lamentations, during the Counting of the Omer, on Chanukah after lighting the candles and more. Let us investigate what we say in this Psalm:

"May Hashem be gracious unto us, and bless us; may He cause His countenance to shine toward us; Selah." We ask Hashem to shine His countenance upon us. His 'countenance' means we see that everything that happens is His mercy.

"That Your way may be known upon earth, Your salvation amongst all nations." We ask for the ability to make Hashem's way known to the entire world.

"Then The nations will thank You…" Everyone will thank G-d, in all the languages and dialects.

"The nations will be glad and sing for joy…" The entire world will be filled with songs of praise to Hashem, all the nations will dance in circles…

The ultimate purpose of the entire world is for humans to believe in G-d. Belief in Hashem means belief that everything is for the best, that there is no bad and that we must thank Hashem for everything - always.

Hashem brought a wondrous light down to the world. Emuna, and the gratitude to Hashem that results from true emuna, are not only this wonderful light, but a wonderful path to a beautiful life – a true Garden of Eden! If a person believes that every trouble in the world is for the best and thanks Hashem with all his heart and with joy, he will see salvation. All that he has to do is believe.

Miracles and Mercy

In order to strengthen our service of thanksgiving, in this chapter we have shared a tiny sample of the miracle stories we've encountered. These are true stories that happened to people who left logic at their doorstep and simply believed that everything is for the best, thanking Hashem for whatever tribulation had come their way. Please keep in mind that the author has heard far more stories than what is written here. We are including stories to encourage our readers to keep thanking Hashem, so that they too will experience miracles.

We explicitly say in our prayers: "We thank You for all Your miracles…the Good, Whose mercy has not ended." A person who thanks Hashem for the miracles achieves "the Good, Whose mercy has not ended." He merits Hashem's endless mercy and sees more and more miracles.

Then he continues to bless and glorify and exalt G-d. "And for everything may He be blessed and exalted…the Hashem of salvations, Selah." The person experiences only eternal salvations, because *selah* means *eternal*. When everyone constantly gives thanks to Hashem, we will see more miracles and salvations, until the complete redemption.

Say Thank You - Experience Miracles

In one of my lectures, I told a story of what I call a 'tiny miracle.' I had a small sore on my finger. It didn't hurt, but it was open and bled intermittently. This went on for some time. On Shabbat, it bled again and then I thought to myself that it might be very hard for this sore to heal naturally. After all, I frequently wash my hands for ritual purposes and I can't use a bandage.

Then, during personal prayer, I devoted a mere minute to thanking Hashem for the sore. The next day, the sore was gone! It simply disappeared without a trace! I call this a 'tiny miracle' because this sore didn't bother me much and I didn't need to perform any type of great spiritual service so that it would go away. All I did was thank Hashem for one minute.

In truth, though, this is really a huge miracle, because the sore was not likely to heal by natural means, which was apparent by the fact that it had not healed for weeks. But immediately after I thanked Hashem for it, it disappeared. All it took was a few words of thanks for it to go away…

Hashem wanted me to strengthen my emuna in Divine Providence over the small things in life that we forget to attribute to Him. Thanksgiving is emuna. This was the teshuva that I had to do for this small sore.

The Disappearing Cut

I have seen a lot of medical miracles, but the following strengthened me tremendously. This story was relayed by an important Torah scholar who learns in Rabbi Ovadiah Yosef's Seminary for Religious Court Judges and who also attends my Torah and emuna lectures. After he heard my small miracle with the sore, he told me the story of a miracle that happened to him:

This man had been suffering for some time from a very deep cut the width of the sole of his foot. The cut was so deep that his muscle tissue was apparent through it and he could hardly step on his foot. A short walk of three minutes took him half an hour due to the intense pain that he experienced.

He heard the Torah lesson on thanksgiving and one evening, he began to thank Hashem for the cut on his foot. He simply said 'thank You' for every step he took and for all its accompanying pain. He asked Hashem for forgiveness as, until that point, he didn't believe his injury was for the best, and thanked Him for half an hour straight. The next morning, he woke up and his foot was fine. The cut was closed and his skin was smooth as if nothing had ever happened. A totally supernatural miracle that is impossible to comprehend!

I saw the miracle on my little finger that was healed after a small amount of thanksgiving. But this story – a serious cut that is difficult to heal naturally closing overnight with new skin replacing the injured – amazing!

Hashem shows us that for every trouble, all we have to do is say thank You. Thanksgiving is the proper teshuva for lack of emuna. It transforms everything into goodness and allows us to experience supernatural miracles. By expressing thanks, a person can actually change nature.

From a Tennis Ball to a Lentil

A gentleman in Miami was suffering from a terminal illness. It was so hopeless that the doctors decided to discontinue chemotherapy. The malignant growth in the patient's pancreas had reached the enormous size of a tennis ball. The patient's daughter came to see my student Rabbi Lazer Brody after one of his lectures in Los Angeles, broke down in tears, and sobbed, "The doctors say that my father has three weeks to live! Here – please help him…" She thrust her cellular phone into Rabbi Lazer's hand.

"H-H-Hello," said a weak voice on the other end of the line. "This is M-Mendy."

Rabbi Lazer told me that he had to take a deep breath. What do you say to a person who apparently has three weeks more to live? He composed himself and said, "Mendy, there's plenty to do." Mendy couldn't get out of bed and couldn't read books, but he could still speak. "Thank Hashem for this disease. Hashem has done a great favor for you, because now you must trust Him only – no one else can help. Thank Hashem for bringing you close to Him. Thank Him as much as you can…"

Mendy's daughter thought that Rabbi Lazer was daft. "Rabbi, are you stoned or something? Thank Hashem for a terminal disease?!? Don't you realize that my Dad is dying?"

Despite the daughter's astonishment, Mendy agreed and began thanking Hashem for a few minutes several times a day. He would say, "Thank You, Hashem! Were it not for this sickness, I'd be playing golf and never speaking to You. Thank You for bringing me close to You."

Eleven months transpired. Rabbi Yosef Nechama, my student – along with Rabbi Lazer Brody - were on another speaking tour in the USA, this time in Miami. A couple in their late fifties came to visit them. The husband looked like a retired football player – tall, husky, sun-tanned and healthy-looking. He handed Rabbi Lazer a manila envelope that contained a CAT-scan image of his pancreas. On it was a dot the size of a lentil.

"I'm Mendy," he smiled. "The dot on that image is my tumor – it has totally shrunk, and hopefully soon, will disappear altogether. The doctors are astonished, but they say that I've beat this disease. I feel great! I have plenty of reasons to continue thanking Hashem every day!"

Rebbe Nachman teaches (Likutei Moharan, II:5) that there are illnesses with no cure. The only way to be saved from them is through emuna. Hence, some illnesses, Heaven forbid, cannot be cured through conventional treatment and medication, but only by strengthening one's emuna.

The Retrieved Motorcycle

The motorcycle of one of my students was stolen. He thanked Hashem: "Thank You, Creator of the world, that You gave me a motorcycle and I have enjoyed using it all this time. Thank You for wanting the motorcycle to be stolen. Surely, You love me and do everything for my eternal good. I am very happy, and thank You very much. Everything that You do for me is only for the best. You, Hashem, know what You are doing in this world. Who knows what miracles will happen? Only You, Hashem, know what danger You saved me from by me not being able to ride my motorcycle now. There is no bad in the world. Everything is good. It's wonderful that my motorcycle was stolen. Thank You…"

While he was thanking Hashem with true sincerity, the police called to tell him that they found his motorcycle. This is a real miracle, as anyone who knows how stolen motorcycles are usually dealt with can testify.

The Penitent Husband

A woman cried to me that for years she had been suffering terrible verbal abuse from her husband. When she began to thank Hashem for her sorrows and rejoice in them, everything changed.

She focused on Hashem and thanked Him that her husband was the rod of reproof in her life, and not a terminal disease or some other unthinkable thing. Her husband soon realized that she was no longer upset by his outbursts. He became ashamed that Hashem was using him for a negative purpose. He decided to change his ways and do complete teshuva. Knowing the thorny nature of the husband, this was an outright miracle.

As long as the woman saw her husband as a grief-producer, he fulfilled his role as expected. As soon as she did not see him as the grief-producer, but rather, focused on the fact that everything is from G-d, his role as grief-producer became irrelevant and he mended his ways. Such is the power of the emuna that everything is for the best.

A Ticket to Salvation

We can tell endless stories like these; they're useful for strengthening emuna. A soldier told me that he wanted to travel to Uman on a furlough, but had no money for the trip. He told himself that it looked like he was not supposed to go, because he did not have the money to get there. He began to thank Hashem: "Thank You very much, Hashem, that I do not have the money to travel to Uman." He went to work, and his friend asked him: "Are you going to Uman?"

"No," he answered.

"Why not?"

"I can't."

"Then take my credit card," his friend insisted. "You are going to Uman!"

That was the small miracle. The bigger miracle was that the army called him and told him that he was to be court-martialed for some misdemeanor and therefore would lose both his furlough and his permit to travel to Uman. He turned to Hashem and thanked Him: "Master of the Universe, thank You very much that I cannot travel to Uman – this time for a different reason, because You have already given me money…" He continued thanking Hashem; then the army called him and told him that the commander decided to postpone the trial.

An Easy Match

I met a person who told me about a thirty-five-year-old man who lived in his neighborhood. He was well-liked by everyone, had a very pleasant nature, enjoyed helping out, and greeted everyone with a smile. But for some reason, he had not yet managed to find a wife. The entire neighborhood prayed for him and looked for a suitable match for him, but to no avail. Then somebody brought him my CD, **Stop Crying**.

He listened to the CD and started thanking Hashem every day for a full hour: "Thank You very much, Hashem, that I still have not found my marriage partner. This is certainly the very best for me. I thank You for holding off my match until now, because You do only what is the very best for me. I thank You for everything. Nothing can be better than this. I thank You with all my heart and am happy with everything that You have done with me until today." Within two weeks, he found his match. Once again, such is the power of thanksgiving.

The Wedding that Saved a Life

One of our students was at a wedding, and saw someone sitting there, depressed. Everyone else was happy and he was down and out. The student approached him and began to talk to him. This man told him what was bothering him: He had a few hundred thousand shekels that he had intended to invest and somebody swindled him, leaving him with absolutely nothing. This sent him into a complete tailspin, virtually destroying his bond with Hashem. He fell into the abyss of depression.

"Listen," said the student. "Believe that Hashem is good and what Hashem did for you is good." At first, the man didn't understand what he was talking about. What did he mean that this was good? What was so good about it? He lost all his money, and that was good? But ultimately, the student managed to convince him to thank Hashem for an hour…

The man thanked Hashem for an hour. Four hours later he got a phone call from the Jewish Agency that they were giving him a six-room apartment, worth more than what he could have bought with the money he lost. They also gave him money to start a business and get back on his feet. All of this within four hours! He called the student and said, "Thank you very much! You saved my life!"

The Son that Got Married

A woman spent fifteen years crying that her son was not yet married. She cried and cried and nothing helped. Eventually, she concluded that she had to stop crying. She turned to Hashem and said, "I will stop crying and will only thank You for all the kindness that You shower upon us and specifically for the fact that my son has not yet gotten married, for surely this is for the best." She thanked Hashem in this way for some time, and her son got married. She stopped crying and merited salvation.

The Divorcee

A divorcee with a number of children told me that she heard my CD **Stop Crying**, and thanked Hashem for an hour for the fact that she had not yet found a husband – and then she met her match.

Sweeter than Sugar

Someone told me that his father had diabetes that had been causing him years of excruciating pain in his legs. Then he listened to **Stop Crying** and began to thank Hashem. The pain disappeared.

Slam on the Brakes!

A heavy, bullet-proof bus lost control of its brakes on the slope going down to Beitar, in the Judean Hills south of Jerusalem. Miraculously, the bus didn't hit anything along the way. Eventually, it crashed into a car that a father and son had exited just minutes before.

"How did you merit this miracle?" they asked the father, whose life and the life of his son were miraculously saved. "I listen to Rabbi Arush's Torah lessons and always thank Hashem. In this merit, Hashem performed such a miracle for me," he answered.

A person who thanks Hashem constantly experiences miracles all the time.

Saved by Gravel

A successful businessman was distant from Judaism. But that wasn't the main problem. The main problem was that he was very abrasive in his interpersonal relations. He was simply a miserable person.

He planned to buy the entire 17th floor of the Azrieli Tower, a prestigious Tel Aviv skyscraper, but a swindler convinced him to invest instead in tracts of land in Romania, promising that the land was zoned for construction. In truth, the land was zoned for agriculture and was a bad investment. The businessman lost a tremendous amount of money and eventually lost all his wealth. He fell deeply into debt and received an arrest warrant for his failure to pay his tax bills.

He tried to borrow money from friends, to no avail. Somebody advised him to take a loan on the "grey market." He was told to go to a lending company that was located in the Azrieli Towers – on the 17th floor – the floor that he was supposed to have bought and could have been his, had he not lost everything…

The businessman entered the loan office, signed some papers and got the cash that he needed. Before he left the building he decided to look around a bit. He went up to the top floors to see what he could see. He went up one floor and then the next and saw that everything was rented out and looked good. He was eating his heart out over the mistake that he had made. Eventually, he got up to the roof and went out to see the view. But then, the door closed behind him and locked. He had no way to get back into the building!

He banged on the door, shouted at the top of his lungs, but to no avail. Who would hear him up on the roof? He looked down from the roof to the street at all the people walking by. He thought that to attract their attention, it would be a good idea for him to throw something down to the street. He thought to himself: What would draw people's attention more than money? He would throw money down, people would look up to see where the money was coming from and they would come up to free him from the roof.

One by one, our businessman threw 200 shekel bills down to the street. But to his dismay, the people hit in the head with the money simply grabbed it and didn't even look up to see where it came from. Nothing seemed to help. Nobody looked up! Our businessman began to panic. He felt that he had nothing to lose and preferred any alternative to dying of hunger on the roof. He decided to throw all his money down. The rain of 200 shekel bills came pouring down on the heads of the people below. The people on the street joyfully chased after the bills floating down onto their heads. But once again, to his dismay, not one person thought of looking upward. Everybody was busy grabbing as many bills as he could.

It was getting colder by the minute and the hapless businessman was at a dead end. He reached the point that even the person farthest from religion reaches when he encounters a major problem. Suddenly, he turned to faith! He stood there, alone on the roof some 40-odd floors above ground level - closer to Heaven than he was used to being - and said: "Master of the Universe, save me! I do not know what to do. Save me!" He prayed from the bottom of his heart. Of course, Hashem heard his prayer and immediately put a new idea in his head. There was a lot of gravel on the roof. Our businessman decided to throw gravel down on the people below, in the hope that somebody would finally look up and see him.

He threw a few stones down below. The people hit on the head with the stones began shouting and cursing, gazing upward and shaking their fists. In no time, somebody called security and complained that there was a man up on the top of the tower throwing stones at the people below. The police came and found him up on the roof. They wanted to arrest him for throwing stones on the passersby. One policeman was willing to listen to him, and he explained what had transpired. "Come with me to the 17th floor," he said, "and you will see that I took out a loan just a few hours ago. After that, I came up here, got stuck and threw all the money down to the street. Nobody noticed me until I started throwing gravel. Look, even you came now!"

The police believed him and let him go. He returned home - without money, and with no idea about what to do about the arrest warrant against him - having had a very eye-opening experience. He sat down and began to think: "What happened here? When I threw down money, nobody looked up. But when I threw gravel, everybody looked up. Hashem is giving me a message. After all, I prayed to Him and it was He Who gave me the idea to throw gravel. That is what saved me."

Then he understood G-d's message to him. It was all an allegory. When Hashem threw him money from Above, when He showered him with riches and success in his business and he was a millionaire, he never once raised his eyes to Him and never once thanked Him! Only when Hashem threw "gravel" his way – when He plunged him into debt and locked him out on the roof - did he remember to raise his eyes to G-d.

This is the common behavior of most people. When there is abundance, they do not look to Hashem and do not thank Him properly. Only when the gravel starts to fly – when troubles arrive - do they remember to look to Hashem and beg Him to heal their lives.

The businessman felt a strong desire to repent. He burst into tears and asked Hashem to forgive him for all the years that he was so ungrateful. He thanked Hashem for the miracle that He had performed for him and for the invaluable lesson that He had taught him. He merited in this way to do complete teshuva. He sat and thanked Hashem again and again for his life and all the goodness that Hashem gave him. And then he thanked Him again. In a short time, he received a telephone call, informing him that the properties in Romania had been re-zoned for construction. He became a billionaire literally overnight! All he said was "Thank You!"

This story overflows with lessons for life. It shows us how Hashem showers each and every person with abundance, life and goodness every minute of the day. Hashem does kindness with us every second, may His Name be praised. Most people do not know to look heavenward until they have a problem. A person should always pre-empt tribulations with Torah and thanksgiving for all the goodness, loving-kindness and salvations which Hashem showers upon him.

Unexpected Income

A certain kollel student was receiving 900 shekels in monthly support from his local kollel. He lived in poverty and prayed and did teshuva to try to increase his income. Nothing helped, until he heard a CD on thanksgiving. He began to spend an hour daily in personal prayer, thanking Hashem for his meager income. He expressed confidence that his poverty was an atonement and thanked Hashem for the fact that everyone in his family was healthy.

He continued in this manner for an hour daily; thanking Hashem and feeling joy with his lot in life. Within a few weeks, a man who he did not know approached him and told him that he was looking for someone who would learn in his father's memory - he would offer a monthly salary to do so. From that day on, he paid him almost 7,000 shekels every month.

The Stroke that Turned to Joy

A man about 60 years old, who was not observant, was blinded by a stroke. While he was in serious condition, a debt collection agency came for a huge sum from the man. They threatened to take all his possessions, which would not even cover the sum of his debt.

The man fell into a terrible depression. One of our yeshiva students gave him the **Stop Crying** CD. He listened to it once and began to thank Hashem; he listened to the CD over and over again. He began to feel joy and thanked Hashem for his troubles.

After a number of hours of thanking Hashem, he burst into tears and asked Hashem to forgive him and have mercy on him. He again thanked Hashem for everything, but asked Hashem to help him. Soon, he regained his eyesight. Then someone came to him and gave him – as a gift – the entire sum that he needed to cover his debt! Here was a man who was light-years away from Torah and mitzvot; thoughts of doing teshuva were foreign to him. As such, this story clearly shows the power of thanksgiving followed by heartfelt prayer.

Saved by a Dream

When I lectured in Ofra, a settlement north of Jerusalem, a woman asked to speak to the audience. She said that she gave birth to a baby boy and the doctors told her that he had just a short time to live. She cried and cried and sorrowfully begged Hashem to save him. She fell asleep and in her dream she was told: "Rabbi Shalom Arush, Emuna, Rabbi Shalom Arush, Emuna." After the dream, this woman began learning the concepts of emuna and her husband came to hear my lectures. Since then, her baby has begun to eat and she sees how Hashem is sustaining him all the time.

Healing from Serious Illness

When I lectured in Beit El, not far from Ofra, a man told me that his wife had been diagnosed with a terminal disease in her blood. The doctors gave her just a short time to live. But they listened to the CDs and thanked Hashem, and she recovered.

The Disappearing Hole

A baby was born to a couple. The hospital staff told them that they suspected that there was a small hole in one of the atria of the baby's heart. The doctors were convinced that they must perform open heart surgery – a very dangerous undertaking, especially for a newborn. They informed the parents that there was not much time to wait, since the hole was growing.

The grief-stricken parents turned to their emuna. They went from one tzaddik to the next to ask for advice and blessings. They appealed to Hashem for mercy but as time passed, the tests only showed worse results. The doctors began to pressure the young couple to do the operation before the situation became too dangerous.

The parents came to me for a blessing and advice. I instructed them to go to the resting place of Rabbi Shimon Bar Yochai, may his blessed memory protect us, amen. Once there, both husband and wife should spend six hours in personal prayer reharding their son. They went to Meron and began their personal prayers. But they couldn't keep it up for six hours. After two hours, they felt that they could no longer continue.

They arrived home and were informed that the hole in their son's heart had dangerously expanded and that they must bring him in for an emergency operation. They drove to the hospital with heavy hearts. The doctors pressured them to agree to an immediate operation. If not – they could begin to bid him farewell…

The wife cried incessantly. Her husband said to her: "After all, we are students of Rabbi Shalom Arush, and he says to thank Hashem for all of our troubles. We have exactly one hour until the operation. Let us thank Hashem for this trouble for an entire hour."

"But how can I say thank You?" the young mother asked through her tears.

"It doesn't matter how," her husband answered. "We have nothing else to do. We will try hard and say thank You however we can, and let Hashem take care of the rest."

The couple sat in the waiting room with tears in their eyes. Their lips were saying thank You, but their hearts were not with them. For an entire hour they made a tremendous effort to believe that this situation was for the best.

After an hour, the baby was wheeled into the operating room. After some time, the doctor came out of the operating room and asked the broken-hearted parents to come into his office. When they entered, he said to them with happiness mixed with embarrassment, "I really apologize for all the unnecessary anxiety that we put you through. We did a cardiac catheterization on the baby and discovered that he doesn't have a hole in his heart, after all. He doesn't have anything! He is completely healthy! As soon as he wakes up from the anesthesia, you can take him home. In the name of the management and staff of the hospital, I apologize for this unfortunate situation."

The Mystery Treatment

Rabbi David Elkayam delivered a lecture, reviewing what he had heard from me about giving thanks and all the wonderful ideas with which Hashem has enlightened us. After the lecture, a well-known, learned woman told him that she had never heard such an inspiring Torah lesson. After hearing about thanksgiving, her entire life changed.

About a week later, the same woman called Rabbi Elkayam. She told him that she was ill with a very serious sickness. Since she had heard his lecture on thanksgiving, she thanked Hashem for the entire week for her health woes.

The following week, she had to go for tests. She took the tests and waited for their results. As the doctor was reviewing the results he saw that…the illness had disappeared! The doctor couldn't believe his eyes!

"What treatment did you take?" he asked her.

"I didn't take any treatments."

"It can't be. Are you sure you didn't take any drugs?"

"I am sure," she answered.

After all, what could she tell him? That she thanked Hashem for one hour daily for her illness?

The Amazing Message

I received a letter from a non-Jewish student who is learning Hebrew and wrote the following letter herself:

*Shalom! I am a 23-year-old student in university and I am learning Hebrew in my free time. I have three Hebrew books by Rabbi Shalom Arush. When I read the book **The Garden of Emuna** (a very nice book!) I felt that this book helps me as well, even though I am not a Jew. It is wonderful to find very important things in which we also believe. But it is very easy to forget them – for example when we have big problems or we are busy with work or school. We forget that "there is no one but Him" and we fall into anger, sadness or hatred of others. I understood that if a person's thoughts are always focused on Hashem – that everything is from Him and is for the best and that we must always rectify our ways; if a person turns to the Creator in prayer and repentance and thanks him – it would bring people true peace…*

I also had a big problem. For three years I suffered and did not know what to do. I prayed a lot, asked forgiveness for *the sins that I did (also for what I did unintentionally) but I did not find a solution. Until I read the chapter **Thank Hashem and be Healed**. Then I tried to thank Hashem for what happened to me. I asked the Creator to give me a solution. And thank Hashem I solved the problem and everything is fine now.*

I just want to thank your Rabbi. It seems to me that he really makes peace and I am happy that there are people like him in Israel. Even though it seems that the situation in the Middle East is very difficult, I believe that it is possible to achieve peace, with G-d's help, through faith in G-d. I listened to a nice song with the words: "We separate in the name of religion and we meet with faith." I will always pray for peace and that there should be no conflicts and no terror and no hatred and no idol worship. May there be only love here and people worshipping Hashem alone.

What can we say about a letter like this? It certainly obligates each and every person to begin working on emuna and thanksgiving. It also gives us great encouragement to pray for the entire world – that everyone will get to know Hashem.

A Letter from Mexico

In a heartfelt letter to our website from Mexico, the writer told of a man in whom a tumor was discovered. He already had an appointment for a biopsy. This man got the CD **Stop Crying**, which was translated to Spanish. He was very encouraged by what he heard and decided to buy 100 additional CDs and distribute them. When went to the hospital for the operation, there was no longer any need for it. In a preliminary x-ray, they saw that the growth had completely disappeared! Thank G-d! After this letter, our website received an order for another 500 CDs.

Giving Thanks for the Thanks

People do not understand the power of thanksgiving. That is why I repeat: Believe that Hashem is good! There was never bad in the world and there will not be bad in the world. It was always the very best; things are now the very best and in the future they will be too. In the past it was the best, now is the best and it will be even better. There is no bad in the world and there will be no bad in the world. Believe it!

In prayers in a quorum, the prayer leader makes the blessings in the name of all the worshippers and fulfills their obligations in this way. The only blessing that the worshippers must say by themselves is the thanksgiving blessing. Everyone says, "We thank You…for thanking You." We give thanks to Hashem for the fact that we are able and privileged to thank Hashem. Not only are we thanking Him, but we also thank Him for the fact that we are thanking Him.

When a person understands what a wonderful gift it is to say thank you, then he says thank you for the thank you. It is impossible to ever thank Hashem enough, so we must thank Him for the fact that we can thank Him!

Chapter Eight:
Overcoming Setbacks

Rebbe Natan of Breslev asks (Likutei Halachot, Choshen Mishpat, Collecting Debts from Orphans, 3) why the Torah was given in the desert - home to snakes, scorpions and windstorms. Wasn't it better to have waited until the Nation of Israel entered the Land of Israel and conquered it? Then Hashem could have given the Torah when the Nation would have peace of mind, in the holy city of Jerusalem, about which the verse says "For from Zion the Torah will come forth."

Rebbe Natan explains how the Torah, given in the desert, teaches us a core principle in serving the Creator: Before we can merit the Torah, we must past the 'desert test.' The entire Nation of Israel had to traverse through the desert on the way to Mount Sinai, enduring all sorts of trials on the way so as to refine itself. In the same way, every individual must go through the 'desert test' – the obstacles that must be overcome – on the way to his personal receipt of the Torah. Rebbe Natan says: "For before a person merits a revelation in Torah or service of Hashem - which are an aspect of the receiving of the Torah – there must first be confusion, doubt and many obstacles, lusts, distractions and the like…"

Every Torah achievement that we attain is a facet of 'receiving the Torah.' For this we make the blessing, "Blessed Are You, Hashem, Who gives the Torah" every day. On the surface, we should make the blessing in past tense: *Who gave the Torah*. After all, Hashem gave the Torah in the past on Mount Sinai. Why, then, do we say "Who gives the Torah" in present tense? When a person learns and comprehends the Torah, he experiences his own personal receiving of the Torah on a daily basis. Every day, the Creator gives the

Torah anew to whoever wants to receive it. In the *Shema Yisrael* prayer, we say: "And these things that I command you today should be on your heart." Our Sages explain that, every day, they should be as new to you as the day they were given on Mount Sinai.

Furthermore, our Sages say that the Torah is available to anyone who seeks it: "The crown of Torah is placed before us, and he who wants to partake of it can come and take." They continue, "However, each person receives the Torah in accordance to his work and effort." Some people receive the book of Torah and put it on the shelf. That is not called receiving the Torah. Other people learn parts of the book, but do not understand what they are learning. That is also not really receiving the Torah. Then there are those who understand but do not fulfill what is written. That is also incomplete reception of the Torah. Receiving the Torah takes place when a person works hard to understand the words of Torah, internalize them and fulfill them!

Without effort, we achieve nothing. A person who thinks that he can take it easy yet still attain Torah will achieve nothing. Receiving the Torah takes work, especially in overcoming the obstacles in the path of acquiring Torah.

Not the Path of Least Resistance

The path of acquiring Torah is strewn with spiritual setbacks, both moderate and severe. Overcoming failure and hardship is the price of Torah; the resilient person who refuses to give up merits new revelations of Torah and lofty achievements in the service of Hashem. Torah is certainly not the path of least resistance.

Outer spiritual forces, tribulations, trials, lusts and negative character attributes sometime overcome a person and envelop him in darkness. He has difficulty finding Hashem, especially when he's fighting to stay afloat in life. So what does such a person do? How does he cushion himself from a dangerous spiritual fall and crashing into despair and depression? Hashem is everywhere, even in the muck and mire of a person's base thoughts. All a person has to do to save himself is to call out to Hashem and seek Him. That way, a near crash-landing becomes the ultimate ascent.

Your Torah

When a whirlpool of negative thoughts inundate a person's mind; when distractions and lusts overcome him with doubt yet he does not despair and calls out to Hashem instead; he ascends to the highest place in the spiritual realm and draws Torah down from there. This is called "receiving of the Torah." Such a person literally receives a very special portion of the Torah in accordance to the trial he withstood without falling into despair.

We can now understand what Rebbe Natan calls "receiving the Torah in the desert." The desert represents the abode of challenging spiritual forces. The Nation of Israel endured many trials that were the spiritual manifestation of the "desert." They were engulfed by all sorts of difficulties from negative spiritual forces. They were challenged in body and spirit with snakes, fiery angels, scorpions, windstorms, thirst, scorching heat and hail. They overcame it all and called out to Hashem, as the Torah says: "And the Children of Israel called out to Hashem." They then merited redemption in the place of negative and impure spiritual forces.

When they searched for Hashem in a place that seemed distant from Him, they merited receiving the Torah, as explained above. This is the concept called "descent for the purpose of ascent." A specific aspect of the Torah is attainable only when one seeks Hashem while encased in his own spiritual desert – where outer spiritual forces abide. A person who manages to overcome these negative spiritual forces and connect to Hashem reveals Hashem's glory in the world.

The Concealed Utterance

Our Sages say that Hashem created the world with ten utterances. In other words, with every detail that Hashem created, the Torah writes: "And Hashem said." For example: "And Hashem said, 'Let there be light' and there was light." Or "And Hashem said, 'Let there be a sky within the water,'" etc. These are the utterances. A close look at the first verses in the book of Genesis reveals that there are only nine explicit utterances. Where is the tenth utterance? The tenth utterance is, "In the beginning, Hashem created." This is called the concealed utterance, because Hashem is not explicitly mentioned as uttering anything. Rather, the utterance is hidden in the words "In the beginning, Hashem created."

This first concealed utterance is the root of all the other utterances and the root of the entire Torah. Within it is cloaked the highest level of Torah that exists. When a person calls out, "Where Are You, Hashem?" he ascends to the level of the concealed utterance, to the root of all the utterances and the root of the entire Torah, bringing the Torah down to this world from the loftiest spiritual heights! It is specifically when a person is experiencing difficulties and he can't find Hashem – there, in the difficult tailspins – that he can attain Torah.

There is a stipulation, though; a person turns a setback into a marvelous triumph only if he does not fall into despair during trying times. This is not easy because one's Evil Inclination takes advantage of hardships and dark periods to break a person's spirit with messages like, "There's no hope for you - you'll never overcome your lusts. Why bother with the whole faith deal? Have a good time and the heck with your spiritual fantasies…" These are propaganda broadcasts from a dire enemy that's out to destroy you - the Evil Inclination. Its purpose is to plunge a person into despair.

When a person ignores and overcomes the Evil Inclination's messages and continues to seek and hope for Hashem's presence, he reveals the diamond-like sparks of holiness that are concealed even in those dark and lowly places. This is a most laudable spiritual achievement.

The Grateful Person

A person who lives life with the understanding that he has to thank Hashem for everything stands stalwart against the Evil Inclination. The most effective spiritual immunity against any message of despair is the deep belief that everything is for the best.

Giving thanks to Hashem and complaining are mutually exclusive. Even when things are askew, the grateful person thanks Hashem that things are not working out according to plan. When he falls, he thanks Hashem for the stumbling blocks. When life is difficult, he thanks Hashem for all the difficulties. When he has to fight off his bodily urges, he thanks Hashem, because he knows that everything is from Hashem and everything is for the best.

One way or another, despair stays far away from the grateful person. No matter what, he yearns for Hashem and seeks Him, despite his journey in the spiritual "desert." He finds Hashem everywhere and constantly ascends to greater heights.

My Special Torah

Once, I was out in the field for a number of hours. I was going through a difficult test of faith and I thanked Hashem for it. In response, Hashem gave me the special gift of a new Torah insight. I had a pen and notepad so I wrote down the thoughts that Hashem sent me. Let me share them with you:

A person who is happy with his troubles – both physical and spiritual – and with his periodic setbacks, his disappointments, and his painful experiences virtually neutralizes any harsh edicts or severe judgments. Since he believes that there is no bad in the world because Hashem is only good and merciful, Hashem responds in kind and treats that person with no severe judgments and nothing but goodness and mercy. Such a person is capable of invoking miraculous salvations.

Hashem guides a person in accordance with his emuna. If a person believes there is no bad, then he will see that there is no bad. If a person believes there is nothing but Hashem, then he won't have to worry about prosecuting angels or anything else.

When a person is fearful, he grants power to the very object of his fear and subjugates himself to that object, Heaven forbid. When a person believes that there is nothing but Hashem, and that everything is purely good and merciful, no severe judgments or agents of severe judgment can be leveled against him.

Initially, when a person builds belief that everything is purely Divine mercy, he believes but does not understand. Afterwards, when he has maintained his strong belief over some time, he begins to comprehend the events surrounding him with his intellect. He receives the attribute of knowledge; to truly know and understand that everything is merciful.

A person with the level of spiritual awareness that everything Hashem does is good no longer needs troubles to learn emuna. The ultimate purpose of our lives on this material planet and all the hardships therein is to teach us emuna and give us knowledge of Hashem. When we strive to learn emuna and knowledge of Hashem on our own, most trials and tribulations become superfluous. They simply disappear!

Thanks and Humility

Humility means accepting suffering with emuna. Someone who revolts and becomes angry when things aren't to her liking exhibits a sense of entitlement, a spoiled character, and arrogance. Since when does the Almighty have to run the world according to some obtuse person's sorely limited logic?

A humble person is a smart person; she knows that difficulties in life are Hashem's way of keeping her on an upright path. If she strays from the path of truth, Hashem is there to "prod" her back to the right path, just as a sheepdog will bark and snap at a straying lamb to return to the flock. The lamb owes the sheepdog sincere gratitude, despite the fact that the dog had to prod the lamb with a little bite in the ankle. Why? Were it not for the sheepdog, the lamb would have strayed off into the woods and ended up as dinner for hungry wolves. By the same token, we must thank Hashem. "Thank You, Hashem, for not letting me stray away from you. Thank You for waking me up. Thank You for not letting me fall prey to the Evil Inclination."

You Can't Outsmart Severe Judgment

Now we can understand why the Sages of the Midrash explain that the Holy One, Blessed Be He, desired to create the world with severe judgment. However, He saw that the world could not exist, so He included the attribute of mercy.

The Creator wanted to run the world in such a way that all people would walk the straight path. One step off the path would bring immediate punishment that would return them to the straight path. This is the meaning of the world being created with the attribute of severe judgment; under the regime of severe judgment, it is impossible to stray from the path of fulfilling the Creator's commandments.

Hashem saw, though, that the world could not exist with these rules. The wonderful knowledge of emuna – within the books of Rebbe Nachman of Breslev in particular - teach us that what Hashem sent down to the world in the last few generations has not yet been revealed. Hashem saw that if, for every move outside the parameters of truth, people would be stricken, then instead of returning to the path they would complain and rebel: "Why should I be stricken?" The moment they would rebel, they would die, for the attribute of severe judgment cannot be outsmarted. If he is not willing to humbly subjugate himself to Divine will and to the Torah's commandments, and he fails to do teshuva, he forfeits his life. Arrogance is thus eradicated in the face of severe judgment.

When we humble ourselves, severe judgment isn't required to humble us. At any rate, the arrogant ultimately discover their nothingness when they die. Why wait for such an irreversible fate? Hashem foresaw how few people could withstand the reign of severe judgment, so He included the attribute of mercy to govern the world.

The Attribute of Mercy

Now that we have gained the wonderful awareness of thanksgiving, we know that as soon as a person encounters any sort of hardship, he should immediately thank Hashem with all his heart: "Thank You very much, Hashem, for this tribulation that returns me to truth. The root of all sins is false pride - thank You for reminding me to be humble!" Immediately after giving thanks, he must return to the proper path. In this way, the world could, indeed, exist under the attribute of severe judgment.

But Hashem knows that this knowledge is still lacking in the world. This knowledge must be acquired with great effort throughout the generations – particularly through tzaddikim who have attained this knowledge by virtue of their struggles, holiness and self-sacrifice. But as long as the people of the world have not attained this knowledge, the world cannot exist with the attribute of severe judgment. That is why Hashem included the attribute of mercy to govern creation.

The attribute of mercy is really for those who do not deserve it. Hashem patiently waits until sinners rectify their mistakes. Under the authority of severe judgment, the sinners would die. Hashem doesn't want that; He wants the world to exist.

He knew that the world would have to wait thousands of years until books on emuna would be published and CDs on thanksgiving would be distributed, and until people would actually study them and pray to fulfill them. And what will be until then? Hashem says: I will leave them alone, for they have good points. Here and there, they try to do mitzvot. The Creator looks only at our good points.

In this way, Hashem continues to keep the world in existence, even when the majority lives erroneously with false pride and illusions of grandeur, as if their own prowess has brought them success. According to the attribute of severe judgment, we know what should be happening, Hashem forbid. But Hashem waits patiently until, little by little, the knowledge of emuna is revealed and spreads throughout the world. Then everyone will truly return to Hashem, know that they are nothing, and that there is nothing but Him. When this is accomplished, Hashem will be able to renew the world with the attribute of severe judgment as He had originally desired, since a world based on severe judgment is the most beautiful world possible, because no one has any blemishes on his or her soul.

Maybe this sounds strange. Who in the world would want to live under the reign of stern judgment? We all would, for living in such a manner is like being in a crime-free world where you don't have to lock your doors.

As odd as it sounds, in an environment of stern judgment, there are surprisingly few stern judgments. Why? Existing in such an environment necessitates humility, and when everyone is humble, there isn't a need for severe judgments or afflictions. Even if we surmise that there could still be a way for people to err and forget that they are nothing, immediately when they receive a blow, they'd thank

Hashem with all their hearts for helping them emerge from their mistake. They would immediately return to the truth, and the entire world would exist in perfect harmony based on the attribute of severe judgment in the most beautiful way possible. There would be a world with no afflictions or sorrow, and void of sin or adultery, jealousy or narrow-mindedness.

In reality, Hashem's attribute of judgment is the greatest mercy of all. With judgment, the world is in a state of wholeness, which is the most wonderful and delightful state possible. To paraphrase the prophet Isaiah, people will be filled with knowledge of Hashem, just like the waters fill the sea.

The Ultimate Purpose

Hashem illuminated my brain with another insight: A person who lives a life of thanksgiving does the initial will of the Creator, fulfilling the ultimate purpose for which the Creator desired to conceive the world!

The Creator wanted the world to be governed with the attribute of severe judgment which, as stated above, is the best and most beautiful possibility. But Hashem saw that there was no choice and that the world would not be able to exist based on severe judgment. Most people live their lives with false pride, certain of their own prowess. The attribute of severe judgment, though, would decimate all of those people in an instant. Hashem has mercy on the world and allows it to continue to exist, along with all of mankind's mistakes and transgressions.

In actuality, there is so much continual suffering in the world because of the attribute of mercy. Without it, we would immediately surrender to Hashem or there would simply be no world. But when Hashem included the attribute of mercy, he curbed the attribute of severe judgment so that it would not judge people with complete severity. Instead it would only strike people once in a while to awaken them – slowly but surely - until they'd completely return to Hashem.

For generations already, the attribute of severe judgment has wanted to strike and the attribute of mercy prevents it from doing so. In this way, the world exists with tremendous difficulties, since there are so many uncorrected misdeeds that have not yet been atoned for.

We can now grasp how the attribute of severe judgment is actually complete mercy. Its purpose is to bring a person to the ultimate goal for which he was created – to totally cling to the Creator and thank Him. The only obstacle that distances a person from the Creator is pride.

The Sacrifice of Thanksgiving: The Best of All

We have learned an amazing thing: A person who lives his life with the understanding that he must give thanks for everything ascends to the loftiest spiritual and personal heights. According to this explanation, we can understand why all the sacrifices in the Holy Temple, except for the thanksgiving offering, will be nullified when Moshiach comes. At that time, everyone will have attained the understanding that they must thank Hashem for everything. They will not have to bring any sacrifices other than the thanksgiving offering, as the rest of the sacrifices correspond to teshuva. The thanksgiving offering is the loftiest of all the sacrifices. When everyone will apprehend the light of thanksgiving, they will happily do teshuva by way of gratitude and they will bring no sacrifice other than the thanksgiving offering.

True Teshuva

The ultimate purpose of a person's life is to learn emuna. Therefore, the main teshuva that we must do is repenting for our lack of, or weakness in, emuna. If a person does understand that he must also do teshuva for a lack of emuna, then he only repents for the outer dimension of the sin. True teshuva necessitates teshuva for weak emuna, as well as teshuva for misdeeds. This explains why the world has not yet reached its rectification. Even when we do teshuva, we are not reaching the root of the problem if we are not doing teshuva for weak emuna.

Many people think if they sinned and then say, "I sinned, I transgressed, I erred," they have done teshuva. Such teshuva is effective only if they atone for a defect in their emuna, which caused them to sin in the first place. The sin itself is the result - not the root - of the problem. It comes to show the person that he lacks emuna. That is why he has failed. The main focus of teshuva is to recognize the lack of emuna that caused him to sin against Hashem in the first place, do teshuva, and rectify it.

In the same vein, people come to me and ask with pain and longing: "When will the Moshiach come?" When I ask them why they want the Moshiach to come, they answer, "What? You don't see all the troubles?"

I answer, "No, what troubles?"

They then look at me like I just landed from Mars. "What, you don't live in this world? You don't hear what troubles abound?"

My explanation: "Hashem has given me a peek at the troubles in the world. Every day I have office hours and people come to cry to me. One has troubles providing for his family, another has marital problems, a third has problems with his children, and another is ill, may Hashem have mercy. I actually am quite aware of the troubles that exist in the world. But I also know that the world suffers from only one problem – lack of emuna! That is the only trouble we truly have."

Complete Salvation

There are countless stories that prove that the only problem a person has is lack of emuna. The following is one of them:

A Jew came to Israel from Iran just to see me. When he met me, he became very emotional. He came to one of my Torah lectures and at the end, told everyone his story. He spoke in Farsi, and one of my students translated what he said.

This Jew was a very successful businessman. He bought a lot of real estate - then the real estate in Iran bottomed out and he lost all his possessions, falling heavily into debt. He dove into despair, depression and great sorrow. His aunt, who lives in Israel, sent him the book **The Garden of Emuna**. He studied the book, and began to understand and see that everything is from Hashem.

In one of the chapters, I wrote that whoever spends an hour in personal prayer for forty days straight will certainly see salvation. This man resolved to give it a try and spend an hour in personal prayer in his language, Farsi, for forty days. **The Garden of Emuna** goes on to elaborate that sometimes a person can merit salvation even before his 40 days are up. The book brings the fourteenth day as an example. When the fourteenth day arrived, he anticipated some sort of improvement. But nothing happened.

He felt confused and doubtful, and was not sure whether or not to continue. Ultimately he overcame his concerns, strengthened himself and continued with the hour of personal prayer – day after day. When he got to the 26th day – nothing happened. Thirty days – zero; then, he reached the 39th day.

The Big Business Transaction

On the 39th day, he got a phone call from his mother. This man had turned off his cell phone because all his creditors were looking for him. His mother called his home and told him that a businessman had been looking for him for many days but could not get ahold of him. She said that he wanted to close a big business transaction with him.

At the end of the 39th day, his cell phone rang and the businessman told him the details of a huge and profitable business transaction that he wanted to make with him. This transaction would cover his debts and put him back on his feet!

"At that moment," the man emotionally said, "I felt so ashamed that I hadn't believed in Hashem and that my spirits were down!"

After that, he did another 40 days of personal prayer and experienced more miracles and salvations. And then he did a third set of 40 days consecutive personal prayer, so that he could come to the Land of Israel and see me.

From Iran and Back

Hashem heard his prayer and he managed to get to Israel via Turkey. Once in Israel, he met a student of mine who is of Persian descent, and he brought him to my Torah lesson in Ashdod, where he told us his story with great emotion.

This Jew went through all the effort to come to Israel – at great personal risk – just to see me, kiss my hand, and get my blessing! And he immediately returned to Turkey and from there to Iran. All in all, he traveled for about 48 hours straight!

I have shared this story as an example of one of thousands of stories that showcase the power of emuna. The Iranian man in this story clearly had troubles. But the moment he connected to emuna and persevered in its path, everything worked out for him. Now he has a sweet path upon which to tread his entire life.

We do not need Moshiach for ourselves. We need him, rather, to reveal Hashem's monarchy over the world. Moshiach will not be coming to solve our problems. On the contrary, when we learn what we should be learning from our troubles, then Moshiach will come! To take care of our troubles, all we have to do is learn emuna.

Daily Redeemer

In the Silent prayer that we recite three times daily, we say, "And He brings the redeemer for the children of their children for the sake of His Name, with love." It doesn't say that Hashem will bring the redeemer in future tense. It says that He brings the redeemer – present tense. At every moment, Hashem brings the redeemer. The world is in the redemption process at every second.

What is the redemption? This deep understanding and study of emuna that we are learning at this very moment is the redemption. Every Torah lesson that deepens our knowledge of emuna is the light of redemption.

Redemption is for the purpose of glorifying Hashem's Name. The entire world will learn emuna and recognize that Hashem is One and His Name is One. Every child will come to know that Hashem is entirely good and bestows only good. We are not waiting for the redeemer to resolve our troubles, pay off our debts or heal the sick. For that, we don't need the redeemer; it is enough to study **The Garden of Emuna** or to hear the CD **Stop Crying**.

If Moshiach must come to solve people's personal problems, he will come with war and death, Heaven forbid. But, if we want him to come to magnify and sanctify Hashem's Name – so that the entire world will know and recognize how good and merciful Hashem is – then he'll come in love and peace.

Simple and Sincere

Rebbe Nachman of Breslev mentions in his famous tale **The Clever Man and the Simple Man** that whenever the simple but upright cobbler would finish making a shoe, it came out triangular - the worst possible shape for a shoe. The shoe was too narrow in the front and squeezed the toes while the back was too wide and didn't support the heel.

Yet the simple man in Rebbe Nachman's story would take the triangular shoe, rejoice in it, dance with it, kiss it and praise it: "What a sweet shoe; honey, sugar, chocolate! What a praiseworthy shoe!"

His wife would see him taking pleasure from the ridiculously unsightly triangular shoe that he made with so much effort, and she would wonder: "Why is he so happy?" She would also try to explain to him that he was not acting logically. "Look at the shoes that others make - attractive and comfortable. And they sell them for a good price, while you sell the shoes that you make for next to nothing."

But the simple man would not be dismayed by her remarks. Instead, he would answer her: "That is his work and this is my work." In other words: The Creator makes everything. The Creator of the world created the other shoemaker and He also created me. One of His creations, for example, is our forefather Jacob; another is Moses, and yet another is just an ordinary fellow. Every person is a creation, made by the Creator. Not only that, but there is a book written about that person. After one hundred twenty years (the lifespan we wish to a person), everyone will see that everyone has a book and his own story.

Hashem Does Everything

Reflecting on this concept that each person is Hashem's unique creation, one of my students was upset because he organized something for the good of the entire yeshiva, yet no one complimented him. The student thought of the simple man from Rebbe Nachman's story; the simple cobbler received no encouragement or flattery - the people laughed in his face. The simple man, however, was not insulted or saddened, and continued to be happy.

Why didn't the simple cobbler break down from society's negative attitude toward him, like the student who was initially insulted because he didn't receive flattery for the good deed that he did? The answer is that the simple man lived emuna completely. He believed that Hashem made the shoe. His work is actually Hashem's work, accomplished through him. Whoever laughs at his work is actually laughing at Hashem's work, Heaven forbid. He ridicules the handiwork of the Creator, as in the Talmudic story (Tractate

Taanit, 20b) of the unsightly individual who rebuked Rebbe Shimon ben Eliezer for commenting that he was ugly, saying: "Go to the Craftsman Who created me and tell Him: What an ugly vessel You have made."

The simple man surmised that Hashem created him with such simple and low intelligence that a three-sided shoe was the best he could produce. If anyone has a problem, he surmised, let them go and tell the Master Craftsman Who molded me that His work is not good. "But please note," the simple man says with utter confidence, "You will be the only one complaining. Because, I, the simple man, am happy with how Hashem created me. I do not question why He made me like this." The simple man's emuna gave him remarkable inner strength to the extent that no one daunted him.

Never Insulted

The simple man was impervious to the ridicule of others because he didn't have any pride that could be hurt or an inflated ego that could burst. If a person feels broken because he is not appreciated, or he doesn't get encouragement – and certainly if he is ridiculed or opposed – it's because he mistakenly thinks that he did the action in question. For that reason, it bothers him when he sees that people think negatively of what he has done.

This, though, is foolishness. In truth, he has done nothing – it is only Hashem Who does. Hashem helps him and gives him the intellectual prowess, strengths and talents that all contribute to a particular deed or accomplishment. Feeling insulted is heresy. Hashem does everything. Whoever laughs at another person is actually laughing at Hashem. If, when a person is ridiculed, he would feel pain because in actuality Hashem is being ridiculed, this would be understandable. But everyone knows that in truth, when a person gets insulted, it is purely personal. And this is total denial of Hashem.

Hashem's Shoe

The simple man had every reason to be happy with the triangular shoe he knew that Hashem made through him. In truth, the triangular shoe that the simple man made with the knowledge that Hashem made it is much better than the most beautiful, high-quality shoe made by a heretic who thinks that he made it.

The Creator gives every person the ability to act in accordance with the tools that he has. This is the reality lived by the simple man. He clearly knew that these were his tools given to him by Hashem to do what he did; in this case, make a triangular shoe. For this reason, he was happy with his lot. When a person does something in accordance with the tools that he has, it is the very best for him and is in line with his soul-rectification.

The student was insulted because he was not living the truth that everything is Hashem's handicraft and that he must be happy with his lot. If he had lived the reality that there is nothing but Hashem, like the holy simple man, he would not have felt slighted even for a minute.

A Honey and Sugar Prayer

The holy, simple man's happiness with his handiwork not only applies to material matters; it applies mainly to spiritual matters. He knew that he must take joy in his service of Hashem at every moment – even if it is lacking and full of blemishes. A person can err and think that in physical matters, he can achieve perfect results. But in the service of Hashem, this is clearly not true. Every servant of Hashem – even the greatest tzaddik – will always see that his service is lacking. As opposed to Hashem, Who is utter perfection and infinite, anything we do will be lacking and blemished.

When it comes to service of Hashem, everyone must adopt the method of the simple man and rejoice in every accomplishment, every mitzvah and every prayer. Dance and sing - what a prayer of honey and sugar! This is the simple man's method. But a person who is not "simple," and is rather full of pride and ego, is sad and broken when he finds the slightest flaw in whatever he does, because he sees himself as the "doer," not Hashem.

The simple man's triangular shoe is a parable for everything that a person tries to do well in life – unsuccessfully. After a person has died, Hashem will not say to him: "Why didn't you do as much as Moses?" Or "Why didn't you do this or that?" Instead, Hashem will show the person how he should have been happy with his lot in life and worked with the tools and talents with which He had endowed him.

Should, Could and Reality

For this reason, people become broken and sad. There is always a large discrepancy between what they understand they should do and what they actually accomplish. For example: A person prays the evening prayers in the usual manner. Afterwards, he thinks that he did not pray the way he should be praying. He becomes disappointed in himself because, in his opinion, he should have prayed better. It is important to understand that just because a person comprehends to what he should be striving, it does not mean that he can attain that particular level immediately. It is mistaken and foolish to think otherwise.

When a person does a certain deed that is not as perfect as he would like it to be, this means that in truth, he has accomplished what he could at that point. This, though, is confusing. Certainly there are many instances in which a person could have done better than what he actually did. So why didn't he do better? What is the explanation?

If a person understands that he could have done better, it is because Hashem gave him this understanding. He does this so that the person will strive to do better and pray for it. Hashem will give him the ability to pray, because prayers must be received by Hashem. If Hashem so chooses, the prayer that he prayed or that he will merit to pray, will be accepted and the person will see an improvement the next time. He must pray with focus and he will begin to experience salvations.

If Hashem still does not wish to accept his prayers, the person will not see any change. He must be patient and simply strengthen his desire while continuing to pray. Meanwhile, he should remember that Hashem performs all of the person's deeds - there is nothing but Him!

We must work hard to eliminate pride and the thought that our accomplishments are due to our personal prowess. Hashem does everything! We must live this truth, just like the simple man did. Then, a person can be happy with whatever Hashem lets him accomplish. If it is a triangular shoe, he is pleased and does not feel bad even when others laugh at him. He has no pride and is happy with his lot even in the face of criticism. After the simple man was promoted to the king's advisor and received wisdom, he remained sincere – everything was equal in his eyes. This is because everything is done by Hashem – with no exceptions.

A person truly has to live the reality that everything is from Hashem. This explains why the simple man says: "And why should we talk about what others do?" To talk about the accomplishments of others means that there is something other than Hashem, Heaven forbid. According to emuna, we attribute our own successes and failures – as well as those of other people – to Hashem alone. That doesn't mean that people are not responsible for their actions – certainly they are! But we must pray for Hashem's guidance and blessing in whatever we do, and desire to do the right thing. The actual outcome is in Hashem's hands.

Self-improvement and True Happiness

From this concept we can now understand how to do teshuva and rectify everything. Let's say a person has a lust for seeing certain movies. At first, he says: "Thank You, Hashem, for my lustful yearning. It reminds me that I need improvement. You made the lust overcome me so that I will not think that I'm perfect and so I'll work on myself. Thank You very much for guiding me in the path of self-improvement. Thank You, Hashem, for my lust for these movies."

In this manner, a person is always improving himself. He views his negative character traits, lusts, and setbacks or other spiritual failures as an expression of the fact that he still has some self-improvement to do. This admission in itself – attainable by the emuna that everything comes from Hashem and is for the very best – is a giant first step in the direction of humility, knowing that none of us is perfect and that we still have plenty of character work to do.

Once we understand that Hashem shows us our flaws so that we can work on them, then Hashem doesn't need to send us additional setbacks, failures, and harsh wake-up calls. The purpose of all the suffering that Hashem sends a person is to teach him that he is powerless without Hashem.

Sin stems from false pride; heresy from when we think we're in charge. But once we learn that everything comes from Hashem, we learn humility. We attribute everything to Hashem, thank Him for everything, and pray for everything. Such a mindset enables us to be happy no matter what. So we see that emuna and humility – the opposite of pride and heresy – are the two most important prerequisites for happiness.

Failure makes haughty people cry and complain, but it brings the humble person closer to Hashem. When a humble person has a setback, he reminds himself that he is nothing without Hashem. If he inadvertently sins, he is happy for the suffering that he receives as a result and thanks Hashem for His rebuke. This is true humility and the rectification of the root of the sin. It is also the only form of true teshuva, because if a person is doing teshuva but does not conclude that he is nothing without Hashem, then he really hasn't done teshuva at all.

A person who understands what we have explained here will no longer need to seek solutions to end suffering through natural means. By accepting Hashem's Will with emuna and thanking Hashem for whatever He does, suffering becomes the catalyst for teshuva and self-improvement. With gratitude, emuna, and teshuva, suffering ultimately falls by the wayside. In this very simple way, a person attains a truly beautiful life.

Chapter Nine:
Abundant Gratitude

The Hebrew word for *thanksgiving* is *hoda'ah*. This word has a number of meanings; one is simply *give thanks*. A second meaning is *admission* – to admit that something is true. Yet another meaning of *hoda'ah* is *confession* of sins. All of these aspects of the word *hoda'ah* are connected, as we will learn.

Let's begin with the connection between *thanksgiving*, which is recognition of the fact that someone has done something good for us, and *admission* of truth. These two meanings are actually one and the same. When a person recognizes that Hashem has performed an act of kindness for him and thanks Him, he is also admitting the truth – that the act for which he is thanking Hashem is an expression of Hashem's Divine Providence, and is only from Him.

When a person believes that everything Hashem does is for the very best, he can consequently thank Hashem for every hardship he encounters in life. Such thanks to Hashem is an admission of the truth on a deeper level. He recognizes that this trouble is from the Creator and that everything is for the best. He does not blame or persecute himself, or anyone else.

One who thanks Hashem for everything, particularly for every hardship, makes a statement: "I believe that this is coming from You, Hashem, and I believe that it is all for the best." These two aspects of thanksgiving – recognition of the truth and recognition of the fact that an act of kindness has been performed for him – bring a person to the third aspect of *hoda'ah*: confession. He confesses the sins that triggered the troubles, as we'll soon see.

Rebbe Nachman of Breslev writes that when a person lives his life with thanksgiving, truth illuminates his speech. In other words, he attains truth.

Before a person begins to thank Hashem for everything, his Evil Inclination overtakes him, and infuses him with heretical thoughts that things are bad for him and that his life is a mess. This person spends his days far from the truth, mired in despair and darkness. He is sure that life is unfair and that everything is a battle.

All of this is false. In truth, everything that happens to him is wondrous Divine Providence from the Creator, fine-tuned specifically for his eternal good. If he would only believe that Hashem is watching over him and everything that happens to him is for his own good, he would not feel pain and hardship. On the contrary, he would feel blissfully close to Hashem.

Since the Evil Inclination has subdued him with negative thoughts, he does not see the emuna aspect of life at all. He can't even turn to Hashem properly, because he'll be begging Hashem to eliminate the bad from his life when, in truth, everything that Hashem has done for him is good.

A person can properly pray only when he believes that his difficulty or deficiency is for his own benefit. Then, he can thank Hashem and ask Hashem to let him understand what he must learn from this particular difficulty or deficiency, and what he must subsequently correct.

Thanksgiving, Admission and Speech

The grateful person knows the truth: Hashem is completely good and merciful, and that everything is for the best. Consequently, the light of truth illuminates his speech. Illuminated with truth, his words of prayer will be full of hope and optimism, and not needless whining and complaining. It's not difficult to understand which type of prayer will be more effective and acceptable.

The most desirable way to request anything from Hashem is through *hoda'ah* – thanks and admission - as in the following manner: "My beloved Father in Heaven, I want to thank You with all my heart, for You are certainly good and merciful to me and righteous in everything You do. And although it is difficult for me to thank You, for the Evil Inclination distorts my heart, I do believe that everything is for the best. And I request of You, beloved Father, that You will open my heart and brain so that I'll be able to thank You with total sincerity."

One cannot thank Hashem with all his heart as long as he lacks emuna. If this is the case, he must ask Hashem to give him emuna that everything is for the best.

Naturally, one cannot connect to Hashem if he does not believe that Hashem is completely righteous. Many people say that they cannot speak with Hashem. That's because they are not content with their lot in life. Such a feeling is actually a lack of emuna. Sadness and discontent are a statement that a person doesn't like the way Hashem is running the world in general and his life in particular. People don't enjoy speaking to anybody who does things against their liking. So without emuna, they won't connect to Hashem at all, much less speak to Him.

A person must therefore contemplate all the goodness that Hashem, in His kindness, has bestowed upon him throughout his life. Think about how seemingly negative things in the past ultimately turned out for the best. Think how many times Hashem has saved us from peril, or how many times He has showered His abundance upon us. When we ponder our lives under Hashem's influence properly, the truth will illuminate our hearts and we'll be able to speak with Hashem.

Gratitude and Paradise

Rebbe Nachman writes that giving thanks is the sublime delight of the World to Come. We can see with our own eyes that when a person begins to live his life with thanksgiving, he experiences paradise in this world. People approach me and tell me that, from the time they began to thank Hashem for everything, they virtually tasted "the Garden of Eden." I tell them, "Of course you do. Your life is now a reflection of the World to Come. This is the light of thanksgiving. You are not mistaken. You have the taste of the Garden of Eden in this world."

Defying Logic

One of my students became ill with a terminal disease. The doctors told him that he needed chemotherapy. He didn't want this treatment because he had heard that chemo takes a severe toll on a patient, such as loss of hair, weakness, and a fragile immune system, Heaven forbid. He said to himself: "I am a believing person who spends an hour daily in personal prayer; I will turn to Hashem."

When he came to me and told me about his illness and that he wanted to strengthen his emuna, I said to him: "With Hashem's help, I'll support any decision you make and I'll pray for you."

He said to me, "I decided not to do chemotherapy."

"It is your decision," I said to him.

"Help me fortify my emuna, Rabbi," he requested.

I said, "You know that I've been teaching extensively about gratitude lately. For one hour every day, thank Hashem. If you can, do an additional daily hour of personal prayer on teshuva."

"I'll do it!" he said to me. "I want to strengthen my emuna."

That's exactly what he did. Every day, he spent an hour in personal prayer, singing to Hashem and thanking Him for sending him the illness. In addition to the hour of thanksgiving, he also did an hour of self-assessment and teshuva. He said to Hashem, "Beloved Father in Heaven, I don't want to lie in bed, weak from chemotherapy. It breaks a person until he can't do anything. Instead of that, let me spend my whole day praying!"

This young man made every effort to mobilize the weapons of prayer and teshuva to win his battle with disease. He even asked his oncologist to call him once a week and remind him of the dangers of his illness. When the professor would call and tell him how serious the illness was and what the test results showed, it motivated my student to pray harder.

The alternative to using the gift of thanksgiving when faced with a test of emuna such as a terminal disease is a life of misery, fear, worry, despair, and questioning Hashem, Heaven forbid. But this student merited to sincerely thank Hashem for the disease. He was happy with his lot because he believed that it was all for the best. By virtue of the disease, he strengthened his emuna and became much closer to Hashem. For this he thanked Him every day.

The young man amassed hours of personal prayer in addition to his daily hour of thanksgiving. And may the Name of the King of Kings be praised – the illness disappeared!

Anyone who lives his life with complete gratitude merits salvation. Thanking G-d means acknowledging and accepting His Divine Providence.

Thoughts of the Heart

One of the basic concepts that I discussed with my student was that when a person is suffering, he must be careful not to allow any negative thoughts about Hashem enter his heart. I told him: "Be sure to thank Hashem with all your heart! Don't think for a moment that Hashem is doing something that's not good – this is a negative thought about Hashem. Hashem does only the very best for a person."

When someone says that something in his life is bad, he is actually saying that Hashem is doing something bad, since everything comes from Hashem. This is certainly a negative thought. Once a person harbors negative thoughts about something or someone, he ends up seeing the object of these thoughts as negative. As a result, a person who thinks Hashem does negative things ends up thinking about Hashem negatively, Heaven forbid!

Such thoughts of course are false. Hashem is completely good. Rebbe Nachman writes (Likutei Moharan, I:64), "Hashem created the world because of His mercy, because He wanted to reveal His mercy. If there would not be a created world, upon whom would He bestow His mercy? Thus, He created the entire creation, from the beginning of the World of Emanation until the end of the central point of the material world, in order to show His mercy." A grateful person lives with the faith that Hashem is completely good, that there is no evil in the world, and that Hashem is merciful.

I taught the young man to say, "Master of the Universe, help me be strong, so that no thought will enter my brain or heart that, Heaven forbid, something is bad. There is no such thing. I thank You for what You have done! You are just and merciful, for You do the very best for everyone. Thank You, beloved Father in Heaven."

The Prime Asset

Personal prayer is a person's prime asset. Once a person speaks to Hashem, thanks Him for his troubles, and asks Him to open his eyes so that he will understand what he must do teshuva for, he'll see the fruits of his efforts in a number of ways. He'll feel relief, be instilled with hope, and won't feel alone. He'll also correct and purify himself, which in and of itself is a lofty spiritual accomplishment. Therefore, the best thing that one can do is to invest as much time and effort in personal prayer as he can.

The faith that everything is for the best mitigates all stern judgments. No matter what trouble befalls a person, if he takes a "time out" and speaks with Hashem, he'll immediately feel better. A person should repeatedly speak words of emuna: "I believe with complete faith that there is no evil in the world and that everything is for the best; Hashem is merciful!" Such a declaration of emuna, even when spoken to oneself, has the power to mitigate harsh judgments and open the gates of prayer.

Amalek Shows Up

Complaining and whining invoke stern judgments. We see this in the Torah when, after the exodus from Egypt, Israel voiced doubts about Hashem's Divine Providence. Hashem sent them Amalek so that they would cry out to Him in prayer. As soon as they asked, "Is Hashem in our midst or not?" – in other words, doubts about emuna entered their hearts - immediately "And Amalek," the symbol of all the evil, Evil Inclination and troubles of this world "came."

In Exodus 17:7, the Torah relates how the Children of Israel tested Hashem's patience. Our Sages conclude that when a person thinks Hashem is not with him, he is actually "testing" Hashem.

The verse that follows on the heels of this one is, "And Amalek came and battled with Israel in Refidim" (Exodus, 17:8). Rashi explains that the Torah relates this chain of events to open our eyes to how Hashem views Israel's complaints: "I am always amidst you and ready to fill all your needs, and you say 'Is Hashem in our midst or not?' Now you will see, the dog will come and bite you and you will cry out to Me and you will know where I Am!"

"This can be likened," Rashi continues, "to a man who took his son upon his shoulders and set out on a journey. His son would see an object and say: 'Father, pick up that object and give it to me,' and he would give it to him, a second and a third time. They met a man and the son said to him, 'Have you seen my father?' His father said to him, 'You do not know where I am?' He threw him on the ground and the dog came and bit him."

When does Amalek appear? When do troubles come? Only when a person begins to ask, "Does Hashem see me? Does He hear me? Does He care about me? Does Hashem love me? Is He with me? Maybe He is not with me?" Amalek immediately puts in an appearance in the form of severe judgments and troubles. A person need not complain a lot – the troubles appear immediately.

A person's questions and doubts stem from his lack of belief that Hashem is good, Heaven forbid. If a person would cling to the conviction that Hashem is good, he wouldn't ask any questions. Such doubts as, "Does Hashem hear my prayers?" are symptomatic of a lack of emuna. Anyone who believes that Hashem is merciful and compassionate knows that Hashem hears his prayers.

It's All Compassion

Rebbe Natan writes that sometimes hardships befall a person and his family, Heaven forbid. At these times, a person must strengthen himself with the faith that everything is for the best. He must be careful at these times not to allow feelings of resentment - as a result of these hardships - distance himself from Hashem, Heaven forbid. He must firmly believe that everything is for the best. If he succeeds, he will not only merit the World to Come, but he'll live a life of inner peace despite whatever outer turmoil he may encounter.

Rebbe Natan writes further that during the time one is suffering, he should not foolishly deceive himself and say that he cannot serve Hashem because of his troubles and suffering. He must know that – on the contrary – all of his troubles are chockfull of Divine compassion. Through them, he will ultimately be strengthened.

Sometimes, a person complains and says, "I can't handle this…how am I able to serve Hashem with all this suffering?" Rebbe Natan addresses this specific point and says that Hashem sends tribulations to bring Israel close to Him and not to push them away, Heaven forbid.

Don't Be Foolish

Rebbe Natan cites the Talmud (Tractate Avoda Zara, 4a): "Rebbe Abba asks: What is the meaning of the verse in Hoshea 7:13, 'And I will redeem them and they spoke falsely of Me'?

Hashem said, 'I said that I will redeem them in exchange for their money in this world, so that they may merit the World to Come, and they spoke falsely of Me.' The Holy One, Blessed Be He gives his children financial hardships for their own good – to redeem them from severe judgments so that they may merit the World to Come, and they complain and speak falsely of Hashem, that He, Heaven forbid, is doing bad to them…"

Sometimes, Hashem constricts a person's finances. The person still has a roof over his head, food and drink, but money is tight. This could be saving him from untold suffering in this world and in the next. Yet, instead of appreciating what Hashem is doing for him, the person complains about Hashem and falsely accuses Him of persecuting him for no reason, making him suffer and not giving him what he deserves.

The Talmud (ibid) continues: "And Rav Papi said in the name of Rava, What is the meaning of the verse (Hosea, 7:15), 'I gave them tribulations to strengthen their arms; and they think bad of Me.' Hashem brings suffering upon a person for his ultimate good, but the foolish person thinks bad thoughts about Hashem."

A person must realize that Hashem does everything for the good. That's why the Gemara calls anyone who harbors bad thoughts about Hashem, "foolish." Don't be foolish!

Do Not Despair

Someone who understands the importance of thanking Hashem for everything and decides to do just that – thank Hashem for the seemingly bad as well as the good –is no longer at risk for sinking into sadness, depression, or spiritual downfalls. Why? It's simple:

A person suffers spiritual downfall when he is dissatisfied with his current spiritual situation; he feels that something is wrong or missing, and he's upset with himself. But when he thanks Hashem for everything – including his spiritual situation – he doesn't falter. Although he'd like to be on a higher spiritual level and is striving as such, he is happy with, and accepting of, whatever Hashem grants him at the moment. He can sincerely say, "Hashem, thank You for my current spiritual level, as low as it may be. Thank you for not giving me a higher level at this time; I realize that this is for the best and for my own good, because if I were at a higher level without proper growth and preparation, I might be fooled into thinking that I'm some big tzaddik, when in actuality, I have so much to correct. Thank You, Hashem! Please enable me to serve You with joy at my current level, and help me grow spiritually and get closer to You!"

A person is sad when things do not work out the way he wants them to. But when he thanks Hashem for the things that aren't the way he likes, he is not sad; on the contrary, he is actually happy. And when he is happy, he connects to Hashem.

Thanksgiving connects a person to Hashem, making it easier for her to ask Hashem for help in bringing her even closer to Him. The very factor that would have once caused her to feel sadness has now become a reason to rejoice and thank Hashem.

One of my yeshiva students once sorrowfully told me, "Rabbi, I am tired all day long. Nothing works out for me."

I said to him, "So thank Hashem that you feel exhausted. Instead of being disappointed and despondent, thank Hashem. Everything that Hashem does is for the very best.

Do not blame yourself and don't blame external factors. Whatever is happening in your life is from Hashem and it is for your eternal good. So say, "Thank You, Creator of the world. You know what You are doing. If You have done this, then it is good. Thank You."

By understanding whatever he has is a product of Hashem's loving-kindness, one exercises humility. By thanking Hashem, he clings to Hashem, and subsequently asks for whatever else he needs with greater ease.

There is Nothing but Him

A student once asked me: "What if I err? Should I thank Hashem for the fact that I made a mistake?"

"Yes," I answered. "Do teshuva, and thank Hashem for the fact that you erred."

"But I failed!" he exclaimed. "I made a mistake!"

"You are correct that you have to take responsibility for your sin," I responded. "But your mistake is that you want to take responsibility for the wrong thing. You are responsible for not wanting to do Hashem's Will hard enough, but the final outcome is, was, and always will be, in Hashem's hands. That's what is hard for you to accept, and that's why you have trouble thanking Hashem for the mistake."

The source of this type of sin is lack of faith and false pride, thinking that one determines the outcome of things; that's forgetting Hashem! A person must appeal to Hashem and beg that Hashem help him overcome his Evil Inclination. The root of his misdeeds is failing to seek Hashem's help and feeling lukewarm about doing Hashem's Will. Because of that, people sin.

With the above thought in mind, one can do genuine teshuva and confess: "Master of the Universe, I sinned, I transgressed, I strayed. Mostly, I am guilty of forgetting to pray for Your help. And because I didn't pray, You didn't help me avoid the misdeed, so that I would wake up, do teshuva and realize that there is nothing but Hashem! You determine everything! Help me desire to do Your Will and to pray for Your help always."

Such personal prayer is a beautiful and readily-accepted form of teshuva.

Teshuva Minus the Unnecessary Crying

True confession necessitates thanking Hashem for everything and knowing that everything is a product of Divine Providence and for the very best. When a person looks at his failures from an emuna perspective, he can do teshuva from love, without unnecessary crying and self-blame.

We must not be too hard on ourselves when doing teshuva – blaming ourselves, thinking that we are worthless, and so forth. True teshuva goes together with the faith that Hashem has a hand in everything. We must stop blaming ourselves and others, and instead use our energies to move forward in emuna and internalize that there is nothing but Hashem. We shouldn't blame natural circumstances, heredity, upbringing, fate, luck, or any of the other reasons for which we might have previously blamed our problems – because there is nothing but Hashem!

Asking Like Jacob

Satisfied people have a low sense of entitlement. We learn this from our forefather Jacob.

Jacob was on his way back to the Land of Israel after an extended stay with his father-in-law Lavan in Aram (today's Syria). Jacob was apprehensive about his impending encounter with his evil brother Esau. He prayed to Hashem and begged Him to save him, prefacing his prayers with the words: "I am humbled by all the loving-kindness..." The Zohar explains that what Jacob was saying was, "I have no right to ask anything of You." Jacob felt that everything Hashem did for him until that point was total loving-kindness he did not actually deserve, and that he had no merits with which to ask for more.

The Torah itself praises Jacob as an "ish tam," a man of perfection. How did he feel so non-deserving? For fourteen years he did not sleep, and learned Torah day and night. He had unblemished emuna too, and he weathered excruciating hardships with perfect faith.

During the twenty years that Jacob worked for his father-in-law, Lavan swindled him repeatedly, going back on his commitments and failing to pay Jacob's salary. It made no difference to Jacob. His faith in Hashem was so strong that he kept mum. He didn't lie or get upset, he did not become arrogant, and he did not get angry. He did not say a single bad word about Lavan. He simply believed that whatever was happening to him was from Hashem.

Let's imagine ourselves being swindled one hundred times. How would we react? What would we do to the swindler? How angry we would be and how many bad feelings would be churning inside us? Not to mention how much forbidden speech we would speak about him! The entire city would know what a swindler Lavan was. What a thief, what a liar!

I am Humbled...

Jacob returned from Lavan's home in Aram after having endured all those trials with emuna and integrity. Yet he asks Hashem to protect him from the evil Esau, saying, "I am humbled by all the loving-kindness," as if he had no merits. How can that be?

The Zohar explains that Jacob prayed in this way to teach the world the proper order of prayer. First, we must praise Hashem and only afterwards make our request. Jacob also taught us that the greatest praise we can offer Hashem is "I am humbled by all the loving-kindness." When a person lives the truth that everything he has is the product of Hashem's loving-kindness and that he deserves nothing, his prayers will certainly be answered. This type of prayer is called "The prayer of the poor man." The Zohar explains that this type of prayer bursts through all the Heavenly gates and ascends directly to Hashem.

Two Alternatives

We have only two alternatives: Either we cling to truth and thank Hashem, or we live in falsehood and complain constantly. When a person thanks Hashem but does not really mean it, he is essentially asserting that he deserves better, but is saying thank you just to be polite. That's a mistake! Thanksgiving is not merely good etiquette; it must be genuine – from the bottom of our hearts.

If Jacob lived his life with the knowledge that he deserves nothing, and that everything Hashem had given him was a wonderful gift, then we should certainly follow suit. The best way to raise children who are appreciative, unspoiled, and blessedly lacking an inflated sense of entitlement, is for the parents to be a personal example of gratitude and humility, just as our forefather Jacob is a shining example for us.

The Dangerously Inflated Sense of Entitlement

An inflated sense of entitlement is ever so counterproductive, for it leads to disappointment and depression every time expectations fail to materialize. What's worse is that the inflated sense of entitlement closes off all sources of abundance. Even when the "I deserve" person asks Hashem for something, he makes his request in a way that reflects his inflated sense of entitlement.

Whenever a person thinks that he deserves some positive benefit, the Heavenly Court makes a quick judgment to determine if he indeed deserves what he is demanding. In actuality, the Heavenly Court generally discovers that this individual has already received much more than he deserves and begins demanding justice. The court then reveals the person's outstanding spiritual debts, and that's bad news…

Humble Requests

Somebody told me that his son was not going on the path that he desired. "Be happy with your lot in life," I said to him. "Look at the good inherent in this situation and accept it with love. This is the child that you deserve and this is surely an expression of Hashem's loving-kindness and mercy. Now say, 'Thank You, Hashem! I deserve this! You are righteous in all that befalls me. This is certainly a part of my soul correction.'"

Through emuna and thanksgiving, a person can approach Hashem with humility. If he has a problematic child, for example, he can say, "Master of the Universe, have mercy on this child. Help him, heal his soul and give him wisdom, understanding and knowledge. Have mercy on him so that he will succeed in life, live a good and beautiful life, and have self-confidence." Ask for whatever you want for the child, but the main thing is to approach Hashem with humility, as if we deserve nothing.

A discontented, broken and sad parent cannot pray. And even if he or she does pray, the prayers will be full of disgruntlement and grievances.

The same principle applies to a person who is experiencing financial difficulties. First he must accept the judgment upon him and thank Hashem: "Master of the Universe, thank You! All that I have until now is due to Your loving-kindness. I deserve nothing! Until today, You have sustained me and done great kindnesses for me. You are righteous in everything that happens to me, and I thank You, Hashem. Surely, my situation now is also an expression of Your great mercy. For if You would give me what I really deserve, may Heaven forbid what would happen to me. Thank You Hashem, I accept everything with love. My financial difficulties are certainly a soul correction and for the very best. But please, Hashem, grant me the merit to do teshuva and show me what I must rectify."

What are You Complaining About?

Our sages relate that whenever a person expresses dissatisfaction, a voice from Heaven bellows: "Look at what he is complaining about!"

Imagine that a husband comes home and finds that everything is upside down - toys are strewn all over the floor, the morning dishes are still in the sink, and worse. He starts to shout at his wife: Why doesn't she watch the children? What has she been doing all day long? A voice rings out from Heaven and says: "Look what this man is complaining about! How many people in North Japan lost the roofs over their heads in the tsunami? How many people would give everything for just one child? How many single people would dream of having a spouse to come home to, and you're complaining?"

Imagine that your teenage daughter returns from school and finds the table set for supper with salads, fresh bread, drinks, and much more. But there's no tuna. She complains: "What? No tuna today?" At that moment, a Heavenly voice roars: "Look what this girl is complaining about! She has everything. All that she is missing is some tuna and she is complaining?" Some people are so hungry that they eat weeds or anything they can find. May Hashem save us from such ingratitude.

Being ungrateful is a person's failure to appreciate his blessings in life; it's also a symptom of weak or no emuna. Nothing invokes more difficulties in life than ingratitude. Whenever you feel like complaining, remember the Heavenly voice that declares, "Look at what my children are complaining about…"

Often, people come to me with their troubles. They cry and cry with no end in sight. I explain to them that their crying closes the gates of prayer. They argue with me and reply, "But the Gemara says that the gates of tears never close!" The Gemara is referring to those who cry with a broken heart out of longing and thoughts of teshuva - not to complainers. In fact, the only reason there are gates in the first place is because the complainers don't appreciate what Hashem does for them. As such, their prayers are not accepted.

A person must resolve never to complain, no matter how difficult his circumstances, Hashem forbid. Indeed, one should always thank Hashem for the seemingly bad as well as the good, remembering that everything in our lives is a product of Hashem's loving-kindness and for our ultimate benefit.

Once a person is happy and appreciative, she can make requests: "Master of the Universe, thank You very much, but nevertheless I ask You to have mercy on me." When a person prays in this order, her prayers are readily accepted since she is happy with her lot. She does not have complaints against Hashem or bad thoughts about Him. She has simple emuna that Hashem is good and righteous. This invokes marvelous Divine compassion.

Once I told a sick woman to thank Hashem for ten minutes every day for all the parts of her body that were healthy: For the fact that she sees with her eyes, hears with her ears, walks on her legs, etc. For ten minutes she should give thanks for the loving-kindness that the Creator does with her. After that, I told her to ask for Hashem's mercy and a complete recovery for her illness: "Creator of the World, have mercy on me, help me. I deserve nothing but I am asking for Your loving-kindness; please heal me." She was soon healed.

The feelings of dissatisfaction that a person has are tantamount to heresy. Whether his dissatisfaction is in the physical or spiritual realm, it is still heresy, as if he is making a statement that Hashem is not running the world in an approvable fashion, Heaven forbid.

Rejoice in Your Lot

The holy Zohar says that if a person is not happy with his lot in life, he is liable to forfeit everything. The person who is happy with his lot, however, gets his portion and the portion of the unhappy people, as well. In other words, the unhappy people lose their portion, which is given instead to the people who are happy with their lot in life.

The Successful Path

There is only one way to succeed in this world, and that is by being happy! This is the way that the Torah teaches us. If a person thinks he understands better than the Torah and the teachings of our great sages, he is welcome to try his own alternative. He'll quickly see that sadness accomplishes nothing. Gratitude and joy, appreciating every tiny blessing in life, is the proven way to success.

When a person is happy with his lot in life, the Creator says: "If you are happy with your lot, you'll now have more things to be happy about!" Abundant gratitude creates a wonderful upward spiral of abundance. Try it – it works!

Chapter Ten:
The Greatest Giving

Our master, teacher and rabbi, the Arizal, of blessed and saintly memory, writes that if a person wants to attain spiritual perfection, he should transform himself from a "receiver" to a "giver." By doing so, he will merit Divine illumination. In other words, he will emulate Hashem, because Hashem is a giver. Such a person will have a monumentally positive influence in both the spiritual and physical realms for himself, and for the entire world.

A person must strive to be like the Creator, as our Sages instruct us: "In all a person's ways, one should know Him – just as He is merciful, so you should be merciful, just as he is forgiving, so should you be forgiving." Clearly, the Creator is only a giver, while the created being is by nature a receiver. When a person overcomes his nature and becomes a giver, he becomes like his Creator in spiritual perfection and therefore becomes a conduit for salvation.

The process of overcoming one's nature from receiver to giver is called complete teshuva. By doing so, a person sheds his self-centeredness, arrogance, and lust for honor and material amenities; he attains a level of inner peace in this world that resembles the World to Come.

Giving and Kindness

Life provides numerous opportunities for giving: One can give charity, help others in need, act lovingly, say a kind word, make others happy, lend an ear, and more. When a person is giving, he should not think about what he should be getting in return; he should think about the other person's needs and how to fulfill them. Doing so helps him overcome his nature.

Prevailing over one's nature by becoming a giver instead of a receiver is especially vital to marital harmony. An alarming number of couples don't understand that marital peace requires effort. They think that their neighbor has marital peace because he's simply lucky enough to have landed such a nice wife. What a myth! A couple merits marital peace by virtue of their efforts. A strong marriage has nothing to do with coincidence or luck. Good results are the product of hard work.

In settings of social interaction – especially in marriage and at the workplace - the primary task is to transform his nature from receiver to giver. The difference between a taker and a giver is night and day. Employers love those who strive to contribute to the company and disdain those who are solely concerned with their salary and benefits. The successful married person's orientation must be what he or she can contribute to the relationship, rather that what they can get. Amazingly, the word *gett* in Hebrew means a "writ of divorce." With this Hebrew play on words, we say those who want to get end up getting a *gett*. If you want to live, then try your best to give. Giving illuminates any environment, especially the home.

Marriage is the main venue for giving. Most giving takes place within the home - not outside of it. When a person gives outside his home, he usually has an ulterior motive – to receive honor, money, status, or a favor in return. That's not really giving. But at home, when a person removes the "mask" he wears in public and acts naturally, then it's genuine when he gives to his spouse and children.

What Can I Give You When Everything is Yours?

Giving to Hashem is a lofty accomplishment. But we're behooved to ask ourselves: What can we possibly give the Creator when everything is His?

The answer is gratitude. Saying thank you is a form of giving. That's why we say "giving thanks" or "thanksgiving." Gratitude is a form of giving specifically when the giver expects no type of reward in return. Some think that giving thanks to Hashem is a kind of ploy - just be thankful and you'll be the recipient of all sorts of miracles. They give thanks to Hashem only because they truly want to receive, and that's not giving at all. Only sincere expressions of appreciation with no ulterior motives constitute true giving. By giving thanks, we bring Divine illumination into the world. We also expedite the full redemption, may it be speedily in our days.

Nothing Could be Better

When we thank Hashem for the uncomfortable and undesirable things that happen to us, we invoke even greater Divine illumination and get a spiritual boost to boot. Such thanks go against the very grain of human nature, which desires to receive and have its own way.

A person is able to thank Hashem for the troubles in her life when she fortifies her emuna and realizes that Hashem does everything for her ultimate benefit. With this in mind, nothing could be better. If Hashem could have done something better for you, He would have done it! After all, He can do the very best, so if this is what He has done, then it is surely the very best that can be.

In truth, there is no bad in the world. Everything is good. A person who has emuna knows that all of life's hardships are intrinsically good. The entire concept of *bad* comes from the fact that the person wants Hashem to fulfill her desires and requests. When that does not happen, she feels bad. But when a person's desire is to live in congruence with Hashem's desires, then the concept of *bad* no longer exists.

Look and See Goodness

A person lacks joy in life simply because he's ungrateful.

Every person must ask himself: Is something that brings me closer to Hashem good or bad? Obviously, it's good. If so, there is no bad in the world. When we look at everything with emuna, we see that Hashem's sole intention is to bring us closer to Him. As such, everything is good.

We all view the world through one of two pairs of glasses - glasses of heresy, G-d forbid, or glasses of emuna. The glasses of emuna see no bad. And, when they can't see the good, they must be cleaned, for they are most likely smudged with heresy.

The understanding that everything that happens comes from Hashem is actually redemption. People suffer because they lack emuna, as Rebbe Nachman teaches. Once we begin to believe in Hashem with complete faith, redemption will come without suffering, hardships or wars; it will come with smiles. Every person on earth will know that G-d is good and the source of all good.

Negative thoughts about G-d, complaints about Him and criticizing what He does create a state of what we can term as Divine exile. We overturn this state of exile when we pray that the truth of G-d's goodwill be revealed and that the awareness of emuna will be spread across every continent on earth.

When Will You Reign?

All of mankind prays for the day when Hashem will rule over the entire earth. But doesn't He do that already? What makes Hashem King of the Universe?

Hashem is surely King, and He'll do what He wants when He wants. But, when we nullify our will and accept His with joy, we crown Him our King and invoke enhanced blessings on ourselves and on the entire world.

The more we conduct ourselves in accordance with Hashem's will, the more we reveal Divine light in the world. An illuminated world is a better world; a place of peace and abundance for all.

The Dark Side

Rebbe Nachman writes, "But when a person has a desire other than the will of Hashem, this creates the kingdom of the dark side." The dark side is the opposite of Divine illumination, characterized by strife, tyranny, poverty, and natural disaster, Heaven forbid.

It's easy to understand how desires that are not in accordance with Hashem's will destroy the world; greed, dishonesty, adultery, and murder are classic examples. Yet, even smaller and subtler desires that go against Hashem's will add darkness to the world for they diminish Divine light - and open the door for dark-side forces to rule the world. Hashem's dominion on earth depends on us doing His will. Hence, we should desire what Hashem desires.

A Difficult Test

Rebbe Nachman cites two difficult tests: Money and children. A person has difficulty with willfully accepting the lack of either. In the meanwhile, if a person lacks money or children, or he has not yet found his soul mate, he should realize that this too is Hashem's will and thank Him for what he's lacking. He must genuinely give thanks and not just perform lip service. He's broke? He should say, "Thank You very much, Hashem, for the fact that I have no money!" He's still single? "Thank You, Hashem, for the fact that I don't yet have a spouse. I thank You from the bottom of my heart. For I believe with complete faith that if I don't yet have a spouse or enough money, this is Your will. This is the very best situation for me and all I want is what You want."

Rebbe Nachman used money and children as difficult examples, but his teaching obviously applies to other desires as well.

Vessels for Abundance

Accepting Hashem's will with gratitude does not mean, however, that a person should not pray for the future. Praying for the future and for all our needs, big and small, is not only permissible but desirable. It's even a mitzvah! First, a person must genuinely thank Hashem for everything that he has - or lacks - until this moment in time, and believe that it is all for the very best and Hashem's will. Afterwards, he can ask Hashem for mercy from this moment on and for the fulfillment of all his needs. The key phrase is thanking Hashem for the past and present while humbly requesting for the future.

The gauge of emuna is the extent that we're happy with our lot in life – the greater the emuna, the more we're satisfied with what we have. That doesn't mean, though, that one need not ask Hashem for more. To be happy with one's lot in life means that he must be happy with whatever he has *until this moment*. Once again, we may certainly ask for more for the future. It is not contradictory to be both happy with the current situation and to ask for more for the future. A person is happy when he believes that everything that has happened to him until this point is Hashem's Divine Providence and that it is for his very best. His prayer requests for more for the future build suitable spiritual receptacles for additional Divine abundance, both material and spiritual.

Giving thanks for the past and present combined with requests for the future come together to form the ideal prayer.

Positive Thinking

If a person feels negative, hopeless and wrought with worry, there's hope: Since everything depends on emuna, if he can bring himself to believe that Hashem does everything for the best, then his life will do a complete turnaround for the better. He'll mitigate harsh judgments and consequently experience much less anxiety. He must simply resolve to strengthen his emuna.

Take five minutes and ponder the principles of emuna. Consider how there's really no bad in the world and that everything is good. Take stock of all the positive things in life that are reasons to thank Hashem – functioning lungs, eyes that see, a heart that beats without the help of a pacemaker, food in the refrigerator, running water, air to breathe – the list is endless. Think about how life's less desirable hurdles are blessings too, whether or not we understand how or why. So let's thank Hashem for whatever is worrying us just as we'd thank Him for our lungs or eyesight. Such sincere gratitude is a true miracle worker! You'll see that all harsh judgments will be sweetened just by thinking that there is no bad and that everything is for the best. Gratitude is the ultimate cure.

If it's difficult to attain such thinking in just five minutes, one should spend time in personal prayer telling Hashem that he aspires to live a life of emuna, believing that Hashem is good, that everything that He does is for the very best, and that there is no bad in the world. Yet even if a person spends just five minutes daily thanking Hashem and pondering His loving-kindness – all harsh judgments will be mitigated.

Nobody's a loser. Life can be burdensome, heavy, and dark, but that's because a person succumbs to fear and negative thoughts – indicators of stern judgments on a person. As we've shown, nobody has to surrender to stern judgments. We can apply emuna on the spot, take a five-minute "timeout" for personal prayer and repeat to ourselves, "I believe that there is no bad in the world. I believe that there is only good. I believe that Hashem is only good and does the very best for each person in general and for me in particular. Therefore, whatever will be, will be for the very best." Repeating this several times can dramatically improve how much better one feels, both mentally and physically.

Such personal prayer is more effective than a pain-killer in getting rid of a splitting headache. How? A tension headache is just another manifestation of a stern judgment. Personal prayer with gratitude mitigates and even neutralizes stern judgments, and it can rid a person of a headache lickety-split. As a person repeats this brief prayer every few minutes, the harsh judgments slide off his shoulders, like a hundred-pound backpack suddenly dropping to the ground.

He'll escape the darkness that surrounds him and instead bask in Hashem's light.

Don't ever forget – think positively - everything is for the best. Whenever you feel the slightest negativity, take a timeout for a few minutes of personal prayer, contemplate emuna and thank Hashem for everything. G-d willing, you'll see amazing results.

Remodeling

People run to remodel their homes, but they'd be much better off if they remodeled their outlook on life. The negative way people see the world won't get anyone anywhere. The emuna outlook, however, will bring inner peace, joy, and much higher fulfillment of potential. We must all strive for a remodeled emuna-outlook on life; for Torah and thanksgiving. This means bringing ourselves to the level where we can sincerely thank Hashem for the things that are the most difficult and painful for us.

This, dear reader, is exactly what Hashem wants! By adapting ourselves to a life of gratitude and emuna, we merit the best blessings, including an end of our exile – both personal and national – as well as true inner peace and miraculous salvations that we never dreamed of obtaining.

Gratitude and Self-Correction

Modern society conditions people to do things for their own advantage, where everything is a product of personal gain, vested interests, and ulterior motives. True spirituality and a genuine relationship with Hashem require the opposite – selflessness - particularly prayer and gratitude, with no expectations in return.

Precisely those prayers whose sole aim is gratitude are most powerful. Ulterior motives weaken and dilute prayers. Therefore, when we thank Hashem for life's difficulties, we shouldn't be doing so as a ploy to rid ourselves of those difficulties. Our thanks should be the product of internalized emuna that helps us believe and realize how everything is for our ultimate benefit.

Prayers of thanks also help us internalize the belief in Hashem's precise Divine Providence over every tiny detail in life. If we had truly spiritual eyes, we'd see how everything was for the best.

Recently, a young lady was about to board a bus to a job interview in downtown Jerusalem. Running from her home to the bus stop, she slipped and twisted her ankle. The pain was so sharp that she could barely walk. Her bus – that comes only twice an hour – passed her by. She was miserable about her misfortune and her swelling sprained ankle. A short while later, she heard that the bus was blown up by a terrorist bomb, only two stops before her destination – the very bus she would have been on had she made it on time! After the fact, she was dumbstruck by the magnitude of Hashem's loving-kindness and doubly ashamed that, at the time, she complained about her misfortune.

When something painful happens to us, we should thank Hashem on the spot.

Our desire for teshuva – penitence and subsequent self-correction – is certainly not an ulterior motive in our thanks for something painful or undesirable. Indeed, Hashem wants us to ponder the intrinsic message that each of life's setbacks convey. For example, if someone gets a headache, before he reaches for the aspirin, he should thank Hashem. Next, he should ask, "Hashem, please let me comprehend the message of this headache. If there's something I did wrong to incur this pain, please help me realize what it is so that I can do teshuva appropriately."

The spiritual awareness and sensitivity that we develop by thanking Hashem and by being in constant teshuva helps us repair our wrongdoing constantly. This ongoing self-correction keeps us spiritually healthy and therefore happy. Just as the body's immune system fights and destroys harmful disease agents and microorganisms when we're not even aware of it, such constant thanks for our troubles, and consequent teshuva and self-correction, maintains the health of our soul.

Don't ever forget that Hashem loves you unconditionally and is doing everything in your life for your ultimate good, with no exception. Thank Him with all your heart and you'll soon see so many additional reasons to express your gratitude.

Chapter Eleven:
The Basis of Good Character

Rebbe Nachman of Breslev teaches (Likutei Moharan, I:5), "A person must say to himself, 'The whole world was created especially for me; therefore, I must assume responsibility for the correction of the world, to correct the world's deficiencies, and to pray for them.'"

A person naturally supervises his own household, or whatever domain for which he is responsible. We all make sure to keep undesirable elements out of our domain, and do our utmost to assure the highest level of quality living that we can. We spend hours maintaining, cleaning and repairing it inside and out.

Rebbe Nachman emphasizes that every person, not just the generation's leaders, must look at the world as his or her own private domain; not from an egotistical point of view, but from one of responsibility. Each individual should do his utmost to make this world a more harmonious and livable place.

At this point, it's easy to say, "What can I possibly do to contribute to the correction of the world?"

Rebbe Nachman answers, "Start praying!" This is something we all can do. To correct the world, all we have to do is pray.

The primary correction of the world that Rebbe Nachman is referring to is spreading emuna and eradicating heresy. Heresy is the darkness of the soul and the root of all the world's troubles. When Rebbe Nachman writes about correcting the world's deficiencies, he is referring to the lack of spiritual awareness and emuna. By praying to

Hashem for the whole world to gain spiritual awareness and learn emuna, a person helps uplift the entire world from transgressing and brings all of earth's inhabitants closer to Hashem. This in itself is a correction of the world.

Praying on Time

Rebbe Nachman differentiates between two types of prayer: Before a Heavenly-court verdict is issued and after a Heavenly-court verdict is issued. In other words, if we pray for something that needs correction before a Heavenly-court verdict has been issued, then we can pray in a normal manner. But once a Heavenly-court verdict has been issued, normal prayer is no longer effective, and the prayers must be veiled within a seemingly mundane story or parable in order to conceal the prayers from those accusing angels trying to obstruct them.

Easier said than done; who can possibly differentiate between situations that are before or after a Heavenly-court verdict has been issued? Rebbe Nachman answers that if a person is on such a spiritual level that he performs a mitzvah without caring about any reward – whether in this world or the next – he'll be able to differentiate. Since such a person derives an enormous amount of joy from the mitzvah itself, he'll know if there's a severe verdict hovering above whatever he's praying for if he feels a constriction of his joy in the performance of the mitzvah.

Severe judgments, decrees, or verdicts create a constriction of joy in the world. A person on a high spiritual level can sense this constriction and therefore know if a harsh Heavenly decree has been issued yet or not. That's why we should pray on time for the world's deficiencies – when our great spiritual leaders tell us to - before Heavenly decrees are issued, making prayer a much more difficult task.

The Greatest Privilege

The spiritual level that Rebbe Nachman refers to seems somewhere on Mount Everest. How many people are willing to forego the rewards for a mitzvah in both worlds, simply rejoicing in the mitzvah itself? The following example shows that such a level is really attainable:

Picture that you're granted the opportunity to be the understudy of, and personal valet for, Moses. Imagine your excitement! Think how you'd run to prepare him a cup of tea exactly how he likes it. You'd be singing and dancing about your unique privilege and good fortune. You'd anticipate the very moment you can shine his shoes or perform some other service for him. And to top things off, you'd get to hear his Torah learning first-hand from the Almighty. Would you be expecting rewards? No way! Every moment with Moses is a thrilling experience that fills you with joy.

Every moment a thrilling experience fills us with joy is how we should feel when we serve Hashem by doing His commandments. We should eagerly anticipate the next mitzvah and the next prayer opportunity. We should ask ourselves, "What else can I do for the King? How can I bring Him greater gratification?"

Those who regard prayer and mitzvot as tiresome obligations are far from the spiritual level that we should all be striving for. Our goal should be to serve Hashem merely for the joy of serving Him, with no ulterior motives or expectations of reward.

The Blessing is Yours

There's a world of difference between our mode of dress in the gym and our mode of dress for an important business meeting with foreign investors or at a formal gathering.

Some people don't understand the importance of a modest and respectable appearance. Yet, in light of our discussion above, if a person considers himself the King's servant in the palace – or even more, the King's son or daughter – then he or she would certainly not parade around in a slovenly or immodest manner. Modesty goes hand in hand with spiritual awareness.

Take the same man and dress him in an honor guard uniform or in patched and tattered clothing; in the uniform, he'll stand erect and walk with dignity. In the shabby clothes, he'll act like a hobo, because he'll feel like one.

When people are dressed modestly, they think and act modestly. Modest behavior not only makes the world much more pleasant for all of Hashem's children, it invokes Divine blessings as well.

Whose Pupil?

The Mishna in Tractate Avot (5:19), commonly known as *Ethics of the Fathers*, cites three characteristics that differentiate between the pupils of Abraham and the pupils of the wicked Bilaam.

Pupils of Abraham	**Pupils of Bilaam**
Humble	Arrogant
Judge favorably	Condemn
Satisfied with what they have	Greedy
Outcome: Inherit the World to Come	**Outcome**: Inherit purgatory

The Mishna seems odd; Abraham was a man of absolute goodness and piety while Bilaam was an evil, money-grubbing soothsayer. Why did our sages find the need to describe the differences between the two and their followers? Isn't it obvious?

The Mishna's comparison between Abraham's pupils and Bilaam's pupils does not intend to describe them per se; rather, it's a diagnostic test for every individual to see in whose footsteps he's following. In fact, you can have two people learning in the same classroom or sitting next to one another in the same synagogue, with one resembling a pupil of Abraham and the other a pupil of Bilaam.

In the same line of thought, the Mishna (ibid, 1:12) also encourages us to "Be a pupil of Aaron – love peace, pursue peace, love your fellow humans…" Even though Aaron the High Priest lived over 3,300 years ago, a person who loves peace and seeks peace wherever he goes is very much a pupil of Aaron.

Character Perfection and the Holy Temple

A person's main challenge in life is character perfection. Every person must evaluate himself: "Who am I? What direction am I taking in life? In whose footsteps am I walking – those of the righteous or those of the wicked?" A person's true character is apparent at home, where his behavior is most natural. Is he stingy with his wife? Is he patient with his children? The character parameters of humility versus arrogance, generous versus stingy, accepting versus condemning are readily evident at home.

Our sages show how character perfection - or lack of it -influenced the first and second destructions of our Holy Temple in Jerusalem. The First Temple was destroyed because of idolatry, bloodshed, and debauchery. The people were unified, so the exile lasted only seventy years. In the time of the Second Temple, people were learned in Torah and observant of most of its laws; however, intramural hate and contentions were prevalent. As such, the exile and diaspora still lingers on after nearly two thousand years.

Many people complain that they cannot fulfill our sages' directive to lament about the destruction of the Holy Temple. They claim, "Is it my fault that the Temple was destroyed? I don't have any idea what went on there!" Our sages refute such a claim and say that if the Holy Temple wasn't rebuilt in our days, then it's as if it were destroyed in our days. In other words, we haven't yet rectified the negative character traits – especially jealousy, hate and contention – that brought about the Holy Temple's destruction.

As such, character perfection is our principle task. The key to good character traits is emuna; until a person strives for emuna, he won't know what is truly good character.

Joy in Mitzvot

Let's return to Rebbe Nachman's teaching that a person who does a mitzvah with complete joy and with no expectation of remuneration in this world or the next is capable of knowing whether a stern judgment has been decreed in a particular situation or not.

Rebbe Natan elaborates on Rebbe Nachman's teaching, explaining that Hashem has no problem granting eternal bliss to every soul without troubling that soul to descend to this material earth. Yet intrinsically, the soul is embarrassed to partake of that which it hasn't earned on its own. The delights of the spiritual world are very different if the soul has earned them, as opposed to the soul receiving them automatically without having earned them first.

We ask ourselves, in light of everything we've learned until now, where does the soul get the notion that it's capable of doing anything on its own, much less earning a place in the World to Come? If a soul does a mitzvah, that's from Hashem! A soul is capable of performing a mitzvah because Hashem gave it the opportunity. As the Rambam teaches in the very first principle of our faith, Hashem alone did, does, and will do every deed. So what's left for the soul?

The soul is rewarded for doing a mitzvah; even more so for doing it with joy and good will. As such, if a person doesn't attain the spiritual level where he performs the mitzvot with joy, then his soul will feel like it's getting a handout in the World to Come – an embarrassment.

It All Depends on Emuna

We attain joy by expressing our gratitude to the Almighty for everything – the good and the seemingly otherwise. We are capable of expressing gratitude for everything only after we've built sufficient emuna. Emuna is therefore the main prerequisite of joy in life.

With emuna, a person casts his own logic, preconceptions, and interpretations of life's events aside. Logic and analysis tell him that a given situation is disastrous, suggesting that depression and despair are the justified order of the day. Emuna tells him to set all that aside, because everything comes from Hashem and it's all for the very best. Therefore, there's no reason for depression, blame, or self-persecution.

Since everything is for the best, say "Thank You, Hashem!" With emuna, give your troubles over to Hashem lap and be happy!

Rebbe Natan says that few people are capable of grasping Divine truths with their intellect; therefore, they must build and rely on emuna. Rebbe Natan says (Likutei Halachot, Hilchot Giluach, 3): "Even if a person has attained a lofty level of scholarship both in the Talmud and religious jurisprudence, as well as Kabbalah and the writings of the Holy Ari, he cannot possess the intellectual capacity to grasp truth in Divine concepts until he is completely free of bodily urges and worldly desires. Indeed, he could cause great ruination and fall deeply, Heaven forbid. Therefore, one must reinforce oneself in emuna and cast intellect aside and depend on our forefathers and the greatest of tzaddikim, for they alone attained the true and complete grasp of the Divine."

According to Rebbe Natan, even the intellectually gifted scholars of Torah should depend on emuna rather than their own intellectual prowess. We must remember that Rebbe Natan wrote this advice for his peers and pupils, who had already attained a high level of Torah scholarship and Divine service. Also remember that emuna means thanking Hashem for everything, because there is no one but Hashem.

The Big Misconception

Ask the average person if he has emuna, and he'll invariably respond, "Of course I do!" Such a person sees learning emuna as an admission that he lacks it. This is a tragic misconception. Furthermore, since he's not striving to attain emuna, he's probably living without emuna; without emuna, life is unbearable misery.

Let's help those who don't realize that they need to strengthen emuna. Let's ask them one question: "Do you experience a high level of joy in life?" Any lack of complete joy is an indication of incomplete emuna; conversely, complete emuna manifests itself in complete joy.

Suppose you're not willing to acknowledge the linkage between joy in life and emuna. What about humility? Can you truly look in the mirror and tell yourself that you're humble? If not, you lack complete emuna.

The same goes for all the character traits; good character is the barometer of emuna. Any deficiency in good character – anger, impatience, inconsideration, or stinginess, to name a few examples – indicates a deficiency in emuna. So rather than delaying our individual betterment with further denial, let's get to work strengthening our emuna!

Rebbe Nachman of Breslev teaches us that emuna is a person's prime emotional and spiritual asset. Imagine other favorable qualities – intelligence, ability, charisma; these are like a check with so many zeros. But, if you don't have a "one" on the left side, you're left with zero. Emuna is the "one" that turns those six zeros into one million; without it, the six zeros remain zero. Or imagine the best mahogany furniture; what good is it if you don't have a house? Emuna is the house.

The Basis of Emuna

The Almighty put our forefathers to extreme tests of faith, which they passed with flying colors. Abraham's emuna was tested ten times, each test progressively more difficult than the previous one. The Torah refers to the tenth trial of his emuna in the episode known as the *Akeida*, where he was asked to sacrifice his son Isaac.

Our forefather Jacob had a life strewn with adversaries, multiple exiles, and many tests of faith.

Joseph – the archetype of the tzaddik – was sold into slavery, framed and falsely accused, and thrown into prison for thirteen years. Yet, he accepted everything with a smile and ultimately emerged to be the viceroy of Egypt.

Moses was accused of murder and forced into exile at twenty years old. Even as the leader of the Jewish people, he had enemies from within and without. Yet his faith never wavered.

From where did our forefathers derive their power? How was their emuna so steadfast?

The answer is simple – personal holiness. Rebbe Nachman of Breslev explains why (Likutei Moharan, I:31): The Divine soul of a person receives its vitality from that person's desire to cling to Hashem. In other words, the more a person strives to cling to Hashem, the more he envelops himself in holiness, and the more he envelops himself in holiness, the stronger his Divine soul.

Abraham, Isaac, Jacob, Joseph, and Moses attained the highest levels of soul development because their only desire was to cling to Hashem.

The desire to cling to Hashem – a completely holy desire – and the desire for debauchery or any other type of bodily lust - completely the opposite - are mutually exclusive. Since our forefathers sought holiness and desired Hashem, their souls were mighty. They had the inner strength to weather the most difficult tests of faith.

Rebbe Nachman further explains that if a person has negative desires - such as personal aggrandizement, lust for material amenities and bodily pleasures - his Divine soul will be vanquished. He may have strengths, but they'll be channeled in the direction of evil. These negative desires are counterproductive to good character development. As such, a person might even be a Torah scholar, but if his desires are not directed toward personal holiness and clinging to Hashem, his Torah scholarship will only fuel negative character traits such as arrogance and lust.

Hence, personal holiness is the fertile ground that enables the seeds of emuna and good character to germinate and flourish.

The Protective Force

Emuna – the pure and complete belief in the Almighty – is a protective force that guards us from all evil. How? If a person believes in Hashem, then he certainly believes in Hashem's commandments. When Hashem tells him to do something, he readily accepts this because he knows that it's truth.

For example, the Torah forbids adultery. A person with true emuna – as we've just learned – develops a strength and vitality of soul and a strong positive character. His bodily urges cannot overcome him, because his soul rules his body, and not the other way around. The person with true emuna would no sooner ponder the neighbor's wife than he'd contemplate jumping off the roof of the Empire State Building. The Torah tells him not to covet the neighbor's wife, so he doesn't even look at her.

Meanwhile, this emuna-oriented person is living a sweet life with marital bliss. His wife loves him and trusts him, because she knows that he doesn't even look at another woman. Consequently, we see how true emuna leads to a beautiful upward spiral of good character development, inner strength and peace, and success in every facet of life.

Stop and think for a moment, and ask yourself a few simple questions: Am I willing to sacrifice so much good for a few ridiculous bodily thrills? Am I willing to cheapen myself and parade around immodestly to make men look at me? Why weaken myself? Why sacrifice inner peace and inner strength for some chocolate-covered poison?

No matter what the cheap thrill or temporary bodily pleasure, it's not healthy – spiritually, emotionally, or even physically. Some people overeat when they're sad. Does that help? Of course not! If they realized that happiness and strength of character come from seeking Hashem and strengthening emuna, they'd be opening the door of the refrigerator so much less. Think of the calories, the pounds, and the flab they'd save! Think of the clogged arteries and the heart attacks that they'd avoid. Any time the body overrules the soul and gets its way, the person walks away the big loser.

Now look at what you gain when the protective force of emuna is applied to life: The good character you develop makes you a more sought-after person - people will anticipate your company. The inner peace you gain has a direct positive influence on your health. Suddenly, the nervous twitches, headaches, and indigestion will become figments of the past. Your enhanced inner strength will help you focus your energies and achieve so much more. Emuna and realization of personal potential go hand in hand.

Fictitious Gains

All blessings in life are received as a result of Divine abundance. Isn't it senseless to think that we can gain anything from going against Hashem's Will?

Take dishonest business dealings, for example. The Torah not only tells us not to steal, but commands us to speak honestly and refrain from misleading people.

Maybe you're wondering how there are dishonest, cruel, and tyrannical people who are also fabulously wealthy. Don't be impressed: An old Hebrew expression says *sof ganav letliya*, in other words, the end of a thief is at the end of a rope. Notice how all the thieves and tyrants never go peacefully to the grave, so don't be jealous of them when things seem to be going in their favor for the time being.

In the White Russian town of Radin, during the time of the Chofetz Chaim, there lived an extremely wealthy property owner. A widow rented one of the shanties he owned on the outskirts of town and eked out a meager living by selling whiskey to travelers and the local peasants. During a bitter winter, few passed by the widow's shack. She barely had money for a bit of bread and couldn't pay the rent. The landlord refused to listen to the widow's pleas for mercy and evicted her, throwing her and her possessions out in the snow.

The entire town was up in arms. What injustice! The landlord was the richest man in town; the loss of a few rubles rent made no difference to him. The townspeople protested to the Chofetz Chaim. After arranging a place for the woman to stay, the Chofetz Chaim told the townspeople to refrain from doing anything against the rich man. Cruel or not, he had the right to do as he pleased with his own property. "But," said the Chofetz Chaim, "There is a Judge of Truth, blessed be His Name. He shall judge…"

Twenty-two years later, a rabid dog roamed into town. It crouched in front of the rich man's mansion. As soon as he walked out the front door, the dog pounced on him and bit him deeply in the leg. The rich man fell sick with rabies and died an excruciating, terrible death.

Apparent abundance of any kind that's obtained by way of transgressing the Torah will not only be short-lived, but it won't carry a blessing. Money earned in a forbidden manner or by causing pain to others will be spent on repairs, doctors' bills and lawsuits, just to name a few of the nemeses that the cruel and dishonest will deal with at some point. Don't be impressed at all by their fictitious and temporary gains.

Reward for Passing the Test of Faith

The Midrash tells about King Yehoyachin (also known as Yachania), who was the last king of the Davidic dynasty at the time of the destruction of the first Holy Temple and the Babylonian exile. King Yehoyachin's unsightly behavior aroused Hashem's wrath to the point where Jeremiah the Prophet said (Jeremiah, 22:30), "Thus said Hashem: 'Inscribe that this man shall be childless; a man who will not succeed in his life; for none of his descendants will ever succeed to sit on the throne or to rule over Judah.'" This was a terribly harsh decree; there would be no more offspring of David to rule over the Jewish people.

Nebuchadnezzar, the Babylonian despot who destroyed the first Holy Temple and conquered Jerusalem, exiled King Yehoyachin together with Mordechai, Esther, and the leaders and wise men of Judea (Esther, 2:6).

Nebuchadnezzar imprisoned Yehoyachin in a cell so small that he couldn't lie down. No one ever emerged from such incarceration alive. Isaiah the Prophet describes Nebuchadnezzar's ruthlessness and says (Isaiah, 14:17), "He made the world like a desert and tore down its cities; his captives never saw home again." As soon as Yehoyachin was thrown into Nebuchadnezzar's prison, it seemed positive that Jeremiah's prophecy would now come true; namely, that Yehoyachin would die childless. How could he father a child from a nine square-foot prison cell?

The wise men of the generation knew that the Moshiach must be a descendant of David. Under the present circumstances, the Davidic dynasty would be felled and the hope for Moshiach would be lost forever! They had to do something.

The Midrash tells us that the wise men approached the elderly nursemaid who raised Nebuchadnezzar's wife, the queen of Babylonia. They urged her beg the queen to convince the king, and allow Yehoyachin to have a conjugal visit with his wife in hopes that there would be a continuation of the Davidic dynasty. The nursemaid succeeded.

Yehoyachin's cell was so tiny that his wife had to be lowered from a rope through a hole in the roof. As soon her foot touched the floor of the cell, she felt a shuddering sensation in her abdomen. "Oh no!" she cried. "I've become a *niddah*, ritually impure!" At that moment, she had received her monthly menstrual period.

Yehoyachin, despite not having seen his wife for so long, refrained from touching her. While incarcerated, he had done some deep soul-searching. He desired to rectify his evil ways. And here he was, being tested: Will he succumb to bodily lusts, or will he refrain – as the Torah commands – from touching his wife during her ritually impure period? Yehoyachin rose above his bodily desires, and decided to adhere to the Torah's commandment.

Yehoyachin's Evil Inclination was probably putting tons of pressure on him, questioning and tempting him with seemingly convincing claims: "What are you doing? Who says you'll ever see your wife again? This is the only chance to save the Davidic dynasty! Who says you'll ever see a woman again?" Yehoyachin didn't listen to any of the Evil Inclination's arguments, girded himself with spiritual strength, and did Hashem's Will.

Yehoyachin's teshuva and resistance to temptation made such an impression in Heaven that all the harsh decrees against him were nullified. As such, after his wife became ritually pure again, she was allowed to visit him once more. From this visit, Shaltiel was conceived.

Shaltiel's son Zerubavel was not only a great tzaddik, but he became Rosh HaGola, the leader of the Jewish people in the diaspora. Zerubavel's sons continued in his footsteps. As such, the Davidic dynasty lived on, thanks to Yehoyachin's success in overcoming a difficult test of faith. The Midrash tells us that when Hashem delivers a Torah discourse in the Upper Worlds, Zerubavel is the one who rises to say Kaddish afterwards. Then, all the souls in purgatory yell out "Amen!" By virtue of their answering "amen" to Zerubavel's Kaddish, the souls in the netherworld are elevated to eternal rest in Heaven.

We have no idea the magnitude of good we create in the world by successfully withstanding a test of faith. As in Yehoyachin's case, each one of us should feel that clinging steadfast to our faith will have a profound effect on all our future offspring, and on the world in general.

Leaving the Bad and Doing Good

We see that a lone but monumental instance of withstanding temptation can be the basis for our future redemption, speedily and our days, amen. Emuna enables us to resist temptation.

King David says (Psalms, 34:15), "Leave the bad and do good." "Leaving the bad" is resisting the temptation to transgress. "Do good" refers to learning emuna, getting close to Hashem, and fulfilling His commandments. Leaving the bad and doing good are a continuous and simultaneous process. We must strive for both.

Emuna is the luscious spiritual fruit that we harvest from our efforts to perfect our character and get close to Hashem. Through emuna, we not only hasten our personal perfection, but the perfection of the entire world as well.

Chapter Twelve:
Gratitude and Trust

As long as a person still has the will to pray, no situation justifies despair. No matter what the predicament might be, prayer can invoke any salvation or overturn any harsh decree. With this in mind, the only "big trouble" that looms is a situation in which a person lacks the will to turn to Hashem in prayer.

Just as we've been in an exile that's both physical and spiritual, so too we are in exile when we lose confidence in prayer's purpose and effectiveness. Since prayer enables us to be in Hashem's presence, the lack of it resembles a harsh decree that exiles a person, banishing him from the King's presence. In that respect, the most unbearable decree of Torah is Hashem's warning (Deuteronomy, 31:18), "I shall conceal My countenance from them on that day;" this is more disparaging than all of the ninety-eight curses that appear in Chapter 28 of Deuteronomy. Our sages say (Jerusalem Talmud, Sanhedrin, 51a), "There was no such difficult hour in the world as when Hashem told Moses, 'I shall conceal My countenance from them.'"

Moses was able to maintain his composure when Hashem uttered the ninety-eight curses, because he knew that with prayer, he'd be able to rescind any curse. But when he heard Hashem say, "I shall conceal My countenance," he trembled like a leaf in a strong wind. The Jewish people can withstand anything as long as Hashem doesn't turn away from them.

Trust in Love

If a person is cast away from the King and no longer welcome in the King's presence, then what can possibly be done? The Slonimer Rebbe, of saintly and blessed memory, says that there is still hope. Trust in Hashem invokes Divine blessings and salvation even during a time of concealment. Someone who trusts Hashem can overturn harsh decrees, because he knows that there is no stern judgment that can't be mitigated.

"Trust" means that a person knows Hashem loves every human unconditionally. The worst criminal can return to Hashem and turn any curse into a blessing, and even salvation, as long as he trusts in Hashem enough to turn to Him. The Gemara promises (Yoma, 86b) that if a person returns to Hashem in love, then his worst transgressions become merits in his favor. The Prophet promises (Jeremiah, 30:7), "This is a time of trouble for Jacob, but from this he shall see salvation."

Your G-d

Rebbe Yechiel Michel of Zlatchov used to say in the name of the Baal Shem Tov that the Heavenly Court can't punish a person who trusts in Hashem. King David declares (Psalms, 26:1), "I have trusted in Hashem, I shall not falter." No evil can befall a person who trusts in Hashem, for King David adds (ibid, 32:10), "He who trusts in Hashem, loving-kindness shall surround him."

Rabbi Levi Yitzchak of Berditchev teaches that the power of trust in Hashem is capable of mitigating all stern judgments. Hashem says in the first of the Ten Commandments, "I am the Lord, your G-d;" this is not merely some statement to make us feel good. Hashem is telling us that He is our own personal G-d. He personally watches over each and every one of us. As such, we can always trust in Him.

Since our trust in Hashem is rooted in the First Commandment, and the First Commandment is the commandment of emuna, through which we believe that Hashem is our G-d, then trust in Hashem is rooted in emuna - the pure and complete belief in Hashem. Our connection with Hashem is both limitless and eternal, just as He is limitless and eternal.

Our job is to internalize the principles of emuna and trust in G-d. Nothing gives a person such confidence and inner strength like a heart full of emuna and trust.

Always With Us

The Rebbe of Avritch writes in his book **Bat Ayin**, that even if a person has complete belief that Hashem created the world, took us out of Egypt, and gave us the Torah – but he doesn't believe that Hashem is with him personally – that person is a heretic. Hashem is with every one of us.

The notion that Hashem is not with us, Heaven forbid, stems from *klipat Amalek*, the impure spiritual force of Amalek. The Torah relates that when the Jewish people doubted whether Hashem was with them or not, Amalek immediately attacked them. Ingratitude and heresy always summon the archenemy Amalek, who is also the archetype of suffering and tribulations.

Unlocking Doors

Emuna and trust comprise the key to unlocking the door of concealment. Rebbe Levi Yitzchak of Berditchev adds that even if a person has done something terrible, causing Hashem to turn away from him, there is still hope. By accepting Hashem with love and joy, a person rectifies the worst transgressions. How?

Transgressions result from a weakness in emuna, because if a person really believes that Hashem is right there with him, he won't sin. Conversely, accepting everything that Hashem does with love and joy – the good and the seemingly otherwise – a person demonstrates that he lives with emuna. This is a wonderful rectification of wrongdoing.

You might ask whether emuna can really unlock the doors of concealment, even in circumstances where our sages said that regular teshuva won't help. It's a good question; the level of emuna where a person is happy with his lot in life and thanks Hashem for everything is the highest and most cogent form of teshuva. When a person returns to Hashem out of love rather than fear of punishment, this is known as *teshuva from love*. This type of teshuva unlocks the doors of concealment, converting a person's worst transgressions into merits in his favor.

Magic Elixir

Gratitude and trust, when mixed together, become a magical spiritual elixir that mitigates all stern judgments. The Gemara (Tractate Berachot, 10a) shows us a magnificent illustration of this principle in the following story: King Chizkiyahu was very ill. Isaiah the Prophet visited him and told him that his days were numbered. King Chizkiyahu answered, "Stop prophesying and leave! I learned from my grandfathers that even if a sharp sword is placed on your throat, don't lose hope in [Hashem's] mercy!"

What does this mean, the "sharp sword is placed on your throat"? Imagine the harshest decree signed and sealed on

Yom Kippur; gratitude, trust and emuna can overturn this too. There's always hope and no room for despair - ever.

We learn trust from King Chizkiyahu. Any person – no matter how low he has fallen – can make a complete turnaround and return to Hashem whenever he wants and under any circumstance. Things might look hopeless, but Hashem has infinite solutions and modes of salvation. Despair and depression are counterproductive. Trust, emuna, and gratitude work miracles.

Oftentimes, the Evil Inclination injects its poisonous propaganda into a person's heart and brain. If it succeeds in reducing a person's mood to the abyss of disappointment and despair, that person becomes neutralized. That's why the Evil Inclination will tell you, "Hey, look what you've done! Look how terrible your sin is! You'll never be forgiven…"

The Evil Inclination is a liar. Anyone sincerely desiring to make a new start in life can at any given moment. It's so simple – Hashem loves every individual; He'll unlock the door for anyone that truly seeks Him. We can always depend on Hashem's mercy – this is the basis of our trust. We believe that Hashem is a loving Father and we thank Him for all His blessings. Soon, all the concealment dissipates…

No Despair in the World

With all this in mind, we can now appreciate what Rebbe Nachman of Breslev always emphasized – there is no despair in the world at all. There's no reason for despair, since emuna, trust and gratitude provide a bright ray of light that guides a person out of the deepest and darkest tunnels in life.

Rebbe Nachman also answers the Evil Inclination's claim that a person's sin is unforgivable. Rebbe Nachman says, "If you believe that you can ruin, believe that you can rectify!" Once again, Rebbe Nachman's teaching is anchored in the Gemara's lesson about the power of teshuva (Yoma, 86a,b).

Hashem gives us a priceless gift called personal prayer. Anyone who spends an hour a day in gratitude, self-assessment, and teshuva attains a lofty level of emuna and trust. Hashem gives us the wonderful opportunity to judge ourselves; when we do so, Hashem doesn't allow the Heavenly Court to judge us. Our sages explain that there is no double jeopardy in Divine jurisprudence – the Gemara says that if there is judgment in the material world, there is no need for judgment in the spiritual world.

Depend on Emuna

Let's take a closer look at the story of Isaiah the Prophet and King Chizkiyahu. There wasn't a holier man that walked the face of the earth than Isaiah the Prophet. Isaiah received the loftiest prophecies. He spoke with Divine inspiration and a spirit of holiness. Yet King Chizkiyahu trusted so much in Hashem's mercy that he could tell Isaiah, "Take your prophecies and get out of here!"

Do you know what that means? Suppose the sky turns dark with heavy clouds, bolts of lightning strike and a voice bellows from the Heavens declaring that all is lost - we don't have to believe it! Our belief in G-d's mercy and loving-kindness overrides everything, as long as our emuna is strong and our trust in Hashem is firm. It doesn't matter what prophets say or how loud the thunder; we can always depend on emuna. Nothing is more conducive to inner peace than trusting in Hashem and depending on His mercy.

Your Own Personal Relationship

So many people are "fair-weather friends." They seek our company when we're healthy, making money, successful, and doing well in our career or business. When things turn sour, the "fair-weather friends" are no longer in sight. Time and again, we see that there's no one to turn to but Hashem. Since that's the case, we are best advised to enhance and strengthen our relationship with Hashem. Personal prayer is the very best way to do just that.

King David nurtured an intimate personal bond with Hashem. In fact, his classic all-time number-one bestseller – The Book of Psalms – is actually the protocol of his personal prayer sessions with Hashem. As such, King David is able to say, "I place Hashem before me always" (Psalms, 16:8). In other words, King David felt Hashem in his life at all times – he always envisioned Hashem's Holy Name before his eyes.

A Turn for a Turn

It's easy to understand why gratitude to G-d and trust in Him are so effective to mitigate harsh judgments and turn hopeless situations around for the very best. The Gemara teaches that Hashem runs the world according to the ATFAT principle (acronym for *A Turn For A Turn*). Let's see how this works:

The best manifestation of emuna is when a person is happy with his lot in life and thanks Hashem for everything. Suppose that the person has a splitting headache; rather than whining and complaining, he opts for the ultimate panacea, and uses his mouth to say: "Hashem, thanks so much for the headache. Please let this be atonement for any wrongdoing

I might have done. Thank You that this tribulation is not so much worse."

Rabbi Yosef Chaim Zonnenfeld, of saintly and blessed memory, head rabbi of Jerusalem in the early 1900s, was walking through the Arab market. Some urchin threw a tomato at him that splattered in his face. The rabbi turned his eyes to the Heavens and said, "Thank You, Hashem, that this was a tomato and not a rock."

We move mountains with gratitude to Hashem, especially when we thank Him for the less desirable things in our lives. Such gratitude is capable of rescinding the harshest decrees.

If a person has no complaints about the way Hashem runs his life, even though circumstances aren't always so desirable, then Hashem has no complaints about that person, despite the fact that some of his actions aren't so desirable. On the other hand, if a person complains about any little inconvenience in life, then Hashem complains about any little misdeed that person might do. That's the ATFAT principle for you.

By accepting the way Hashem runs the world, we virtually neutralize severe judgments. When we sincerely thank Hashem for whatever He does, severe judgments transform into favorable ones.

No More Worry

Rabbi Mordechai of Lachovich used to say that the only justified worry a person has is the worry about why he's worrying.

Worry is the opposite of emuna. A person that worries doesn't trust Divine Providence and, as a result, forfeits it. Anyone who worries should ask himself the following questions:

1. Why am I worrying?

2. Why do I lack emuna?

3. Why don't I believe that I'm in good hands?

4. Why don't I believe that Hashem is watching over me at all times?

As soon as we sense the slightest bit of worry, we should immediately strengthen our emuna and trust in Hashem. When emuna is steadfast, there is no longer any reason to worry. All we have to do is remember the first of the Rambam's Thirteen Principles of our faith: "I believe with full and complete belief that the Creator blessed be He is Creator and Director of creation and He alone did, does, and will do every action." Since everything comes from Hashem, there's no longer a need for us to worry!

The more a person trusts in Hashem, the less he needs to worry. Not only that – the more a person trusts in Hashem, the less he'll have to exert himself.

People often ask me how many hours they need to commit to making a living. I cannot really answer that question unless I know the person well, because the stronger their emuna and trust in Hashem, the less effort they have to invest in running after income.

Belief in Prayer

Rebbe Natan of Breslev cites a major reason that a person's prayers remain unanswered: In addition to believing in G-d in a general fashion, one must believe that He hears and answers our prayers. The stronger one's belief in the power of prayer, the more he will see the effectiveness of his prayers.

A person's lack of belief in prayer is in effect a lack of belief in his very self. The question, "Who am I that Hashem should listen to my prayers?" is misplaced humility. Even worse, it's a lack of belief in Hashem, because Hashem readily helps the meek and the weak. Therefore, belief in oneself and belief in the power of our prayers are integral parts of emuna, the full and complete belief in Hashem.

Don't Forget Hashem

Almost everyone has a general belief in G-d, but when he finds himself under stress, he forgets about Hashem.

A person with a dangerous illness once came to the Neshchizer Rebbe, of blessed and saintly memory, requesting a blessing for a complete and speedy recovery.

"I doubt that you'll get better," said the Rebbe, shrugging his shoulders.

The sick person was appalled. "Why does the Rebbe answer me like this? The Rebbe gives everyone else blessings. Why not to me, too?"

"I'll tell you a story," said the Rebbe. "An elderly couple lost their life savings, a bag full of golden coins. They came to the holy Koznitzer Maggid and asked for a blessing that their loss should be found. The Maggid refused to give his blessing. The husband took a gold coin out of his pocket and offered it to the Maggid, asking, 'Now will the Rebbe give me his blessing?'

"The Maggid refused. 'You can have my blessing for one hundred gold pieces,' he said matter-of-factly.

"The wife was flabbergasted. She said to her husband, 'One hundred gold pieces? Is this a holy man or a horse trader? Who needs his blessing? Let's get out of here! This is what we deserve for not trusting in Hashem. Come, my husband – let us do some deep soul-searching and fully repent. Let's turn to Hashem for help, and not to flesh and blood!'

"At that moment, the Maggid chimed in, 'Now I can help you! As long as you forgot about Hashem and thought that I can do miracles on my own, nothing would help. But now that you trust in Hashem, you have my wholehearted blessing that you'll recover your loss.'"

The Neshchizer Rebbe then said to the sick person, "By the same token, as soon as you trust Hashem for your recovery, then my blessing will benefit you. Hashem is the doctor, not me!"

The Tzaddik's Blessing

In light of this story, one might wonder how asking for the blessing of a holy man is called "forgetting Hashem"? The fact that a person recognizes the spiritual powers of a holy man - isn't that recognition of Hashem?

Let's review what is written in **The Garden of Emuna**:

1. Everything is from Hashem – a person must believe that Hashem made him sick.

2. Everything is for the best – sickness is no exception.

3. Everything has a purpose – a person should look for the message that Hashem is conveying to him by way of the sickness, such as the ATFAT principle within the sickness
   (Example: A person with an earache realizes that his ear started hurting

after he listened to slander about someone else). The sickness should stimulate teshuva and prayer.

A tzaddik's blessing is certainly worthwhile, but it is not a replacement for a person's own efforts and obligations. A visit to a tzaddik is especially helpful when a person receives advice on how to improve his service of Hashem.

The tzaddik's blessing is most effective when the person's motive is to get closer to Hashem. But, if a person is merely seeking relief from his current tribulation, then the tzaddik's blessing won't do much.

A haughty rich man once threw a gold coin to Rebbe Natan of Breslev so that Rebbe Natan would pray for him. Rebbe Natan picked up the coin and threw it right back. "What do you think?" asked Rebbe Natan. "I'm not one of your factory workers! You think you can hire me to pray for you by throwing a coin at me? If you had the slightest desire to repent and get closer to Hashem, I'd be the first one to help you, but you can't hire me to do all the work for you!"

We must seek the blessings and wisdom of holy individuals and spiritual leaders to get closer to Hashem, and not simply to seek temporary relief of whatever's bothering us. Truly, the greatest benefit of seeing a tzaddik is to obtain advice as to how each of us individually can attain enhanced spirituality and closeness with Hashem.

The Conditional Blessing

A tzaddik is not doing a person any favor by granting that person an unconditional blessing. Let's use an example we mentioned earlier and explain why:

A person listened to some forbidden gossip. Shortly thereafter, he received a painful earache. Not having done any soul-searching, he made no connection between listening to the gossip and the earache.

Imagine that the tzaddik gives the person a blessing and prays for that person's complete and speedy recovery. By virtue of the tzaddik's piety and righteousness, let's suppose that his prayer is answered. As a result, the person's ear no longer hurts. But is that a blessing in the long run?

Hashem sent the earache so that the person would do appropriate self-evaluation, make a connection between the earache and the transgression of listening to gossip and slander, and consequently do teshuva, thereby rectifying the misdeed. But now, the person is left without the earache, yet he still has a nasty blemish on his soul which, if it continues to go uncorrected, could lead to additional and more severe problems in the future. The tzaddik's unconditional blessing, therefore, does no one any favors.

The blessing of a righteous individual is wonderful when it complements a person's own self-evaluation, teshuva, and prayers. The true tzaddikim preface their blessings with advice on what a person might do to rectify the problem at hand. Once again, a person's own efforts, together with the tzaddik's guidance and blessing, are a winning combination.

Women's Wisdom

Serious damage could result from a tzaddik's blessing to a wicked person. Suppose that the wicked person was ill and, as a result of the tzaddik's blessing, the wicked person became healthy without changing his evil ways. This could become a terrible defamation of Hashem's name, Heaven forbid. We can now understand why Queen Esther refused to intercede at first for the Jewish people, who wanted her to ask King Achashverosh to rescind the harsh decree against them. She didn't want them to think that they could mend their misdeeds – which led to the harsh decree in the first place - by means of lobbying and political activism. Queen Esther was a brilliant woman; she wanted the Jews to trust in Hashem rather than trust in the fact that a Jewish queen dwelled in the King's palace.

Esther realized that the evil decree and Haman's plot of genocide were the wake-up calls designed to stimulate a sincere prayer and penitence process among the Jewish people. Without their prayers and complete penitence, her efforts would be counter-productive. But when she told Mordechai to instruct the Jews to join her in fasting and prayer for three whole days and three whole nights – and they did – then a miraculous series of events led not only to the rescinding of the harsh decree, but to the downfall of their enemies.

Trust in Hashem, prayer and teshuva have been - and always will be - a template for salvation and success.

Chapter Thirteen:
Redemption the Easy Way

The Zohar explains that Moses was not only the first redeemer, but he'll be the last redeemer as well. With regard to the first redemption, the Exodus from Egypt, the Torah comments, "They [the Israelites] did not listen to Moses due to impatience and hard work." Moses came to redeem the nation of Israel with a message of emuna, thanksgiving, happiness, and dancing. All of the other Tzaddikim of that generation sought to expedite the Redemption through harsh means, such as fasts and self-afflictions. They did not accept Moses's concept that emuna, gratitude and joy would hasten Redemption more than anything else. The children of Israel subsequently did not listen to Moses, because they weren't convinced of the power of positivity.

To this day, many people believe that Judaism is a stringent hellfire-and-brimstone faith, Heaven forbid. This is an utter misconception. Judaism's awesome power lies in its positivity – emuna, gratitude, and joy. So many people harbor the false impression that Hashem wants us to preoccupy ourselves with fasting and self-suffering – certainly not! Simple faith and gratitude invoke the Divine compassion that will hasten the imminent Redemption, speedily and in our days, amen.

Let's bring this concept to life: Imagine that Moses walks into the main synagogue in Flatbush or Miami on a Tuesday evening, and declares, "Behold! I have come to redeem you, Hashem has sent me."

The Jewish people say to him, "Please, sir, what do we need to do for the Redemption? Tell us and we'll do it!"

Moses speaks into the microphone on the rabbi's podium and says, "All you need to do is smile, be happy, give thanks to Hashem, keep the Torah and mitzvot with joy, and strive to constantly strengthen your emuna. Singing and dancing in between will help things along..."

Some people start catcalling from the crowd: "Hey, you're an imposter! You can't be the Redeemer! If you would have said that we must fast at least twice a week, not sleep all night, immerse ourselves in freezing water, roll in the snow, and be in a state of absolute remorse all day long, we would have believed that you were the Redeemer. The Redemption requires hard work and suffering! Your flower-child message of joy and gratitude belongs in Greenwich Village, not here! You can't trick us! Get out of here, you're not the Redeemer!"

Rebbe Nachman of Breslev teaches that people's deficiency in emuna prevents them from getting close to Hashem via means of positivity. Like their forefathers who were slaves in Egypt, they feel compelled to perform backbreaking "hard work" in order to make any spiritual gain. They don't believe in Hashem's mercy; particularly that Hashem can bring them close even without all their self-flagellation, long faces and suffering.

Rebbe Nachman explains, (Likutei Moharan, II:86): "Understand, that due to the fact that the world is filled with people who lack emuna, that therefore they must fast, in other words, tasks of 'hard work.' This is because it is certainly understood that it is possible to serve Hashem through every mundane action, because 'Hashem does not come with unrealistic expectations of His creations (Avodah Zarah, 3).'" Rebbe Nachman explains that "mundane actions" such as saying grace after a meal with joy, or maintaining a positive outlook when things don't go exactly as we'd like them to, are in effect more cogent that all types of stringent actions that could lead to sadness and depression. In fact, serving Hashem with emuna, gratitude and joy renders harsh stringencies superfluous.

The Path of the Tzaddikim

Here's a reminder of Rebbe Natan's monumental teaching that we should all strive to internalize: "If every person would really listen to the voice of the true tzaddikim, and walk in the path of emuna and cling to the fact that Hashem does everything for the good, and give praise and thanks constantly to Hashem, whether for the good or for the seemingly bad, then all pain and suffering and all exiles would be completely nullified, and we'd have the ultimate Redemption already!"

It's really surprising: Why don't we listen to the tzaddikim and go in this path? Doesn't it seem easy and pleasant, and a wonderful way to go? By taking this path, Rebbe Natan guarantees the end of exile and suffering! So where are we? Why aren't we all busy reinforcing our emuna and expressing our gratitude to Hashem?

The answer is that we still haven't freed ourselves of the slave mentality that is characterized by "impatience and backbreaking work" (Exodus, 6:9). Emuna frees us from this age-old spiritual slavery. The spiritual freedom of gratitude, thanksgiving and joy is the pleasant and painless path to Redemption.

The Service of Gratefulness

Hashem desires to bestow goodness upon all His creations. He wants them to enjoy abundance, success, happiness and everything good. However, if a person lacks emuna, Hashem cannot give that person the highest good, because emuna is the spiritual receptacle for Divine blessings.

A person who lacks emuna suffers disappointment from everything that doesn't go according to his wishes and expectations. He thinks that Hashem torments him at random, or for no reason. G-d forbid we should ever think such a confused thought! Such people destroy their own hope. They also fail to understand what Hashem wants from them.

If we would only have a little more patience – with emuna – we would see that everything that happens to us is for a good reason and for our ultimate good. Not only that, but we would learn that there is a tremendous lesson to learn from each situation. The seemingly bad situations in life always take us to greater spiritual gain and ultimate redemption. The prophet says (Jeremiah, 30:7), "A time of suffering came upon Jacob, and from it he was saved." The suffering itself brought the salvation. When we understand how to come close to Hashem through whatever happens to us in life, and when we understand how to utilize life's challenges to strengthen our character (which in itself is the greatest salvation), then we'll actually thank and praise Hashem for the suffering that caused us to improve!

"Why Did You Make Things Worse?"

Hashem sent Moses to Pharaoh to seek freedom for the Israelites. But rather than freeing the People of Israel, Pharaoh worsened their conditions and made them work even harder. Moses seems to complain to Hashem (Exodus, 5:22), "Why did You make things worse for them?"

Hashem answered Moses (Exodus 6:2) "I am Hashem."

Rashi elaborates that Hashem spoke to Moses from the concept of Elokim, the Holy Name that signifies judgment, because Moses asked why He had made the situation harder for the Jews. After Moses appealed to Pharaoh, the wicked troublemakers Datan and Aviram confronted Moses, challenging, "Why did you go before Pharaoh in the first place!?! Pharaoh now is making life even more difficult on us – more abuse, more slavery!" That's when Moses turned to Hashem and asked, "Why did You make things worse for them?"

Moses certainly did not agree with Datan and Aviram that the apparently worsened situation warrants complaint, G-d forbid! A tzaddik like Moses would never think that anything Hashem did was bad, G-d forbid. On the contrary, Moses certainly believed that everything was for the good, including the intensification of the slavery and suffering. Through following the awesome path of gratitude and thanksgiving to Hashem, Who was about to redeem them at any moment, Moses knew that the intensification was only expediting the liberation of the Jewish People. Not only that, but they would leave Egypt amidst formidable miracles and with mind-boggling wealth.

Moses's point in questioning Hashem was different than what it seems to be on a superficial level. What Moses can't understand is how Hashem allows such wicked people as Datan and Aviram to make a stand against him? They would challenge him at every turn against the truth, causing the Jewish people to doubt the true tzaddikim who teach them emuna, in such a way they would actually delay and prevent their complete redemption.

Let's review Rebbe Natan's amazing teaching, the foundational concept upon which this entire book is built (and most indicative of Rebbe Natan's awesome spiritual awareness): "If every person would really listen to the voice of the true tzaddikim, to walk in the path of emuna and cling to the fact that Hashem does everything for the good, and give praise and thanks constantly to Hashem, whether for the good or for the seemingly bad, then all pain and suffering and all exiles would be completely nullified, and we'd have the ultimate Redemption already!"

Look and see how deep these words reach! Rebbe Natan is assuring us that through having the emuna that everything is for the good, and through being grateful for everything, whether good or seemingly otherwise, all our troubles and exiles would be nullified on their own, and we'd merit the Ultimate Redemption!

Rebbe Natan continues:

"The main delaying factor in the path of Redemption, whether private or general, is the increasing amount of antagonists, who are like Datan and Aviram who opposed Moses. The Satan and those from the Dark Side intensify their efforts to prevent our gratitude to Hashem. Evil strives even harder to heighten suffering, G-d forbid. When two people fight against one another, just as one seems to be winning, immediately the other exerts more effort. So too, as a person comes closer to his redemption, like in the Exodus from Egypt, the pain and suffering intensify."

The antagonists of every generation, like Datan and Aviram, oppose the true tzaddik and cause many to go astray from the path of emuna, and deny that everything is for the good. Without the basic tenet of emuna that everything Hashem does is for our ultimate benefit, one cannot possibly express gratitude.

Despite the instigation of Datan and Aviram, Hashem chastised Moses for his question. He said to Moses that all things considered, He is Hashem and certainly He will fulfill His promise with mercy, in the merit of our holy forefathers, and in the merit of Aaron and all the righteous people who follow the path of emuna with simplicity.

Ticket to Paradise

It's hard for people to believe that they can merit their own private redemption by clinging to simple emuna and expressing their gratitude to Hashem. They doubt that a daily hour of personal prayer can be a ticket a ticket to Paradise and the World to Come.

I once spoke to a person at his daughter's housewarming party, explaining to him the merits of a daily hour of personal prayer. He said to me, "You know what? I'll take it on! And when I say I'll do it, I mean it!"

After a while, I saw him again. He approached me and said, "From the time I committed myself to an hour of daily personal prayer, my life has become Paradise!"

A daily hour of personal prayer mitigates stern judgments. It's as if Hashem says to a person, "If you set aside an hour a day for personal prayer, you are showing Me that you desire My proximity in your life. You show Me that you are doing your best to do My will. If this is so, then I don't need to judge you – it's enough for Me that you are judging yourself." The whole purpose of life's difficulties is to awaken a person from his spiritual slumber. But since a person who engages in personal prayer is awakening himself for that hour, then Hashem waits patiently for him to correct what he needs to correct.

No Harsh Judgments

Life "without harsh judgments" means that we see everything as being for the good, and that everything is the product of Hashem's mercy. When we talk about judgments being mitigated, it doesn't necessarily mean that everything goes smoothly. It could be that a person still has problems and difficult challenges. Living "without harsh judgments" means is that a person sees those problems as merciful, while recognizing Hashem's mercy in everything. Such an individual sees that everything is for the good, realizing that Hashem is helping him accomplish his mission in life and attain his ultimate goal. What could be better?

As to the concept of a person's path in life, I once explained to a group of Air-Force pilots that if a plane tries to take off – but it's not on its designated runway – a tragedy could occur. By the same token, when a person is not on his designated "runway" – his specific path in life - it's also a tragedy. Everyone can take off and elevate to the highest heights, but each person must be on their own runway – their individual life path – the path of emuna.

Don't Hide Your Countenance from Me

During trying times, it's not easy to believe that everything is for the best. As with the Egyptian exile, it's common for there to be increased darkness and difficulty before the light at the end of trouble's tunnel.

Moses accepted the difficulties in his own life with perfect emuna, but it hurt him to see his fellow man suffer. What's more, it hurt him to see that the Jewish people had difficulty in internalizing the emuna that everything Hashem did was for their ultimate benefit.

As such, Hashem answered Moses: "Yes, I understand your anguish and concern for the suffering of your fellows. But, it's your task to teach them that everything I do is for the very best!" We learn this from the passage in Exodus 6:2 where Hashem's Name of Judgment – Elokim - narrates and says, "I am Hashem" – Hashem, the ineffable Name of Mercy. Hashem is telling Moses that despite how difficult it may be to comprehend, he and the People of Israel must cling to the belief that everything is for the very best! In other words, everyone must strengthen their emuna.

Rebbe Natan writes that people's agnosticism stems from a concealment of the truth. However, if the truth that everything is for the best was apparent to everyone, then the entire concept of free choice would lose all meaning. Therefore, we have spiritual resistance. We are not forced to believe; we must seek emuna on our own accord.

The Long Way is the Short Way

Modern society has conditioned people with two expectations: The first is a sense of entitlement and the second is a desire for instant gratification. As such, if they encounter any difficulty in life, and then seek a solution through prayer, they think that Hashem owes them an immediate snap-of-the-fingers salvation. Such folks frequently lose faith, especially when their difficulties become even more acute after praying.

Hashem is omniscient – He knows that the short and easy way is rarely the best way.

Increased difficulties after praying are tests of faith. Do we really believe that Hashem hears our prayers? Do we really believe that He can solve our problems? If our prayers were answered instantly, we would never strengthen our emuna. We would be in big trouble in an even bigger crisis. In weightlifting, muscle fiber is not strengthened unless it withstands pressure; the same goes for emuna: It is also not strengthened unless it's tested. Just as the biggest muscles are developed from the greatest exertion, our emuna is reinforced through successfully withstanding difficult tests of faith.

The lesson we learn from the slavery and subsequent Exodus from Egypt is that increased difficulties oftentimes precede salvations. This should not discourage us. On the contrary, life's difficulties are an incentive to strengthen our resolve and seek an even closer connection to Hashem. If we don't give up, we emerge with both strengthened emuna, which is a priceless asset for posterity, and salvation as well. The long and difficult way in this world is the short and easy way to the World to Come.

Priceless Gifts

Rebbe Nachman explains the phenomenon of why life becomes even more difficult when a person begins to pray. Just as a tangible commodity has a monetary price tag, whatever we pray for has a spiritual price tag that is comprised of two factors – the number of prayers and the amount of desire. Hashem knows that once a person prays a certain amount of prayers, his prayers are liable to become rote, routine, and diluted of intent and passion. Hashem therefore sends obstacles in our way; we must now appeal to Hashem with increased fervor to overcome the obstacles. This also lets us know that we still have work to do.

Here's an example: A person prays to overcome his anger, yet he seems to succumb to anger with even greater frequency and intensity than before he started praying.

He asks himself, "What's going on here? I've been asking Hashem to help me control and uproot my temper, yet I get even angrier than I did before!"

Hashem is hearing this person's prayers and taking them very seriously. Hashem knows how much prayer is required to truly uproot anger. Hashem says, "Fine, My son. I'll help you overcome your anger if you really want to. But first, I don't want you to fool yourself; I'll show you your true current level and you'll see just how much work you have to do and prayer you must invest to accomplish your goal." The person then sees that he really hasn't done much about his anger, and he soon finds himself begging Hashem for a half hour every day in personal prayer just to overcome this one problem. That, of course, is exactly what Hashem wanted.

Now, take your own problem, whether it's anger, overeating, a bad habit, or whatever, and plug it into the prayer-and-subsequent-difficulty template. Hashem will enable you to understand just how much hard work and prayer you'll need. If you don't lose heart, you'll see miraculous gains. Patience, desire, and perseverance are the key words. We've seen people time and again who've made phenomenal personal gain by praying to overcome a negative character trait for a half-hour a day for ninety days straight. It's not easy, but it's more gratifying than anything. Few things strengthen our emuna more than seeing our prayers answered, especially when we prayed for something that seemed impossible.

A woman came to me with a terrible overeating problem. She had tried virtually every diet, every specialist, conventional and alternative medicine, every pill and every herb. Nothing worked and she just continued to gain weight. I explained to her that only Hashem can help her, suggesting that she commit to an hour a day of personal prayer, half of which should be devoted to her overeating problem. She did. Sure, she had her ups and downs. But, after every binge and failure, she strengthened her resolve. She began walking for an hour a day while talking to Hashem. Within a year, she had lost 80 of her original 250 pounds and now weighed 170 pounds. Her entire self-image and joy in life took a dramatic turn for the better.

Life is More Beautiful

Life is truly more beautiful with emuna. A person's prime struggle in life is against the Evil Inclination's constant attempts to show life as being negative and hopeless. A person must struggle to keep his or her nose above the stormy waters of sadness and depression that are forever trying to drown a person's optimism and peace of mind.

One bright beam of emuna, knowing that Hashem does everything for the very best, is enough to shatter the Evil Inclination's mirror of gloom. Take that bright beam and add it to a daily hour of personal prayer, and wait and see how life becomes so much more beautiful.

Path in Life

Rebbe Nachman writes (Likutei Moharan, I:7) that the lack of emuna perpetuates the exile. Rebbe Nachman is referring to the lack of emuna that everything Hashem does is for the very best. He adds (ibid, I:4), "When a person knows that all the events of his life are for his ultimate good, then life resembles paradise." Rebbe Nachman did not write that paradise is having life go according to the way we think it should.

Every human has his or her designated path in life. Life's trials, obstacles, and difficulties are designed for our ultimate benefit, for three important reasons:

1. To help direct us on our true path in life;

2. To facilitate accomplishing our mission on earth;

3. To and aid in the rectification our souls.

When we know that something that seems negative helps us accomplish these three objectives above, it's no longer negative! Here are a few examples:

- An undergraduate student had a dream of becoming a lawyer, but he wasn't accepted into law school. By virtue of his amazing command of foreign languages, he was accepted into a graduate program in international relations. After receiving his master's degree, he began a wonderful and gratifying career in diplomatic service of his country. Today, he praises the day when he wasn't accepted into law school.

- After dating for several months, a young woman yearned that the successful electrical engineer propose marriage to her. Not only did he fail to propose, but he broke up with her and married someone else. Two years after his marriage, he died of a terminal disease. Today, the "heartbroken girlfriend" has been happily married for over twenty years and is a grandmother already. Not only that, but she and her husband run a successful and satisfying business together.

- A young man was riding a motorcycle. He encountered an oil-slick in the road, but was riding to fast to avert it. He went flying off the bike and broke two ribs, a collarbone, and an elbow. In the hospital, he met a nurse who after his recovery, became his wife and beloved partner for life.

The stories are endless, but in every case, we see after-the-fact how Hashem does everything for the best, to guide us along our designated path in life. With emuna, we need not depend on hind-sight to know that everything is for the best! Suddenly, there's no more negativity and life becomes paradise! Consequently, the knowledge that Hashem does everything for the best becomes our own personal Redemption.

The Messianic Era

Everybody is eagerly anticipating Moshiach, the Messiah. The twelfth of our thirteen principles of faith is that we believe that Moshiach will come, and that we await his arrival whenever he comes. Everyone believes that life will be so much better after Moshiach comes. Let's examine that…

Our sages teach that once Moshiach comes, everyone will accept the reign of Hashem. But basically, the world will remain the same. The sun will rise and set daily, and mortals will continue to be born and die until a much later stage when all the dead will be revived. People will still farm, run businesses, learn Torah, and perform mitzvot. So what's the big difference that everyone is looking forward to?

Once Moshiach comes, everyone will realize that Hashem did, does, and will do everything for the very best. Therefore, once Moshiach comes, people will be constantly expressing their gratitude to Hashem.

Dear reader, do you understand the ramifications of the previous paragraph? Once you read this book and internalize its message, and you too understand that everything in your life is for the very best and you thank Hashem accordingly, then your personal Moshiach has arrived already! The exile of your soul has terminated!

Will He Come, or Not?

Together with the happy expectation of Messianic Days, when everyone will attain spiritual awareness, are the horrifying times that the Gemara associates with his arrival. Our sages were terrified of this period. Some of our leading sages said (Gemara, Sanhedrin, 98b), "Let him come and may I not see him!"

Shortly before I completed this book, I attended a meeting of several of this generation's spiritual leaders with a hidden tzaddik who has chosen to remain concealed from the public eye. They were discussing how the times seemed so indicative of Moshiach's imminent arrival. The hidden tzaddik yelled, "May he not come!"

The other rabbis in the room were horrified. "Why shouldn't he come?" they asked. "We are all so eagerly looking forward to Redemption."

"You don't understand what a price we'll have to pay," said the hidden tzaddik, who left this physical world before this book went to press. "You can't imagine the level of calamity, natural disasters, and wars…you don't understand…I survived the Holocaust; I know how terribly difficult things will be."

Surely, the hidden tzaddik was talking about a scenario of Moshiach coming while people continue to live their lives with their usual crying, complaining, and lack of emuna. But, if they take Rebbe Natan's advice which we mentioned earlier in this chapter, and begin a life of emuna and gratitude, then all suffering will be null and void! Rebbe Natan said, "If every person would really listen to the voice of the true tzaddikim, to walk in the path of emuna and cling to the fact that Hashem does everything for the good, and give praise and thanks constantly to Hashem, whether for the good or for the seemingly bad, then all pain and suffering and all exiles would be completely nullified, and we'd have the ultimate Redemption already!"

If we listen to Rebbe Natan, and we internalize the emuna that Hashem does everything for the best and thank Him accordingly, then Moshiach will arrive with singing and dancing in the streets.

Anyone who has ever resolved to reinforce their emuna, while striving to replace any trace of whining, complaining and ingratitude with daily personal prayer and thanksgiving, has seen major miracles. You can too.

The Greatest Privilege

The classic book of Jewish ethics **Duties of the Heart** states: "Even if a person reaches the pinnacle of Divine service and soul rectification, and purifies his character traits to the extent that he resembles an angel, and loves Hashem like an angel does, he still won't reach the level of those who help others find the upright path."

Helping other people learn emuna and gratitude is the greatest spiritual investment that can be, because a person who helps others receives constant spiritual dividends and credit for their worthy deeds.

A person once approached me after one of my lectures and said, "Rabbi, how fortunate you are! You've written books that have saved who-knows-how-many marriages and suicides. Your book saved my life too!" I told him that his rewards can quickly and easily be greater than mine – all he has to do is distribute this book to his friends, family and acquaintances.

There's no charity in the world that compares to spiritually reinforcing others. With a sum of money, we are able to save a person from hunger by buying him a loaf of bread or whatever. But, by helping people learn emuna and thanksgiving, we are not only helping them during every moment of their lives in this world, but we are helping their future in the World to Come as well.

May we all pray for the day when everyone attains spiritual awareness and learns emuna, realizing that everything comes from the Almighty and that everything is for the very best. Once everyone learns emuna and gratitude, we will certainly see the day when the lion grazes with the lamb and people beat their swords into plowshares, speedily and in our time, amen.

With unlimited gratitude to The Almighty for enabling us to complete this sbook. Thank You, Hashem!

Glossary

Amalek (Biblical) – evil grandson of Esau; nickname for the Yetzer Hara, the evil inclination

Baal Teshuva (Hebrew) – spiritually awakened Jew

Brit mila (Hebrew) – ritual circumcision

Chassid (Hebrew) – literally "pious person", but alludes to the disciples of the Chassidic movement, founded by Rabbi Yisroel Baal Shem Tov in the early 18th Century CE

Dinim (Hebrew) – the spiritual forces of severe judgments that are created by a person's misdeeds.

Emuna (Hebrew) - the firm belief in a single, supreme, omniscient, benevolent, spiritual, supernatural, and all-powerful Creator of the universe, who we refer to as God

Emunat Chachamim (Hebrew) - the belief in our sages

Epikoris (Greek) – skeptic, heretic

Epikorsis (Greek) – heresy, skepticism

Gemara (Aramaic) – The 2nd-5th Century CE elaborations on the Mishna, which serve as the foundation of Jewish law

Geula (Hebrew) – the redemption process of the Jewish people

Hashem (Hebrew) - literally means "the name," a substitute term for The Almighty so that we don't risk using God's name in vain.

Hitbodedut (Hebrew) – personal prayer

Kabbala (Hebrew) - Jewish esoteric thought

Kedusha (Hebrew) - holiness

Mishna (Hebrew) – The oral elaboration of the Torah as given from Hashem to Moses, finally codified by Rabbi Akiva, his pupil Rabbi Meir, and his pupil Rabbi Yehuda HaNassi, 1st-2nd Century, CE

Mitzvah (Hebrew) – a commandment of the Torah; good deed.

Mitzvoth (Hebrew, pl.) – literally, the commandments of the Torah; good deeds

Moshiach (Hebrew) – Messiah

Parnassa (Hebrew) – income, livelihood

Pidyon Nefesh (Hebrew) – literally "redemption of the soul"; a monetary donation that is given to a tzaddik as atonement for a person's soul

Shabbat (Hebrew) – Sabbath, day of rest

Shalom Bayit (Hebrew) – literally "peace in the home", marital bliss

Shmirat Habrit (Hebrew) – literally "guarding the covenant"; male holiness in thought, speech, and deed, particularly the use of one's reproductive organs only in the performance of a mitzvah

Shmirat Eynayim (Hebrew) – "guarding the eyes," or refraining from looking at forbidden objects, particularly at a woman other than one's wife

Shulchan Oruch (Hebrew) – Code of Jewish Law, compiled by Rabbi Joseph Caro of Tzfat, late 16th Century CE

Tallit (Hebrew) – prayer shawl

Talmud (Hebrew) – Jewish oral tradition, comprised of the Mishna and the Gemara

Tanna (Aramaic) – Mishnaic sage, 1st – 2nd Century CE

Tefillin (Aramaic) - phylacteries

Teshuva (Hebrew) – literally "returning," the term that refers to the process of atoning for one's misdeeds

Tfilla (Hebrew) - prayer

Tikkun (Hebrew) – correction of the soul

Tikkunim (Hebrew) – plural for tikkun

Tzaddik (Hebrew) – extremely pious and upright person

Tzaddikim (Hebrew) – plural for tzaddik

Tzedakka (Hebrew) – charity

Yetzer Hara (Hebrew) – evil inclination

Yetzer Tov (Hebrew) –inclination to do good

Yir'at Shamayim (Hebrew) – literally "the fear of Hashem," a term for sincere piety

Zohar (Hebrew) - the 2nd-Century C.E. esoteric interpretation of the Torah by Rebbe Shimon Bar Yochai and his disciples

In loving memory of our
Mother & Grandmother

Zelda K. Cooper

Thank you so much for always
Being a role model in teaching us
Gratitude!

With love, honor, and respect.
We miss you!

Peter, Karen, Rachel and David

Cooper

Easton Pa.

May 2011Iyar5771

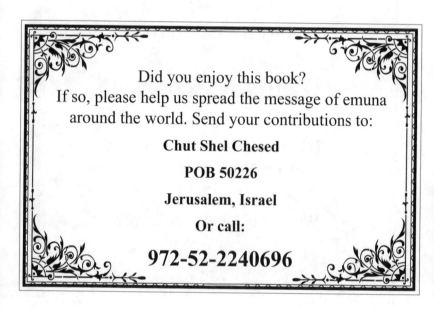

Did you enjoy this book?
If so, please help us spread the message of emuna around the world. Send your contributions to:

Chut Shel Chesed

POB 50226

Jerusalem, Israel

Or call:

972-52-2240696

Dear reader!

The book You have just finished reading has changed the lives of many. Please note that this book is the outcome of a wonderful enterprise that is dedicated to the goal of spreading Jewish wisdom and emuna to hundreds of thousands of people around the globe.

We turn to you, dear reader with a request to become a partner in this enterprise by contributing to our efforts in spreading emuna around the world.
For your convenience please fill in the form on the back and send it to us.

With blessings always
"Chut Shell Chessed" institutions

"Chut Shell Chessed"
p.o. 50226
Bucharim mail box office
Jerusalem zip code: 91050
Israel

Support The Important Work of "Chut Shel Chessed"
Thank you for supporting "Chut Shel Chessed".

Recommended Operation
Support Levels:

$ 15.60 (30¢/week) ☐

$ 26.00 (50¢/week) ☐

$ 39.00 (75¢/week) ☐

$ 52.00 (1.00$/week) ☐

Other Amount: $ _____

Recommended
Support Levels:

$ 100

$ 250

$ 500

$ 1000

Please include your email address,
We will keep you informed about

E-mail address: _____

Name: _____

Street address: _____

City, State, Zip: _____

Phone: (_____) _____

Contribute by Credit Card:

Credit Card Type:

☐ Visa   ☐ MasterCard   ☐ Discover   ☐ American Express

Credit Card #: _____

Expiration: _____ (Month / Year)

Cardholder Signature: _____

Contribute by check :
send a check to the address listed on the back of this card